Achieving Blackness

Achieving Blackness

Race, Black Nationalism, and
Afrocentrism in the Twentieth Century

Algernon Austin

NEW YORK UNIVERSITY PRESS
New York and London

NEW YORK UNIVERSITY PRESS
New York and London
www.nyupress.org

Library of Congress Cataloging-in-Publication Data
Austin, Algernon.
Achieving blackness : race, Black nationalism, and Afrocentrism in
the twentieth century / Algernon Austin.
p.   cm.
Includes bibliographical references and index.
ISBN-13: 978-0-8147-0707-4 (cloth : alk. paper)
ISBN-10: 0-8147-0707-6 (cloth : alk. paper)
ISBN-13: 978-0-8147-0708-1 (pbk. : alk. paper)
ISBN-10: 0-8147-0708-4 (pbk. : alk. paper)
1. Black nationalism—United States—History—20th century.
2. Afrocentrism—United States—History—20th century. 3. Black
Muslims—United States—History—20th century. 4. African
Americans—Race identity—History—20th century.   I. Title.
E185.625.A97   2006
305.896'07300904—dc22   2005030046

New York University Press books are printed on acid-free paper,
and their binding materials are chosen for strength and durability.

Manufactured in the United States of America

c 10 9 8 7 6 5 4 3 2 1
p 10 9 8 7 6 5 4 3 2 1

Contents

Illustrations

Tables

Preface

I believe that I am acting in accordance with the will of the
Almighty Creator by defending myself against the Jew, I am
fighting for the work of the Lord.   —Adolf Hitler

The above quotation is from Adolf Hitler's *Mein Kampf*. It
was quoted on the website of the white supremacist organization, the
Aryan Nations, in 2004. The racial ideology expressed by Hitler and
contemporary white supremacist groups highlights the problems with
the understanding of race used by many scholars today. Many scholars
un-derstand racial ideologies as erroneous biological ideas about groups
that can be distinguished by physical appearance. However, much white
supremacist thought is based on religious, not biological, ideas. The
Ku Klux Klan is a white Christian organization. The Christian Identity
movement, which is linked to neo-Nazi organizations like the Aryan
Nations, is, obviously, Christian also. The religious ideas of these organizations are heterodox, but they do not pretend to be scientific. Much
white supremacist thought identifies Jews as a race although Jews are
not physically distinguishable from non-Jews. White supremacist ideology does not fit comfortably within many scholars' understanding of
race as a biological pseudoscientific concept.

This mismatch between the scholarly conception of a racial ideology
and people's racial ideas is not limited to extremist groups. It is also present with regard to the racial ideas of more moderate Americans. Scholars have overemphasized the work of individual philosophers, naturalists, and scientists in studying racial ideology. Since race is socially created, we need to study social groups, not individual scholars. We need
to examine how race is understood in social relations, not in a treatise.

While philosophers, naturalists, and scientists tend to place their racial ideas in a biological framework, average Americans tend to be less

biologically minded and much more eclectic in their racial reasoning. Scholars have overestimated the power of science and secularism in popular thought. Many Americans are not convinced of biological evolution, for example. As numerous white supremacist organizations have shown, racial ideas are compatible with religious ones. One goal of this book is to bring about a reconceptualization of race so that the scholarly conception of race is a more useful and accurate one for studying social life. I use the racial ideologies of black nationalists to show that their racial ideas also draw on more than biological theories and that their racial categories are not always defined by differences in physical appearance.

This book addresses problems in the thinking of scholars who see race as socially constructed. While it does not directly address the errors in thinking that race is merely biology, these errors should become clear as one reads the book. To say that race is merely an acknowledgment of human biological differences is another way of abstracting the idea of race from social relations. The racial ideology of Nazi Germany, for example, was not mainly preoccupied with obvious physical differences. The Jewish population was not readily identifiable by appearance, which is why the yellow Stars of David were a useful means of identifying them. It would also be a complete misunderstanding of Nazism to assert that Nazism was about Tay-Sachs disease, because this disease is much more prevalent among European Jews than among other groups. Unfortunately, some recent discussions of race and medicine would lead one in this direction.

The discovery that the heart disease drug BiDil is effective specifically for black Americans has again raised the question of the relationship between biology and race for some. In November 2004, the *New York Times* journalist Nicholas Wade wrote about a special issue of *Nature Genetics*[1] on race and genetics. He stated that many geneticists believe that "Race . . . does have a genetic basis." Wade misunderstood the conclusions of the geneticists. They argued that the social concept of race "is far too simple"[2] to describe our genetic diversity and that the connection be-tween race and biology "is generally quite blurry because of multiple other non-genetic connotations of race, the lack of defined boundaries between populations and the fact that many individuals have ancestors from multiple regions of the world."[3]

The geneticists are aware of the fact that social definitions of race are not genetic definitions. How one is defined racially for social relations has never been based on a genetic test. In the United States, it has been possible for individuals with three white grandparents to be black. The way blackness is defined in the United States is not the way it is defined elsewhere. The fact that *some* social definitions of race are imperfectly *correlated* with *some* genes does not make race fundamentally about biology.

This book is the culmination of a very long process. Too many people have assisted me in too many ways for me to even attempt to list them all. I would like to single out a few people who have helped in this last stage of the project. Joseph P. McCormick, II allowed me to see an unpublished preliminary report from his survey of women attending the Million Woman March. Mary Ann Clawson, Roberta Gold, Lorelle Semley, and Dara Strolovich all provided useful comments on specific chapters. Mary O'Kicki helped me make the entire book clearer and better organized. Victoria Stahl and Allynn Wilkinson helped me prepare images for the text. I am grateful for all the help that I have received.

I am also grateful for permission to use material. A version of chapter 2 was previously published as "Rethinking Race and the Nation of Islam, 1930–1975" in *Ethnic and Racial Studies* 26(1): 52–69 (2003). Additional information about *Ethnic and Racial Studies* is available at http://www.tandf.co.uk/journals.

I am grateful to Third World Press for granting me permission to use Don L. Lee/Haki R. Madhubuti's poem "The New Integrationist" in chapter 3. The poem was originally published in *Black Pride* in 1968 by Broadside Press. The current full acknowledgment is as follows: "The New Integrationist," from *Groundwork: New and Selected Poems of Don L. Lee/Haki R. Madhubuti from 1966–1996*, copyright © 1996 by Haki R. Madhubuti, reprinted by permission of Third World Press, Chicago, Illinois.

Contents

1

Making Races

I've heard that most people in Kizimkazi [on the East African island of Zanzibar] claim to be Persian. . . . To me the people look about as Persian as Mike Tyson.

When I was growing up, we used to say, "If you're light you're alright, if you're brown get down, if you're black get back." It's taken my people fifty years to move from Negro to Black to African American. I wonder how long it will take the Swahili to call themselves African.　　　　　　　　　—Henry Louis Gates, Jr.

In the PBS documentary series, *Wonders of the African World*, Henry Louis Gates, Jr., who heads the W. E. B. Du Bois Institute for African and African American Research at Harvard University, is perplexed and disturbed by many of the people he meets along the Swahili coast of East Africa. Many Swahili claim an Arab or Persian identity. To Gates, these people are racially confused and ashamed to acknowledge the blackness that is written on their faces. He informs the Swahili he encounters that "if you came with me back home to Boston, Americans would say that you just look African to them," and not Persian or Arabian.[1]

Are the Swahili racially confused and self-hating, or is Gates simply confused about what race is? Different societies have defined blackness differently. We could turn the tables on Gates and imagine a black person from Africa or Latin America questioning Gates on his classification of Du Bois as black. To someone from Brazil, Du Bois's relatively light complexion, hair texture, and facial features (not to mention his French and Dutch ancestry, education, and refined manners)[2] would exclude him from blackness. In Brazil, Du Bois would be classified as a mulatto or, because of his class background, possibly as white. He would definitely not be classified as black. It is easy to imagine a Brazilian interviewer wondering how long it would take Gates to realize that Du Bois did not look like Mike Tyson.[3]

Gates has written theoretically on race and is a leader in the field of African American Studies.[4] He is among the most prominent scholars who argue that race is socially constructed. Gates's comments on the people of Zanzibar are illustrative of important problems in the current scholarly thinking about race. Although there is an almost universal consensus among academics that "race is socially constructed,"[5] there is a lack of consensus over what "socially constructed" actually means. For some, social constructionism derives from poststructuralist theory; for others, it emerges from new insights in the study of human genetics; and for yet others, it is based on basic sociological theory.[6] This lack of clarity over what social constructionism means leads scholars to vacillate between constructionist positions and biologically reductionist ones.

This book is a sociohistorical examination of blackness in the United States. To understand how blackness can vary by social context and over time despite the fact that the physical appearance of blacks for the most part does not change, one needs to understand what race is and how it is socially created. The understanding of the social construction of race articulated here is based on basic sociological theory. Sociologists have long argued that people's beliefs and understandings shape human behavior. This statement is merely a specification of how and why cultural ideas matter in studying social life. Collective human behavior is what produces the human-made reality that is society.

The sociologist William I. Thomas argues, "If men define situations as real then they will be real in their consequences [for men's behavior]."[7] For example, if I believe that baby formula is better for my baby than breast milk, I will provide baby formula for my baby. But if I believe that breast milk is better for my baby than formula, I will provide breast milk. As American beliefs on this issue have changed, social practices have changed accordingly. Breast-feeding declined with the marketing of baby formula and then increased, following the growing awareness of the benefits of breast milk. The reality of how Americans fed their newborns changed.[8] Baby formula sales were affected. Breast pumps were created. People's changing beliefs had a real and clearly visible impact on social life.

As this example illustrates, on one level it does not matter whether the beliefs are true or false. It does not matter whether formula or breast milk is better for children, because people's behavior follows what they believe to be true. When people believed, incorrectly, that formula was better for babies, they relied increasingly on formula. False ideas can be as effective in shaping people's behavior as true ones.

The sociologist Herbert Blumer makes a similar but slightly different point about cultural ideas and behavior. Blumer states, "Human beings act toward things on the basis of the meanings that the things have for them." Blumer and his students also pay attention to how people can learn to view things negatively or positively through their socialization.[9] For example, in some time periods in some societies, it has been deemed inappropriate and sometimes even illegal for a woman to breast-feed in public. At other times or in other societies, a woman breast-feeding in public would elicit no response, positive or negative, from others.[10] In one society, people are offended by public breast-feeding; in another, people are indifferent. The act of breast-feeding is the same but people's reactions to it depend on the meanings that breast-feeding has for them. Again, cultural ideas shape social behavior.

The sociologist Oliver C. Cox provides an eloquent application of these basic sociological principles to racial relations. He states, "For the sociologist a race may be thought of as simply any group of people that is generally believed to be, and generally accepted as, a race."[11] He continues:

> Here is detail enough, since the sociologist is interested in social interaction. Thus, if a man looks white, although, say in America, he is everywhere called a Negro, he is, then, a Negro American. If, on the other hand, a man of identical physical appearance is recognized everywhere in Cuba as a white man, then he is a white Cuban. The sociologist is interested in what meanings and definitions a society gives to certain social phenomena and situations.[12]

In other words, it is ultimately the shared meanings and definitions that create race—not biology. If some of the Swahili are defined in their society as members of an Arab race, then they are Arabs. Their physical appearance is irrelevant. Social definitions have social consequences. For part of Zanzibar's history, all the elites were Arabs, Muslims segregated themselves from non-Muslims, and Africans could be enslaved by Arabs. Class and status were determined by these social definitions, not by physical appearance.[13]

Although scholars now agree that race is socially constructed, the idea that biology or physical appearance determines race—as opposed to shared meanings and definitions—is still quite common. The most common definition of a *racial group*, or more precisely a *racial category*,[14] is a category of people who are defined as racially different based on physical differences in appearance. Richard Schaefer defines a "racial group" as "those minorities and the corresponding majorities that are classified according to obvious physical differences."[15] In their popular work on the social construction of race, *Racial Formation in the United States: From the 1960s to the 1990s*, Michael Omi and Howard Winant describe race as a concept *"referring to different types of human bodies"* and "invok[ing] biologically based human characteristics (so-called 'phenotypes')."[16] In their comparative study of identity construction, Stephen Cornell and Douglas Hartmann define race "as a human group defined by itself or others as distinct by virtue of perceived common physical characteristics that are held to be inherent."[17] All these authors take a social constructionist position on race, yet all their definitions of race rest on biology.[18] However, biology is not socially constructed. Shared meanings and definitions are. To begin to understand the problems with these definitions of race, we need to see clearly that shared meanings and definitions determine racial relations, not differences in physical appearance.

The Complexity of Making Races

In July 1999, Benjamin "August" Smith went on a violent rampage, shooting six Orthodox Jews, five black men, and two Asian men. In August that same year, Burford O. Furrow, Jr., shot five people at a Los Angeles Jewish community center. Richard Baumhammers's rampage in April 2000 left a Jewish woman, three Asian men, and one black man dead. Baumhammers wounded another Asian man. He interrupted his killing spree twice to vandalize two synagogues. In April 2001, Leo Felton and Erica Chase were arrested for planning to destroy the Holocaust Memorial Museum. Felton was also reported to be planning to assassinate Rev. Jesse Jackson, Steven Spielberg, and other famous blacks and Jews. Felton and Chase were convicted in 2002 of planning to incite a "racial holy war."[19] All these violent individuals were white supremacists and they all had ties to white supremacist organizations.

They all considered Jews to be nonwhites. In their quest for a racially pure and white America, they were willing to kill blacks, Asians, and Jews.[20]

If one accepts a biological conception of race one must define the actions of white supremacists against blacks and Asians as sociologically different phenomena from their actions against Jews. Their actions toward Jews would have to be defined as "ethnic relations"—behavior motivated by cultural difference—while their actions toward blacks and Asians would be seen as examples of racial relations because of a difference in physical appearance. It is not uncommon for scholars to make this type of distinction. For example, Stephen Cornell and Douglass Hartmann deny the claim made by Hutus and Tutsis in Central Africa that their conflict is racial. Although Cornell and Hartmann cite evidence that the groups believe each other to be different races and to be physically different, they insist that the conflict between the Hutus and Tutsis "is ethnic rather than racial" because "outside observers have found these [physical] stereotypes difficult to confirm."[21] Richard Schaefer writes,

> The Jewish people are not physically differentiated from non-Jews. True, many people believe they can tell a Jew from a non-Jew, but actual distinguishing physical traits are absent. . . . The wide range of variation among Jews makes it inaccurate to speak of a "Jewish race" in a physical sense.[22]

Schaefer concludes that Jews are an ethnic group because "Jews share cultural traits, not physical features."[23] Therefore, the white supremacists' attacks on Jews are ethnic relations, not racial relations.

Many white supremacist organizations, however, define Jews as nonwhite.[24] The white supremacists discussed above were clearly willing to treat Jews as they treated other nonwhites. Cox's view that a racial group is whatever group is defined as such gives us a more accurate understanding of the motivation and behavior of white supremacists. This view would also give us a better understanding of relations among the Tutsis and non-Tutsis in Central Africa. In Congo, for example, however similar in appearance Tutsis may be to the rest of the population, they are seen as racially different. For example, although the Congolese parliament member Enoch Ruberangabo and his ancestors have been in the Congo for over a century, he is still not accepted by many

Congolese as Congolese because he is a Tutsi. Over 80 percent of Congolese say that Tutsis cannot be Congolese. Many quote the saying, "Even if a log lies in a river for one hundred years, it doesn't become a crocodile." Many Congolese do not accept Tutsis no matter how much the Tutsis self-identify as Congolese.[25] The difference that is constructed is racial, not cultural.

As with non-Tutsis in the Congo, for white supremacists in the United States the difference that they perceive between whites and Jews is racial, not cultural. White supremacists despise ultraorthodox Jews *as well as* highly assimilated Jews. If anything, they despise culturally assimilated Jews more than other Jews because they see Jewish participation in mainstream organizations as evidence of Jewish plots to take over or corrupt the country.[26]

The belief in racial difference can exist even when there is no difference in physical appearance. If a group believes Jews to be a separate and evil race, they will treat Jews as a separate and evil race. If Hutus and Tutsis believe each other to be separate and evil races, great violence between the groups becomes possible. Hutus and Tutsis have been killing each other since the 1950s.[27] Physical appearance does not determine whether or not a group is believed to be racially different. People's behavior is shaped by their beliefs, not by physical appearance.

Racial Categorization

A close examination of how we place people into racial categories reveals the importance of meanings and definitions in making race. It is common for people to say that race is skin color, but in fact we do not decide people's race by the color of their skin. Skin color plays a small and inconsistent part in racial categorization. First, skin color is only one aspect of physical appearance. Hair texture, the shape of eyes, noses, and lips, and facial structure are all important parts of physical appearance used in racial categorization. Second, even when one examines all aspects of physical appearance, one sees that it is used inconsistently. In the United States, there are at least four different types of criteria used for racial categorization: physical appearance, ancestry, geography, and racialized conceptions of culture. An examination of the 2000 Census racial categories and how people classify themselves reveals the application of these four criteria.

PHYSICAL APPEARANCE

As sociologists often note, in defining racial categories, specific physical markers are selected while others are ignored. The 2000 Census defines whites as "people having origins in any of the original peoples of Europe, the Middle East, or North Africa."[28] It is possible to distinguish Scandinavians from Arabs, for example, based on physical appearance. However, these physical differences were not deemed important by the makers of the Census.[29] Differences in appearance exist among whites but they were not considered socially important in 2000.

In the early twentieth century, there were Americans who argued for distinguishing Northern Europeans from other "white" populations. In 1922, a respected journalist, Kenneth L. Roberts, wrote:

> The American nation was founded and developed by the Nordic race, but if a few more million members of the Alpine, Mediterranean and Semitic races are poured among us, the result must inevitably be a hybrid race of people as worthless and futile as the good-for-nothing mongrels of Central America and southeastern Europe.[30]

Roberts's views were simply a reflection of the eugenicist thought of the time. Harry Laughlin, the important eugenicist, argued:

> Racially the American people, if they are to remain American, . . . can successfully assimilate in the future many thousands of Northwestern European immigrants. . . . But we can assimilate only a small fraction of this number of other white races; and of the colored races practically none.[31]

The America Laughlin wishes to preserve is of the Nordic race. In 1924, the Johnson-Reed Immigration Act codified eugenicist thinking into law. The Act drastically limited immigration from Southern and Eastern Europe.[32] Some peoples, such as Greeks, Italians, and Poles, who are regarded as white today, were seen as physically and racially different in the past.

Just as the white category can be divided, it is not difficult to divide all the other 2000 Census categories based on physical appearance. Southeast Asians and Northeast Asians can be distinguished. West

Africans can be distinguished from East Africans.[33] However, physical distinctions are only made when they are socially useful. In Asia, it is more common for physical distinctions to be made within Asian populations. In Africa, it is more common for physical distinctions to be made within African populations.[34] In the United States, it is not useful to make these distinctions. Physical differences are used as a racial marker, but social groups only select the physical differences that they find socially useful. Other differences are ignored. Even with physical differences, therefore, it is ultimately social factors, not biological ones, that determine whether or not they are socially recognized.

ANCESTRY

Physical appearance is only one element in racial categorization. No system of racial categorization relies only on physical appearance. For example, for most of U.S. history, there have been black people who physically looked "white." Not only have there been hundreds of thousands of these individuals, but many of the most prominent blacks were "mostly white" in appearance. This is a consequence of ancestry being used for racial categorization in the United States. The "one-drop rule" meant that anyone with any known black ancestry or "one drop of black blood" was defined as black regardless of appearance.[35]

Arabian in Zanzibar is also a racial category based on ancestry. If one's father was defined as an Arab, then one was an Arab even if one's mother was African. Just as the "one-drop rule" produced blacks who were physically indistinguishable from whites, the ancestry rule in Zanzibar produced Arabs who were indistinguishable from Africans.[36] The same type of racial categorization found in Zanzibar also exists in the Sudan. Dunstan M. Wai writes:

> While the physical appearance of the Arabs in the Sudan tends to make them deceptively defy any racial classification, the fact is that visible signs of racial or ethnic identification are irrelevant to them. . . . What matters most is their Arab ancestry and their ability to corroborate the claim to it. Hence, though most of them have dark skin pigmentation and not quite straight hair, they feel no less Arab than their brethren in Arabia or Egypt. . . . The question of whether conspicuous racial differences are based on biological heredity or on social and cultural tradition is of no importance and relevance to most of the Arab Sudanese.[37]

Fig. 1.1. The original caption that accompanied this 1863 photograph stated, "These children were turned out of the St. Lawrence Hotel, Chestnut St., Philadelphia, on account of color." These children were black slaves traveling from New Orleans. It was not their actual physical color that blocked their entry to the hotel; it was their blackness. Blackness is not skin color or biology; it is a social definition. It is possible to look "white" physically and be black socially. The occasional "white" slave was not too surprising in the antebellum South. (Photograph by J. E. McClees/Hulton Archive/Getty Images, #3207203)

In the Sudan, ancestry, not appearance, determines race. Ancestry is not an uncommon method of racial categorization. The American Indian racial category in the United States is also defined by ancestry. Individuals of any physical appearance have been legally recognized as American Indian if they had ancestors who belonged to an American Indian nation.[38] When the ancestry of only one parent is used, physical appearance can vary widely. In these cases, ancestry counts for racial categorization and physical appearance does not.

Fig. 1.2. Walter White was the head of the civil rights organization the NAACP from 1931 to 1955. As F. James Davis has stated in *Who Is Black?* many prominent blacks have been completely or mostly "white" in appearance. In his autobiography, *A Man Called White*, Walter White tells of his father George White's experience with racism. Like Walter, George could also pass for white. After being hit by a car, George was taken to a whites-only hospital. When it was revealed by a relative that George was black, George was removed from the hospital in the middle of receiving medical treatment and sent to a dilapidated blacks-only hospital. If racial relations were driven by physical appearance, "white"-appearing blacks would be treated as whites, not as blacks. Race is not skin color. (Photograph by Carl Van Vechten/Yale Collection of American Literature, Beinecke Rare Book and Manuscript Library/reprinted by permission of the Van Vechten Trust)

GEOGRAPHY

In addition to physical appearance and ancestry, geography is also used for racial categorization. The Census Bureau defines Asians as "people having origins in any of the original peoples of the Far East, Southeast Asia, or the Indian subcontinent."[39] South Asians are Asian not because they are very similar in appearance to East Asians but because they are from what is defined as the same continent. South Asians actually look physically very different from East Asians. Many South Asians lack the eye fold which is prevalent among East Asians and have a different facial structure. South Asians tend to have more body hair than East Asians. Their skin color is often much darker than that of East Asians. In fact, some of the darkest people in the world are South Asian.[40] It is not physical appearance that places South Asians in the Asian category, but geography.

Wisely, the Census Bureau defines all its racial categories by geography and not by physical criteria. Recall, whites are defined not by skin color but as "people having origins in any of the original peoples of Europe, the Middle East, or North Africa." Black refers "to people having origins in any of the Black racial groups of Africa." American Indians are "people having origins in any of the original peoples of North and South America (including Central America), and who maintain tribal affiliation or community attachment."[41] The Census Bureau could not use skin color because within each racial category there is in fact a range of skin color. Blacks cover the entire range of human skin color from "white" to "black." The "one-drop rule" means that "whites" can be black. Since South Asians can have "black" skin, the Asian category also covers the entire range of skin color. Whites probably cover at least a third of the range of skin color since it includes populations from Northern Europe to North Africa. The fact that skin color overlaps for all racial categories means that by itself it is a completely unreliable means of categorization. By defining racial groups by geographic origins, the Census Bureau produces a far more reliable method of racial categorization.

CULTURE

The Census Bureau defines Hispanics as an ethnic group, not a racial group. However, 40 percent of Hispanics define themselves as a racial group. The majority of Americans who checked "Other race" on the

Census were Hispanic. Although the Census Bureau is correct that Hispanics vary a great deal in appearance, many Hispanics still see themselves as a race. Undoubtedly, many non-Hispanics also see Hispanics as a race. What the Census Bureau sees as a cultural category is racialized in common thinking.[42]

This idea of making a cultural category into a race is not a new development. In 1880, the U.S. Census Bureau listed "Chinese" and "Japanese" as separate racial categories,[43] although it is doubtful that Americans could tell the groups apart based on their biological characteristics. In 1930 and 1940, the Census had a racial category called "Hindu."[44] Although South Asians were "called 'Hindus' in America, only a small fraction of the Asian Indian immigrants were actually believers of Hinduism. One third were Muslim, and the majority were Sikhs."[45] "Hindu" was a racial designation, not a true cultural marker. In Nazi Germany, the cultural categories of Aryan and Jew were racial categories.[46] For many people, racial categories are also perceived as markers for cultural boundaries. It is more sociologically accurate and informative to say that race is a belief in the *embodiment* of culture[47] than that race is the recognition of differences in physical appearance.

To begin to grasp what race is we need to see that racial categorization relies on physical appearance, *and* ancestry, *and* geography, *and* racialized conceptions of culture. The U.S. system of racial categorization was patched together over time in response to social factors and it continues to change today. It blatantly disregards physical appearance for many people because biology does not determine race. Whenever biology interfered with humans' desired organization of people into races, biology was readily discarded. Human beings make races, not biology.

Ideas of Essential Difference

How people decide who belongs in the black racial category is different from their understanding of what blackness is. Racial categorization is different from people's ideas about the nature of racial differences. Ultimately, what makes a group a racial group is the *belief* that they are *essentially* different from another group. Racial essentialism means that groups are seen as possessing an essence—a natural, supernatural, or mystical characteristic—that makes them share a fundamental similarity with all members of the group and a fundamental difference from non-members. This essence is understood in racialist thinking as being immune to social forces. It does not change with time or social context. In essentialist thought, blacks in the United States share a fundamental similarity with blacks in the African nation of Malawi, for example, and blacks today share a fundamental similarity with blacks in ancient Nubia thousands of years ago.

It is important that we be aware of, and distinguish between, what can be empirically determined to be true and what people may *believe* to be true. Although people may believe that the members of a racial group are essentially the same, the fact is that aside from general human similarities racial categories contain diverse individuals and people vary culturally over time and place. However, racial relations are shaped by people's beliefs about race, not by these facts. There are no racial essences, but people believe in racial essences.

Racial essences are racial because they are passed on to offspring. Sometimes both parents need to have the same essence for it to be passed on to the child; sometimes only one; sometimes only the father or only the mother. In the racial ideology of the United States, blackness was seen as being transmitted by either black parent; in Zanzibar, Arabness could be transmitted only by the father. Because race is an essence, an invisible inner characteristic, one does not have to look a particular way to be of a particular race. One only needs to possess that essence.

Essentialism should not be reduced to mean only biological essentialism or beliefs about genes. Religious ideas have been a source for racial essentialism. In Genesis 9 and 10, Noah curses Canaan, the son of Ham, and proclaims that Canaan would be "servant of servants." Jewish religious texts state that Noah told Ham "your seed will be ugly and dark-skinned," and that Canaan, son of Ham, "was cursed" and "darkened the faces of mankind."[48] This "Curse of Ham" has been used to define blacks as the descendants of Canaan, as essentially different from whites, and to justify racial slavery from the seventeenth to the nineteenth centuries.[49]

Religious understandings of racial difference need not be as textually specific as the "Curse of Ham." In the 1970s, a white respondent told an interviewer that blacks were the way they were because "That's how God made them." The respondent added, "Well, it goes back to the Bible, where the good angels were colored white, whereas the devil is black. Black was related to evil."[50] Some people who are religious may simply assume that since God made the world, racial categories are God's will.

White supremacists use interpretations of the Bible espoused by the Christian Identity Movement to justify their racial theories. The Christian Identity Movement argues that "Jews are the descendants of Satan, and white Anglo-Saxons are the true Israelites, God's chosen people."[51] The idea that God made racial differences has been a common basis for racial essentialism resting not on biology but on theology.

Cultural ideas have also been a basis for racial essentialism. Sociologically, one's culture is a product of one's social context. If a child is raised among Americans, she will be culturally American; if she is raised among the Chinese, she will be culturally Chinese. On the other hand, as Mary Waters writes, "The common view among Americans is that ethnicity is primordial, a personal, inherited characteristic like hair color."[52] It is common for people to think about culture in essentialist ways. If an American couple adopts a Chinese baby, they may think that they have to expose the child to Chinese culture because at some level Chinese is the "true" culture of that child even though it is completely ignorant of Chinese culture. Chinese is the child's "true" culture not sociologically through socialization but *essentially*, through a biological understanding of cultural inheritance.[53]

Racial ideologies about essential difference have been based on religious ideas and essentialist notions of culture in addition to pseudobiological theories. In the history of racial relations in the United States, biological essentialism actually has the shortest history. William Julius Wilson provides a useful summary of this history:

> Ideologies justifying forms of racial exploitation in both South Africa and the United States have shifted back and forth from cultural to biological racist arguments. In the seventeenth and eighteenth centuries in the United States, the "rationale" for racial domination was primarily belief in black cultural inferiority but was replaced by biological racist arguments in the nineteenth and early twentieth centuries. As the United States entered the latter third of the twentieth century, biological racism declined and was supplanted by cultural racism.[54]

The earliest form of racial essentialism, the essentialism on which slavery rested, was religious and cultural. Winthrop Jordan observes that

"Christian," "free," "English," and "white" were used as synonyms in the late seventeenth century.[55] He adds:

> The term *Christian* itself proved to have remarkable elasticity, for by the end of the seventeenth century it was being used to define a species of slavery which had altogether lost any connection with explicit religious difference. In the Virginia code of 1705, for example, the term sounded much more like a definition of race than of religion.[56]

In the late seventeenth and early eighteenth centuries, the term "Christian" did not merely sound like a racial term; it *was* a racial term. It was not based on individuals' actual religious practices. "Christians" were whites.

Biological essentialism only became important around the end of slavery. By the mid-twentieth century, biological essentialism had declined in popularity and cultural essentialism was again the way many people explained racial differences.[57] While cultural essentialism may have been less popular during the nineteenth and early twentieth centuries, it is doubtful that the form died completely. A study of how Americans explained racial differences in the 1970s found three modes of essentialist thinking: biological, supernatural, and cultural. (There were also many Americans who did not employ essentialist ideas to explain racial difference.)[58] The earliest essentialist ideas about racial difference were supernatural and cultural. Biological essentialism developed in the nineteenth century. Today, all three modes continue to exist.

Racial Stereotypes

Defining race by physical appearance directs our attention away from the many important nonbiological aspects of race. As stated previously, racial categories are defined not only by physical appearance but also by ancestry, geography, and an essentialist notion of culture. People's understanding of why races are different can rest on theological and cultural ideas, in addition to biological ones. Perhaps the sociologically most important aspect of racial ideology—racial stereotypes—is not mainly about physical appearance. Racial stereotypes are the basis for racial discrimination.

Much of the sociological power of race rests in the biological, psychological, and cultural stereotypes about racial groups. The biological stereotypes referred to here are not the characteristics used for racial categorization or for the essentialist explanations of racial difference. A white manager in the 1950s, for example, remarked that blacks were excellent "for work . . . that requires stamina and brawn—and little else."[59] This manager had a biological stereotype of blacks, namely, that they were strong; and he had a psychological stereotype of blacks, that they were stupid. He would probably have hired blacks for the simplest manual labor but not for work that required intellectual ability. Stereotypes such as these would help account for differences between blacks and whites in the economy.

It is important to realize that the manager did not say that he disliked dark-skinned workers or that he liked light-skinned ones. Racial relations are not a simple dynamic of attraction to, or repulsion from, physical appearance. In this example, the racial stereotypes would have made this manager seek out blacks for some work and reject them for other types of work. Similar stereotypes about blacks' athletic ability may help them to be selected to play particular sports while at the same time hindering them from becoming coaches and managers of teams playing those same sports. Racial stereotypes collectively can be simultaneously inclusionary for some social positions and relationships and exclusionary for others.[60]

To say that one group looks different from another does not make a race. If I say that the members of Group A are taller than those of Group B, I am not defining racial groups. I am just describing the natural world. If I am able to popularize stereotypes about tall people, then I am on the way to making a race. (One of the racial markers that supposedly distinguish Hutus from Tutsis is height.)[61] A physical description alone is simply a physical description. Stereotypes attached to bodies are justifications for differential treatment. Biological, psychological, or cultural stereotypes are necessary to make a race.

In white supremacist racial ideology, Jews are stereotyped as desiring to dominate, exploit, and destroy whites. If people believe this about Jews, they will be inclined to discriminate against Jews or even work for their extermination. The fact that Jews are not physically distinguishable from non-Jews is of no significance. If people believe the negative stereotypes about Jews, they will make an artificial marker—a yellow star, for example—to identify Jews by sight, if they feel this to be necessary. Stereotyping is necessary for making races but physical differences are not.

Race is socially constructed in part by ideas of essential and heritable difference. Racial categories can be defined by physical appearance, ancestry, geography, and an essentialist notion of culture. In racialist thinking, people understand racial differences as emerging from biological processes, as ordained by God, or as a manifestation of an essential cultural difference. People do mix and combine these different modes of explaining racial difference.[62] In racialist thinking, racial groups are stereotyped as possessing different biological, psychological, and cultural characteristics. Racial discrimination is based upon these ideas of inherent biological, psychological, and cultural difference. The fact that these ideas are false is of little consequence for understanding social relations, because "If men define situations as real then they will be real in their consequences [for men's behavior]."[63] The patterns of human behavior that follow from racial ideologies create a social reality.

Three Dimensions of Race

While racial ideology is necessary for people to begin thinking in terms of race, political and economic conditions set the stage in which racial ideologies become useful to develop. Peoples who differ in appearance can interact without the idea of race developing. When Africans, Middle Easterners, and Europeans interacted in the ancient Mediterranean world, they did not develop a race concept.[64] When American Indians first encountered Europeans and Africans, American Indians did not develop a race concept.[65] Nor did Europeans and Asians develop such a concept when they encountered each other in ancient Central Asia.[66] Even in the American colonies, race did not develop immediately. For the first two generations, Africans and Europeans were able to interact as equals. There were class and other inequalities, but not racial inequality.[67] Race was developed subsequently as a means of solving the problem of a labor shortage and of justifying differential treatment of African laborers from European laborers.[68] However, once racial thinking exists, it becomes a social force on its own.

Race is a multidimensional phenomenon. It has at least three dimensions: racial ideology, racial identity, and racial social structures or racial structures. These three dimensions refer to the cultural, psychological, and social structural aspects of race respectively.

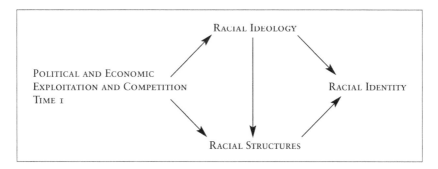

Fig. 1.3. A Field Context of Racial Relations, Part 1

Figure 1.3 is a simple model of the relationship of the political and economic context and the three dimensions of race.[69] It delineates a situation where political and economic exploitation or competition leads to the development of racial ideologies and racial structures. Racial ideology encompasses all the associated meanings and definitions around race. This includes the essential ideas of racial difference, the ideas about racial categorization, the racial stereotypes, and any other racial ideas. In other words, racial ideology refers to all the cultural ideas about race.

Racial structures refer to the practices of racial discrimination, racial organizations, and racial institutions. Racial structures can refer to social structures which are explicitly racial, as were many Jim Crow practices, organizations, and institutions, or to social structures which are racialized because, while not overtly racial, they have underlying racial logics and discriminatory effects. Racial inequality is often the direct result of the racial structures in a society.

Living in a society with racial ideologies and racial structures often leads people to develop racial identities. Identity provides an answer to the question, "Who am I?" Racial identity is as much social as it is individual because it also answers the questions, "Who is like me?" "Who is not like me?" and "To which group do I and don't I belong?" People come to think of themselves as members of a racial group and to see others as such. Racial identity refers to the psychological dimension of race.

Mere contact between groups who differ in appearance does not produce race. A fully developed racial formation requires racial ideology, racial structure, and racial identity. A philosopher or scientist may write a racist tract, but a text does not create race. If the ideas of the racist tract come to be embraced by members of a group, a racial ideology is created. If members of a group begin to treat people differently or live their lives differently based on the tract, then a racial structure has formed. If the members of the group begin to think of themselves in terms of the racial categories of the tract, then racial identities have formed and a full racial formation has been established. The pinnacle of all racial formation is the racial state. Adolf Hitler did not create races when he wrote *Mein Kampf*, but he did create races through his leadership of Nazi Germany. Nazi Germany was a racial state.[70]

The model I have presented in Figure 1.3 is actually too simple. The relationships between all the elements are more complicated. Each arrow should be two-headed, and each element should directly point to each other element.[71] This overdetermination accounts for the durability of racial conflict. One can, for example, effectively diminish biological theories of racial difference (racial ideology), but when people with strong racial identities see racial inequality (racial structures) and develop explanations for why it exists, they are likely to develop new cultural theories of racial difference. The existence of the other dimensions can help re-create or reinforce a weakened dimension. This is not to say that ultimately race cannot be unmade. It is just difficult to do so, and it requires sustained effort.

Once race comes into existence, it develops a life of its own. In a society where there is racial inequality, where people have racial identities, and where people believe in racial ideologies, the ingredients for continuing political and economic conflict exist even if the original political and economic conditions that created race have changed significantly. For example, although the need for slave labor was important to the development of race in the United States, once race was part of American society it continued to shape social relations even after the need for slave labor had passed. Figure 1.4 illustrates these relationships.

Race is sociohistorical because ultimately it is not about physical appearance. Blackness is about meanings and definitions, and about social practices and social identities informed by those ideas. The meanings and definitions of blackness change over time and from place to place. The racial structures that restrict and shape black social life change with time and place. Black people's identities change with time and place because their sense of who they are similar to, and who they are different from, changes. Thus, blackness has a sociohistory.

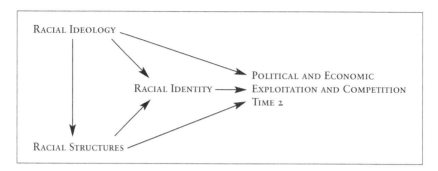

Fig. 1.4. A Field Context of Racial Relations, Part 2

This study focuses primarily on racial ideologies of blackness as articulated by black nationalist movements from the 1930s to the end of the twentieth century. Its secondary focus is on the effects of these ideologies on racial identities and racial structures. I will repeatedly turn to how these racial ideologies were incorporated into schools as one structural manifestation of race.

While scholars usually examine variations in racial meanings and definitions by examining different societies, there are also important variations in meanings and definitions within the United States. Some scholars have noted that there have been regional variations in the racial formation of the United States.[72] There are even more complex variations. Whether Hispanic is seen as a race or not (and whether Latino is seen as the only acceptable term for the group) varies in complex ways in American society.[73] White supremacist movements in the United States cannot be understood by assuming that they see "white" Jews as white, although most other Americans do. It is important to examine the variations in the meaning of race within societies as well as those between societies.

In all the case studies presented, although the emphasis is on racial ideology, I will move back and forth between racial ideology, racial structures, and racial identities. In chapter 2, I will show how the Nation of Islam's Asiatic conception of blackness did not use physical appearance as a means of categorizing individuals. This racial ideology also changed the racial identity of the members of the Nation of Islam. They saw themselves as belonging to the same racial group as people from the Middle East and Asia.

Chapters 3 and 4 address the racial structural concerns of the Black Power movement. In examining the Black Power movement I show that racial stereotypes are not merely attempts at description; they are also prescriptive. During the Black Power era, activists made new assertions about what "Black" people, as distinct from "Negroes," are like. These racial stereotypes became new norms for blackness which directed how black people should behave. Black Power activists were interested in changing not only black people's more personal, social behavior, but their political and economic behavior as well.

Chapters 5 and 6 examine Afrocentrism and the Afrocentric-era black nationalism of the 1980s and 1990s. Afrocentric scholars use essentialist ideas of cultural—not biological—difference between Africans and Europeans to define blackness and whiteness. Afrocentric ideology is an important example of nonbiological racialization. Some people assume that because black nationalists are capable of offending whites, black nationalist politics is a radical, progressive politics. When we examine Afrocentric-era black nationalism carefully, we see that it was both racially and politically conservative. Some of the largest black nationalist movements of the twentieth century have been racially and politically conservative.[74]

Chapters 7 and 8 are concluding chapters. Chapter 7 describes some of the broad patterns of change in black nationalism in the latter half of the twentieth century. I examine black nationalist attitudes in the general black public to show that black nationalism does not represent the political consciousness of the black lower class. I also continue to show that the Afrocentric era of the 1980s and 1990s is an important era in the history of black nationalism in America. Chapter 8 continues to examine the race concept. We see that the race-as-biology and ethnicity-as-culture perspective among social scientists is untenable. Race is not about biology, and ethnicity is not about culture.

Black Nationalism in the Twentieth Century

The term black nationalism is applied to a wide range of phenomena. John H. Bracey, Jr., August Meier, and Elliott Rudwick define black nationalism as "a body of social thought, attitudes, and actions ranging from the simplest expressions of ethnocentrism and racial solidarity to Pan-Negroism or Pan-Africanism." They add that "between these extremes lie many varieties of black nationalism, of varying degrees of intensity."[75] Black nationalist sentiments or activism can be directed to different areas of social life. Black nationalists in the nineteenth and early twentieth centuries worked toward creating or relocating to a separate black nation. Other twentieth-century black nationalists worked toward establishing black control of organizations and institutions that served black communities, but were less interested in a separate nation for black Americans. Some artists, intellectuals, and other activists give primacy to asserting and celebrating black cultural difference over more political concerns. Important work has been done on black nationalist sentiments in black public opinion. Black nationalism in American life ranges from nation-building to ethnic politics to cultural nationalism to public opinion.[76]

To capture this range, a conception of black nationalism has to have some breadth. Of course, scholars also need to be clear that nation-building is not cultural nationalism and activism is not public opinion. Once these points are kept in mind, the extent of black nationalism in American life can be appreciated without misconstruing its social significance. This range of forms and arenas for black nationalism is fairly typical for a minority nationalist movement within a state. Québécois nationalists, for example, have struggled for a separate state (nation-building), for more power for the Québécois *within* Canada (ethnic politics), and for the preservation of the French language in Québec (cultural nationalism).[77]

In addition to exploring racial ideologies of blackness, this study also examines issues and debates in the study of black nationalism in the twentieth century. In chapter 2, we will see that while the Nation of Islam was antiwhite, it was not problack, as is commonly assumed. The Asiatic blackness the Nation of Islam articulated was a shift of identity away from Africa and toward the Middle East. Therefore the Nation of Islam should not be seen as a Pan-Africanist organization, as some scholars have argued. In chapter 4, I make clear that the differences between "cultural" black nationalists and "revolutionary" black nationalists in the Black Power era have been greatly exaggerated. If one's understanding of the "cultural" black nationalism of Black Power is based on sources other than Black Panther Party propaganda, one sees that "cultural" nationalists and "revolutionary" nationalists were more similar than different. In chapter 5, we see that Afrocentrism is rooted in American social thought. It was shaped positively and negatively by the conservative ideologies of the 1980s and 1990s. It is too often assumed that the black lower class is black nationalist. In chapter 7, I show that this is incorrect. In fact, the 1990s were notable for the strong support of black nationalism among the black middle and upper classes. Across the history of black nationalism in the twentieth century, the more explicitly political black nationalist concerns have declined over the twentieth century, while the cultural concerns have increased.

2

Asiatic Identity in the Nation of Islam

When a detective asked Ugan Ali, an official in the Nation of Islam in 1932, whether he had "taught a colored man named Robert Harris or Robert Karriem," Ali shouted, "We are not colored—nobody colored us! We are Asiatic!"[1] From 1930 to 1975, thousands of black Americans entered an organization called the Nation of Islam and were transformed into members of the Asiatic race, a people who traced their origins back to Mecca, Saudi Arabia.

To understand this Asiatic racial identity, we have to be able to see racial identities as social products and not as something determined by biology. Just as the "black-looking" Kizimkazis did not have black identities, the "black-looking" members of the Nation of Islam did not have black identities either. They had an Asiatic identity based on an essentialist idea of religion. Members of the Nation of Islam believed that their ancestors were Muslims from the Middle East and that their true religion was Islam. They also believed that this heritable essence made them fundamentally and permanently different from whites who by nature could not be Muslims. This belief in an essential religious difference therefore created a racial boundary.

Racial categorization based on religion or culture is not unusual.[2] When racial slavery began in the American colonies in the late seventeenth century, "Christian" became a racial term for white. "Christian" referred to a racial essence, not an observable practice, because blacks were increasingly practicing Christianity.[3] In 1930 and 1940, the U.S. Census Bureau used "Hindu" as a term for South Asians, regardless of religion.[4] The Nazi regime made the cultural and religious terms Aryan and Jew into racial terms. In the United States today, many Latinos and non-Latinos consider Latinos to be a race and not simply a cutural category. The last two examples are particularly important because the cultural or religious term does not refer to a particular physical appearance, as is the case with the term Asiatic. Religion and culture can be believed to be heritable essences.

By emphasizing physical appearance, the current sociological conception of race prevents us from seeing the possibilities for common racial identities in spite of differences in physical appearance. It also leads us away from examining the power of racial ideologies and racial identities to produce cultural differences. The assumption that black Americans could only have black racial identities has led to a misunderstanding of the Nation of Islam. Many scholars define the organization as Pan-African,[5] as seeking greater identification and unity with Africa, when in fact the organization faced toward Mecca, not Africa.

Studying the "First" Organization

The name "Nation of Islam" refers to two separate organizations.[6] The "first" Nation of Islam was founded in 1930 and existed until 1975.[7] The "second" Nation of Islam was established in 1978 and is led by Minister Louis Farrakhan. Although Farrakhan reclaimed much from the original Nation of Islam, over time he has moved the organization toward a more orthodox Islam in terms of its ideology and practices.[8] These transformations culminated in Farrakhan officially renouncing the racial ideology of the "first" Nation of Islam.[9] The following discussion and analysis deals with the "first" Nation of Islam.

The characterization of the Nation of Islam presented here is based on its central teachings. It would be incorrect to assume that every member of the organization believed exactly the same thing and had a single motivation for joining the Nation of Islam. Like any large organization, we should expect a degree of complexity. Not every Catholic, for example, believes and follows all the teachings of Catholicism.[10] To understand the Catholic Church, however, one must understand the teachings of Catholicism. Also, a number of nonreligious factors may strongly influence whether one is involved in a church,[11] but religious factors may also play an important part for many. As in any other faith, one should expect to find a variety of beliefs, practices, and motivations among the members of the Nation of Islam. But it would be incorrect to conclude that the central religious teachings are of no consequence. The emphasis in this chapter is on the religious teachings of the organization and not on detailing differences between individuals in the organization.

The Nation of Islam was *not* founded by a black American, although all its other members were black Americans. Although the Nation of Islam hid and distorted the background of its founder, Fard Muhammad, he was never said to be of African descent. Fard Muhammad's father was Pakistani and his mother was a white New Zealander.[12] In the theology of the Nation of Islam, Fard Muhammad was said to be the incarnation of Allah and from Mecca, Saudi Arabia. These facts are the first serious problems for the idea that the organization was Pan-Africanist and problack in a conventional sense. The founder and Allah both point members to the Middle East, not to Africa.

Elijah Muhammad, a black American, was the direct disciple of Fard Muhammad. In 1934, Elijah Muhammad became the leader of the Nation of Islam and the "Messenger of Allah."[13] The organization Elijah Muhammad built was a rigid, hierarchical, "military theocracy." As "Messenger of Allah," Elijah Muhammad's teachings were treated as the word of God.[14] The organization did not hesitate to punish members who did not rigidly follow the teachings and commands of Elijah

Fig. 2.1. Fard Muhammad was the founder of the Nation of Islam and, according to the teachings of the Nation of Islam, the incarnation of Allah. Although Fard Muhammad had no African ancestry and could pass for white, in the racial ideology of the Nation of Islam, he was of the same race as black Americans—Asiatic. Fard Muhammad did not create an organization which relied on a conventional American definition of blackness because such an organization would have had to exclude him as a person without African ancestry. ("The Savior," *Muhammad Speaks*, 16 August 1963, p. 14. Reprinted by permission of *Muslim Journal*.)

Muhammad out of religious devotion. There have also been allegations that the organization physically assaulted and even assassinated individuals who were believed to pose a serious threat.[15] For most members, however, Elijah Muhammad's words were gospel. The racial teachings of Elijah Muhammad cannot be regarded as merely one viewpoint in the Nation of Islam. They were the ideology of the organization itself.

Racial Ideology

The idea that black Americans are Asiatics was central to the religious teachings of the Nation of Islam. Elijah Muhammad told black Americans, "You are not a Negro. You are members of the Asiatic Nation, from the Tribe of Shabazz. There is no such thing as a race of Negroes."[16] The first catechism lesson an initiate into the Nation learned was the answer to the question "Who is the Original Man?" Initiates recited, "The Original Man is the Asiatic Black Man, the Maker, the Owner, Cream of the Planet Earth, and God of the Universe."[17] They also learned that the members of the "Original Nation" in the United States included American Indians and, globally, all people of color.[18]

According to the theology of the Nation of Islam, humanity is divided into two races: whites and Asiatics. Whites are people of Western European descent and Asiatics are everyone else. As Asiatics, black Americans are descendants of "the Original Man," a race of Asiatic god-scientists known as the Tribe of Shabazz who lived in the Nile Valley of Egypt and Mecca, Saudi Arabia.[19] According to the Nation of Islam, Asiatics are Muslim by nature; their original language is Arabic; and their original home, Mecca.[20]

Although Fard Muhammad was said to be Arab and could pass for white, he was seen as "a member of the black nation" and as "racially identical" to black Americans.[21] The fact that American Indians and Arabs were presented as being of the same race as black Americans indicates that the Nation of Islam's notions of race differed from those of most other Americans. The term "black" was used in two ways: "black" could refer to all nonwhites, that is, Asiatics, or it could refer specifically to a black race in the more conventional American sense. For example, Elijah Muhammad would teach that "the Truth of the white race and kind will make all *black* mankind hate them, regardless of their color—*black*, brown, yellow or red,"[22] or that "if you are a so-called Negro or red, or *black* or an Indian or any member of the aboriginal *Black* Nation you are an un-American."[23] In both these examples, "black" is used as a designation for skin color *and* for a notion of race that includes all non–Western Europeans.

Nor was white defined simply in terms of skin color or physical appearance. Fard Muhammad was "white" in terms of physical appearance but he was part of the Asiatic Black Nation. Many, if not most, Middle Eastern Muslims look "white,"[24] but they are still Asiatic. Asiatic was not defined fundamentally by any physical criteria. A person of any physical description can be Asiatic. Just as someone can look "white" and yet still be black, someone can look "white" and be Asiatic. On more than one occasion, Elijah Muhammad indicated that the peoples of Eastern European nations that had long histories of Islamic influence were Asiatics.[25]

The difference between the racial meanings and definitions of the Nation of Islam and those of the general American public has caused the organization to be misunderstood. Even C. Eric Lincoln, an important scholar of the Nation, failed to understand why members of the Nation objected to his book, *The Black Muslims in America*. The book popularized the term "Black Muslims." For two years, the most prominent Minister in the Nation of Islam, Malcolm X, attempted to squelch the term.[26] Members of the Nation never referred to themselves as "Black Muslims" and that label does not make sense within their ideology. "Black Muslim" is problematic for several reasons. Its least offensive reading made it redundant since only "Black" people —Asiatic blacks—could be Muslims according to their theology. A more disturbing interpretation suggested that the members of the Nation of Islam were different from other Muslims. Because the organization saw itself as part of the world community of Islam,[27] this idea was unacceptable. The term also implies that whites can be Muslims, which was highly offensive to the Nation, being in direct conflict with its theology.

Members of the Nation of Islam were also upset at Lincoln's characterization of the organization as a type of social protest organization.[28] As the name Nation of *Islam* suggests, the primary identity of the organization was religious. The organization was apolitical in that, in spite of its militant rhetoric, it waited for Allah to bring about social change. Elijah Muhammad prophesied that Allah would destroy America. Therefore he could argue:

Allah is sufficient for all our needs. This is why I do not have to beg
from our oppressors or march on their Capitol with my hat in my hand.
For how can I on one hand preach the doom of the oppressive system
and then with the other hand ask alms of the oppressor.[29]

Justice, he argued, would come to black Americans "only through Divine and not through civil government."[30] Although the Nation engaged
in a range of nonreligious activities, religion was central to the organization.

Although Africans were Asiatics, the Nation of Islam clearly privileged Arabia over Africa. The early teachings of the Nation of Islam
presented Africa as a part of Asia and argued that the name "Africa"
was a tool used by whites to divide people of color.[31] Africa was clearly
part of the Asiatic world, but Mecca was the privileged location within
the Nation's religious teachings.[32] Elijah Muhammad instructed his followers that Mecca was "the ONLY HOLY SPOT on our planet."[33] While
the centrality of Mecca is merely part of being a Muslim, in other ways
Arabia was privileged.

The Original People were said to look like Arabs or South Asians
and those Original People who moved into Africa were said to have
declined in their level of civilization.[34] As a minister for the Nation
of Islam, Malcolm X taught that before the Original People "wan-
dered down into the jungles of Africa," their "hair [was] like silk, and
originally all our people had that kind of hair." He explained that after
living in the jungles of Africa, "our hair became stiff, like it is now,"
and "we undertook new features that we have now."[35] Master Fard
Muhammad saw Africans as a people who had "strayed away from civilization and are living a jungle life."[36]

Africans were considered to be less civilized than the Original People,
but they were still Asiatics and still superior to whites. The Nation of
Islam taught that white people were genetically engineered by Yakub,
an evil member of the Tribe of Shabazz, to rule the Earth for six thousand years. The white race was seen as inherently evil and inferior. After
being expelled from Mecca and deprived of the superior Muslim civilization, some of these whites evolved into apes. Members of the Nation
believed that, in time, white civilization would be destroyed by the
Mother Plane—a giant circular plane—built by Allah in Japan.[37]

The Nation of Islam's racial ideology rested on an essentialist idea of
religion. What distinguished Asiatics from whites was not appearance

but the belief that Asiatics were Muslims by nature. Elijah Muhammad recognized differences in people's appearance, but "black, brown, yellow or red" people were all members of the Asiatic Black Nation, *a single racial category*. Even physically "white" people like Fard Muhammad, "white" Middle Easterners, and "white" Eastern Europeans could be Asiatic. Although Asiatics were Muslim by nature, fear and deception by whites and religions started by heretical nonwhites caused some Asiatics to forget their Muslim nature, Muhammad argued.[38]

In essentialist thinking, forgetting that one is a Muslim is quite different from not being a Muslim. White people cannot be Muslims even if they try because they are not Muslims by nature.[39] Blacks are "truly" Muslim even if they practice another religion. Black Americans' "true" religion was something they had inherited from their ancestors, the Tribe of Shabazz, irrespective of whether blacks practiced Christianity or some other non-Islamic religion. Although one's practices should conform to one's racial essence, the essence is believed to exist even if there are no externally observable indicators of it.

Asiatic Culture and Identity

The point of racial categorization is never simply about making physical distinctions, even when the categories are defined strongly by physical appearance. Racial categories are perceived to be socially useful because races are believed to differ on socially relevant criteria. Races are stereotyped as having important and permanent differences in physical abilities, "culture and character."[40] Although racial stereotypes are supposed to be merely descriptive of racial characteristics, they can also function like self-fulfilling prophesies. Groups can work to become their stereotype.

Identity can produce stereotypical cultural behavior. For example, a born-again Christian, upon taking a new, strong Christian identity, may begin watching Christian television, listening to Christian music, and shopping in Christian bookstores. The cultural behavior follows the adoption of the identity. Racially, a black American who begins to associate blackness with being African may adopt an African name and African clothing, and build African rituals and customs into her life. In the Nation of Islam, members worked to incorporate Asiatic culture into their lives to match their Asiatic racial identities. Racial identities can foster the production and development of a stereotypical racial culture.[41]

Asiatic culture was formally and informally part of the life of the Nation of Islam. An Asiatic racial identity mainly meant the adoption of Arab and Islamic culture. In lesser, but still significant ways, the remainder of the Asiatic world was also incorporated. There were aspects of Arab culture that were mandatory but individual members also worked to create and imbibe Arab and non-Arab Asiatic culture themselves.

The most important cultural practice was Islam. Islam in the Nation of Islam was an idiosyncratic mixture of ideas from orthodox Islam, Christianity, and other sources. But Louis Lomax argues that the fact that Elijah Muhammad was allowed to make the hajj "must be accepted as the final verdict" on the status of the organization as a sect of Islam.[42] Many other scholars also agree that the organization was a sect of Islam, albeit a highly unorthodox one.[43] Over its history, the organization slowly adopted orthodox Islamic practices. In the 1950s, Elijah Muhammad encouraged his followers to read the Holy Qur'an and to pray five times a day.[44] In 1959, Muhammad made a pilgrimage to Mecca. On his return, he renamed his "temples," "mosques." In 1970, he instructed members of the Nation to observe Ramadan according to the Islamic calendar.[45] Orthodox practices were allowed only if they did not contradict the original teachings of Fard Muhammad.[46] However unorthodox, the Nation of Islam always saw itself as part of the Islamic world.

Arabic, as the "original language," had a prominent place in the Nation of Islam. Members of the Nation of Islam always greeted each other with the Arabic phrase "As-salaam alaikum" (peace be unto you) and were greeted in return by "Wa-alaikum salaam" (and unto you be peace). The opening prayers of meetings were often said in Arabic and followers would face east toward Mecca. Most adults knew little Arabic beyond the greeting, but the Nation worked to change this situation by having Arabic taught in its schools. After proving themselves within the Nation, followers would lose their "X," which replaced their "slave" name, and gain an Arabic name.[47]

Dietary practices also reflected the Asiatic identity. In accordance with Islamic law, members of the Nation of Islam were required to abstain from pork. Beyond this, a wide variety of foods were forbidden, including black American "soul food" such as collard greens, black-eyed peas, cornbread, and catfish.[48] When Nation members chose to eat

SHABAZZ **Restaurant & Bakery**
WE SERVE ASIATIC STYLE and AMERICAN COOKED FOOD
HOME OF THE ORIGINAL BEAN PIE
12434 SUPERIOR AVENUE
CLEVELAND OHIO
PHONE 681-9841

Figs. 2.2 & 2.3. In 1971, when the Salaam Restaurant advertisement was originally published, Black Power activists were increasingly adopting African names, clothing, and traditions to assert their new African identities. The Nation of Islam, however, continued to celebrate the Arab identity of their restaurant and chef. In 1972, the Shabazz Restaurant continued to make clear that the Nation of Islam is an Asiatic—not a Pan-African—organization. (*Muhammad Speaks*, 1 January 1971, p. 12 and 4 February 1972, p. 27. Reprinted by permission of *Muslim Journal*.)

out, they would most often go to restaurants owned by the Nation. In the 1970s, the Nation's Salaam Restaurant in Chicago advertised that in their restaurant one could "enjoy our authentic Arabian cuisine prepared by our Arabian chef in the splendor of the Crescent Room."[49] The Shabazz Restaurant and Bakery in Cleveland boasted "Asiatic Style" food.[50] When members of the Nation of Islam did not go to restaurants affiliated with the Nation, they often went to Chinese restaurants, their Asiatic kin.[51]

The newspaper of the Nation of Islam, *Muhammad Speaks*, reinforced an Asiatic orientation among Nation members. All adult males in the Nation of Islam were required to sell the paper.[52] The paper could be found in all members' homes. *Muhammad Speaks* was also used as a source of current events in the Nation's schools and required reading for teachers in the schools.[53] The paper placed special emphasis on the news of the nonwhite world. As the editors of *Muhammad Speaks* stated, they made a point "of bringing to our readers African-Asian news of significance."[54] One way they did this was by publishing a "series of articles dealing with China and its relationship to Africa."[55] Cartoons printed within *Muhammad Speaks* made fun of black American Christians who did not wish to identify with the "black" nations of Africa *and* Asia. Although the newspaper covered Africa and Asia generally, it paid particular attention to Islam in Africa and Asia. *Muhammad Speaks* published articles such as "Islam Broke Christianity's Iron Grip on African Life"[56] and featured photos of mosques in Africa.[57] The paper also ran a number of articles on Muslims in China.[58] The focus on Islam in Africa and China indicates a strong Islamic identity— not a Pan-African one.

Many of the editors and writers for *Muhammad Speaks* were not members of the Nation of Islam but were black leftists. Some analysts, therefore, see the paper as a voice for an anticolonialist leftist politics. While there is some truth to this perspective, *Muhammad Speaks* was also a voice for the conservative, Asiatic Nation of Islam. Elijah Muhammad may have allowed editors a degree of freedom, but it was clear that he was the ultimate authority. The paper was required to devote a certain amount of space to religious and Nation of Islam news. The opposition to European colonialism expressed by black leftists in the paper fit comfortably with the Nation's teachings. The Nation could, of course, celebrate the defeat of whites by Asiatics. Both the anticolonial and religious articles could be assimilated into an Asiatic interpretation, but the religious articles do not fit comfortably into an anticolonial interpretation. The attacks on black Christians and civil rights activists, the celebration of Islam over Christianity in Africa, and the detailed discussion of Islam in China make sense to an Asiatic reader, but they go against the class-based unity among people of color encouraged by black leftists.[59]

In addition to the Asian and African themes, *Muhammad Speaks* printed articles about other people of color when they were available. Letters by a Mexican American and an American Indian who were inspired by the Nation's teachings were printed as articles in the paper.[60] *Muhammad Speaks* reinforced Nation members' sense of connection with the Asiatic world.

Members of the Nation of Islam took this Asiatic identity to heart. During the 1930s, in a discussion of home furnishings, a member told a sociologist that "when [black Americans] go home to Mecca, we will be able to get really good furniture, just like all our people who live there use."[61] In the 1930s, Fard Muhammad used the promise of returning blacks to the Paradise of Mecca to bring blacks into the organization.[62] In 1950, Hatim Sahib found that Nation members would do their best

Figs. 2.4 & 2.5. These are just two of several cartoons asserting the racial sameness of Africans and Asians. According to the teachings of the Nation of Islam, Africans and Asians were all members of an Asiatic race. The only people who were not Asiatic were whites. (*Muhammad Speaks*, "Brotherhood of Black Nations" cartoon, 25 November 1966, 14, and "Confusion in America" cartoon, 24 February 1967, 14. Reprinted by permission of *Muslim Journal*.)

34

to study the Qur'an, learn Arabic, and consume whatever they could of Arab culture. Sahib observed that "some of the members keep Arabic records in their homes and enjoy listening to them. In their rooms they keep some of the scenes and pictures of Arabian or Islamic buildings or life. In the home of each member is a big picture of the national or some other board on which the name of Allah is written in the Arabic language."[63] "The national" that Sahib refers to is the flag of the Nation of Islam, which is a modification of the Turkish flag.[64]

Members of the Nation truly believed that they were Asiatic, as the writer Peter Abrahams discovered. In 1960, he observed that a woman whom he had at first identified as black had a very different racial identity. Abrahams came to realize:

Emotionally, psychologically, this woman has been transformed from an American Negro and all that this means, to an Arab and all that that means. As I listened to her it became clear to me that there was absolutely no room for doubt in her own mind. She was an Arab.[65]

When asked to indicate their race on official documents, members of the Nation listed "Asiatic." Essien-Udom encountered a member of the Nation who listed "Asiatic" for his race and "Muslim" for his nationality on a college application.[66] Malcolm X also listed "Asiatic" as his race on his draft card.[67]

The Asiatic identity of Dr. Leo P. McCallum led him to travel to Egypt, Kenya, Nigeria, Pakistan, India, Hong Kong, and Tokyo. Dr. McCallum stated that "were it not for the identity-giving doctrine of [Elijah Muhammad]," he "would [have] undoubtedly followed the tourist lanes of the white man into Europe and the like—into countries and areas which are neither *mine* nor occupied by *my own kind*."[68] Elijah Muhammad's teachings were successful in having Dr. McCallum, a black American, see the people of India, Hong Kong, and Tokyo as "his own kind."[69]

The Asiatic identities of the members of the Nation of Islam led them to build more aspects of their "true" Asiatic culture into their lives beyond the formal requirements of the organization. They rejected "soul food" for Asiatic cuisine. They celebrated the successes of Islam in Africa *and* Asia and saw South Asians and East Asians as their racial brethren.

Asiatic Relations

Although the Nation's theology professed unity and harmony among all Asiatics,[70] the actual dealings between members of the Nation and with other Asiatics were more complicated. Interaction with orthodox Muslims often highlighted to members just how different Fard Muhammad and Elijah Muhammad's teachings were from orthodox Islam.[71] However, in many cases the Nation was able to surmount sectarian differences because it was sincerely dedicated to being part of the Islamic world.

Aside from Fard Muhammad, other nonblacks have had close relationships with the Nation of Islam. One prominent individual was Satokata Takahashi, a Japanese nationalist who was able to kindle pro-Japanese sentiments among a number of black nationalist and religious organizations in the 1930s and 1940s. For these organizations, Japan would be the force to liberate the colored peoples of the world.[72] At one point, Takahashi was a roommate of an officer of the Nation[73] and he married a former member of the Nation.[74] Elijah Muhammad declared that Takahashi was sent to teach blacks that "the Japanese were brothers and friends of the American Negroes."[75]

Pro-Japanese sentiments were evident among Nation members during World War II. Members stated that in addition to their general objections to serving in the U.S. military, they could not go to war against the Japanese because the Japanese were fellow Asiatics. When Elijah Muhammad's eldest son was sentenced for violating the draft, he announced, "I hope the Japs win the war. Then all the Negroes will be free!"[76] The fact that the Nation purchased fish for its restaurants and stores from a Japanese food company in the 1960s[77] and had over 3 million dollars in assets in a Japanese bank in the early 1970s[78] may also be indicative of their feelings of kinship with the Japanese.

Despite teachings of commonality, Middle Easterners and Asians were generally not allowed to worship in the Nation's mosques and become members of the organization.[79] The justification for excluding Middle Eastern Muslims was that the services were for those who were ignorant of Islam.[80] Malcolm X explained the exclusion of Middle Easterners by making allegorical reference to the history of black oppression in the United States. He told a group of Muslim students from Persia:

> If a lion is in a cage, his roar will be different from the roar of the lion who is in the forest. That is why you couldn't get in our temple. Both

the lion in the forest and the lion in the cage are lions. That is what matters. Lions love lions; they hate leopards.[81]

We should note that although these excuses may not be very convincing, they do not rest on a denial of kinship with Asiatic peoples.[82] White visitors, on the other hand, were denied entrance to mosques on the basis that the "meeting is for the victims of whites not for whites themselves."[83]

Although formally excluded from mosques, some Middle Easterners did gain access to the Nation. In 1950, Jamil Diab, a Palestinian, was recruited to teach Arabic in the Nation of Islam's schools. He did this and more. He instructed Elijah Muhammad in some aspects of orthodox Islam and spoke at the Nation's annual Saviour's Day celebrations which commemorate Fard Muhammad. Diab later broke with Elijah Muhammad, set up a competing Islamic organization, and condemned the Nation for teaching race hatred.[84]

Before he broke with Elijah Muhammad, Diab provided access to the Nation for Hatim Sahib, a Saudi Arabian sociology student at the University of Chicago. Prior to his contact with Diab, Sahib had visited the Chicago mosque of the Nation and been refused entry. Through Diab, Sahib was able to become fully integrated into the Nation. Like Diab, Sahib became an all-purpose instructor for the Nation. He lectured, gave instruction in gymnastics, taught women how to cook Arab foods, and did whatever else he could to make himself useful to the Nation.[85]

Abdul Basit Naeem, a Pakistani Muslim, was a faithful friend and admirer of Elijah Muhammad.[86] Naeem was the editor of *Moslem World & the U.S.A.* and *The African-Asian World*. Naeem published two very favorable articles about the Nation in *Moslem World & the U.S.A.* in 1956 (he went on to write almost a dozen more articles).[87] In the process of writing these articles he was introduced to Elijah Muhammad and they developed a friendship. Naeem served as editor of Muhammad's first widely disseminated publications, *The Supreme Wisdom*, vols. 1 and 2. For both volumes, Naeem also wrote the Introduction. Naeem made the arrangements for Muhammad's pilgrimage to Mecca and his tour of the Middle East and Africa. Naeem served the Nation of Islam in his capacity as a columnist for the Nation's newspaper, *Muhammad Speaks*.[88] Another Pakistani Muslim, Muhammad Abdullah, also became a close friend and advisor to Elijah Muhammad.

Abdullah was also a religious instructor to Wallace Muhammad, Elijah Muhammad's son.[89]

In addition to these particular close relationships, members of the Nation visited the Asiatic world and individuals from the Middle East, Asia, and Africa visited the Nation. In 1959, Elijah Muhammad, accompanied by his sons Herbert and Akbar, made the hajj. On this trip, Muhammad visited nine countries in the Middle East and North Africa. Akbar Muhammad studied at Al-Azhar University in Cairo, Egypt.[90] Dr. Leo P. McCallum and Herbert Muhammad provided reports for the Nation's newspaper, *Muhammad Speaks*, describing their tour of the Middle East, Asia, and Africa.[91]

By the 1960s, the Nation of Islam was known in the Islamic world through the publicity the Nation received in the U.S. press, in the Islamic press,[92] from members' travels in the Middle East, and through connections with individual Muslims like Naeem. Malcolm X also had connections with Middle Easterners at the United Nations and the Nation of Islam had some contact with the former president of Egypt, Gamal Abdel Nasser.[93] Muslims from around the world made visits to the Nation of Islam and participated in the Nation's events. For example, in 1962 the Director of the Arab Information Service and the Consul of the United Arab Republic (Egypt) participated in an African Freedom Day Celebration held by the Nation.[94] In 1963, officers from a Pakistani ship docked in San Diego visited the Nation's "Muhammad's Mosque" in that city.[95] In 1964, a school of the Nation received guests from Kabul University in Afghanistan and from the Ministry of Education in Iran.[96] In 1965, an Egyptian professor from Al-Azhar University came to the United States to study the schools of the Nation.[97] In 1967, Sudanese and Pakistani Muslims arranged to meet with members of the New Haven Mosque.[98] These are only a few of the contacts between the Nation and Muslims and other Asiatics from overseas.[99]

The contact the Nation had with the Asiatic world was not always pleasant. Questions of doctrine would often arise. Tynetta Deanar, a member of the Nation, was put on the defensive when she met Muslim women from Pakistan. She had to justify the Nation's view of whites as the devil.[100] Akbar Muhammad, one of Elijah Muhammad's sons, after being confronted daily with an alternative version of Islam at Al-Azhar University in Egypt, began to move away from his father's organization.[101] In the 1950s, the Federation of Islamic Associations of the United States and Canada stated that it did not recognize the Nation of

Islam as Islamic. Conflicts with Middle Eastern orthodox Muslims, like the Federation, were minor annoyances in comparison to those with organizations that were also interested in gaining black American recruits. These battles were vicious and on one occasion led to violence.[102]

Although its unorthodox version of Islam repeatedly caused the Nation of Islam trouble, the leaders of the organization persisted in maintaining their connections with the wider Asiatic world. This persistence was based in large measure on the belief that they shared a racial commonality. In 1960, Malcolm X made this point to an Arab audience. He stated,

> Arabs, as a colored people, should and must make more effort to reach the millions of colored people in America who are related to the Arabs *by blood*. These millions of colored peoples would be completely in sympathy with the Arab cause![103]

The University of Islam

> We were taught that Asians and Africans, people of color, are all the same but that Caucasians gave us different names to try to divide us. I didn't question where all this information came from or whether it was accurate. As a little X, I was only supposed to learn it by heart, which I did.
>
> In the Muslim schools children are taught that we were kings and queens *in Asia* while white men still were running around uncivilized and naked in caves.   —Sonsyrea Tate

The elementary and high schools of the Nation of Islam, which were called the University of Islam, imparted an Asiatic identity to its younger members.[104] Although much of the University of Islam's curriculum was based on the state public school curriculum, the religious, moral, and language instruction all revealed its Asiatic identity. In the 1960s the University of Islam adopted more African-centered themes, but the schools could never be described simply as Afrocentric.

From its founding in the 1930s, the Nation of Islam was firmly committed to racially separate education. Each mosque was encouraged to begin a school as soon as it had the resources to do so, and members of the mosques were required to send their children to the schools. The first University of Islam was established in Detroit in 1930. In 1934, a second University of Islam was established in Chicago. By 1965, there were eight Universities of Islam, although only three provided full-time instruction. The remaining five only offered Saturday classes. In 1975, there were twenty-four Universities of Islam. The growth of the University of Islam paralleled (but did not equal) the growth of mosques.[105]

Students traveled to the University of Islam on buses owned by the school. Upon arriving at school, the students lined up outside and waited to be inspected. The inspection served two purposes: security and decorum. The Nation of Islam was intensely concerned about security (possibly due to the past death threats directed at Elijah Muhammad). Students were searched for weapons as well as for food, candy, and indecent literature. They were also inspected to see that they were clean, neat, and wearing the proper uniform. Girls were required to wear brown, beige, or blue jumper dresses and matching headpieces. Boys were required to wear blue, brown, or gray suits. Students who were not appropriately attired were sent home.[106]

Students attended school for four hours a day for fifty weeks of the year. The school year began on the first Monday in March after the Saviour's Day celebrations. (Saviour's Day is the birthday of Master W. Fard Muhammad.) There was a two-week break in the middle of the school year at the end of August. Students also had U.S. national holidays off as well as Saviour's Day.[107]

Classes began with a salute to the Nation of Islam's flag, known as "the national." In the 1950s, the schools were decorated with the flags and histories of Islamic countries in Asia and Africa. Non-Islamic African countries were not featured.[108] Here again, we see a strong Islamic identity which includes Islam in Africa, but no general Pan-African identity.

The curriculum of the University of Islam was basically the same as that for students in public schools. In addition to the state public school curriculum, University of Islam students studied Arabic, the religious teachings of the Nation of Islam, and aspects of the history of Islam in Arabia. Students also learned esoteric "Actual Facts" and catechism lessons that were required of members of the Nation.[109] This curriculum was supplemented by trips to local museums, zoos, and businesses owned by the Nation of Islam or individual members. Field trips took place on Tuesdays when there were no academic classes at the University of Islam.[110]

The University of Islam's curriculum and its texts from the 1950s show no evidence of black American or African studies. In his 1959 study Essien-Udom observed that "although the history of the Black Nation is supposed to receive greater emphasis, there was no special course devoted to it."[111] Essien-Udom's mistake was to think that the "Black Nation" referred to black Americans and Africans. Essien-Udom did find evidence of special attention to the *Asiatic* Black Nation in the University of Islam's attention to the Islamic world.

In the 1960s, the University of Islam introduced black American and African studies materials. Christine Johnson, the director of the University of Islam from 1960 to 1966,[112] was crucial to the inclusion of African and black American material in the curriculum. Johnson authored the more Muslim- and African-oriented reader, *Muhammad's Children*, which replaced *Dick and Jane*. Johnson's interest in black American and African studies preceded her joining the University of Islam and remained after she left.[113] Without Johnson, Afrocentric content may never have become part of the curriculum.

University of Islam education prioritized instilling traditional, conservative morals and values which were said to be Muslim values. The elimination of stereotypic black behavior—which the Nation of Islam saw as slave behavior—was central to the mission of the Nation. The University of Islam counteracted laziness with strict discipline and rote learning. Dirtiness was counteracted by cleanliness inspections at the beginning of the day. Black uninhibitedness was replaced with an emphasis on the restraint of all passions. Students were taught to dress conservatively, to suppress their sexuality, to save money rather than spend it, and to be silent as much as possible. "Islamic economics" taught students that "black men should own their own land, produce their own food and have their own industries." To enforce the rules of the University of Islam, any adult was permitted to use verbal and, if necessary, corporal punishment.[114] Education in the University of Islam was aimed at eliminating what were perceived to be black American characteristics and replacing them with Asiatic ones. It was not a celebration of what they perceived as blackness but a move away from blackness.

The Nation of Islam was also repulsed by the prominence of sports and the arts in black American life. The leaders saw these activities as a waste of time and as encouraging blacks to slavishly entertain whites. As one Nation of Islam Minister stated: "There is too much play among our people already. Our children don't need to play. They need to study." Sports, music, art, and poetry were not taught at the University of Islam. Gymnastics for physical fitness was acceptable for students to pursue. Boys learned martial arts training as part of being male members of the Nation of Islam. Students were allowed to pursue artistic activities on their own time.[115]

The University of Islam was also very conservative with regard to gender roles. Sex segregation began in second grade to prevent "sweethearting while education is supposed to be going on." Birth control and homosexuality were both considered sins. Girls were taught to be good wives and mothers and were discouraged from pursuing higher education. Instead of gymnastics, girls of sixteen years or older studied home economics while boys in this age group studied martial arts. Boys were taught that it was their duty to protect black womanhood, which often meant enforcing numerous restrictions on females' free movement in society.[116] Women were encouraged to take leadership roles in the University of Islam because teaching was seen as their special domain. This view was probably based on the idea that educating children was one aspect of child rearing.[117]

Whites were not allowed to teach in the Nation's schools.[118] The Chicago school did, however, have a Palestinian and an Egyptian principal.[119] On one occasion, Abdul Basit Naeem, the Pakistani Muslim, delivered the keynote address at the school's graduation ceremony.[120] Although the students of the University of Islam consisted of only black Americans, the 17 July 1964 issue of *Muhammad Speaks* proudly reported that the parents of two Pakistani children had applied for admission to the school to learn "true Islam."

Education in the University of Islam was Asiatic education. Students learned Arabic, the history of Islam in Arabia, "Islamic economics," and "Muslim values." They also learned the religious teachings of the Nation of Islam of which the Asiatic racial ideology was an integral part. If there were any doubt about the seriousness of these ideas of racial kinship, the presence of a principal or a visitor[121] from the Middle East served to dispel it.

The Nation of Islam and Pan-Africanism

C. Eric Lincoln observed, "so long as the movement keeps its color identity with the rising peoples of Africa, it could discard all its Islamic attributes—its name, its prayers to Allah, its citations from the Qur'an, everything 'Muslim,' without substantial risk to its appeal to the black masses."[122] Lincoln was correct in noting that an Asiatic identity is not necessary for a successful black religious or nationalist organization. Religious leaders and black nationalists, before and after the founding of the Nation of Islam, have had successful organizations with more conventional notions of black identity. But in locating the identity of the Nation in the African independence movements of the 1950s and 1960s, Lincoln ignored the ample evidence of its identification with the Middle East and Asia. He also missed the more important point that the Nation was successful *and* it defined black Americans as Asiatics. The Asiatic identity was accepted and believed in by many black American members.

Lincoln was also unaware that the teachings of the Nation of Islam were ambivalent about Africa. Ancient African civilizations were celebrated because they were believed to be the creation of the Original People. Newly independent African nations were celebrated because the liberation of any Asiatic people from white domination was seen as a good thing.[123] Celebrating the Original People or Asiatic liberation from white domination is not the same as celebrating an African identity. Elijah Muhammad did not celebrate such an identity. Muhammad saw non-Muslim Africans as uncivilized. He stated:

> Some of us rise up boasting of Africa. I say first get yourself civilized and go there and civilize Africa. . . . We love African people like we love you, in a way. Not quite as much, however, because they have been free and they let England, Germany and other European countries go over there and rob them. The devils put them back into the jungles and took over their country. I dare them to let us get a country. They certainly won't push us out of it.[124]

Muhammad saw black Americans who were not Muslims as less than completely civilized. He saw Africans as even worse than black Americans. Although black Americans had their faults, he still considered black Americans as superior to Africans.

On another occasion, Elijah Muhammad stated:

> I have been preaching to the Black man in America that we should accept our own; and instead of the Black man going to the decent side

of his own, he goes back seeking traditional Africa, and the way they did in jungle life and the way you see in some parts of uncivilized Africa today. They are not using barber's tools, shears and razors to keep themselves looking dignified as a civilized people should look. The Black man in America accepts the jungle life, thinking that they would get the love of Black Africa. Black Brother and Black Sister, wearing savage dress and hair-styles will not get you the love of Africa. The dignified people of Africa are either Muslim or educated Christians. But Africa today does not want Christianity.[125]

Again, it is clear that Muhammad saw traditional Africans as backward. In his view African Muslims and even Christians, who the Nation regularly disparaged as "slaves" to whites, were more civilized than traditional Africans. The celebration of African traditions in the Black Power movement disturbed Muhammad. In 1968, Muhammad forbade members of the Nation from wearing traditional African clothing or hairstyles.[126]

The Nation of Islam cultivated an Asiatic identification among its members throughout its history. The Nation's story of genesis located black Americans as descendants of the Tribe of Shabazz whose original home was the Holy City of Mecca. Black Americans were seen as being Islamic by nature, with Arabic their original language. The importance of this Islamic identification is clearly reflected in the name of the organization. Many scholars have concluded that the organization was Islamic, however unorthodox. Fairly regular visits from Muslims around the world and regular coverage of the Asiatic world in *Muhammad Speaks* were just two of the ways in which an Asiatic identity was reinforced.

These points force us to complicate our understanding of the Nation as a black nationalist organization. It is correct that a great deal of the organization's time was directed to addressing issues specifically about black-white race relations in the United States. The Nation did advocate loudly for black social separation in America.[127] Members of the Nation of Islam were somewhat effective at building small black businesses.[128] Socially and economically, particularly as viewed from outside, the Nation was a black nationalist organization, but religiously it was not.[129] Religiously, the organization located its members in a multiracial community (from an external perspective) unlike that of religious black nationalist organizations such as the African Orthodox Church or the Shrine of the Black Madonna.[130]

The Nation of Islam was not a Pan-Africanist organization, as some have argued.[131] During the late 1960s when many black nationalists adopted African names, started studying Swahili, wore African clothing, and were ideologically Pan-African, members of the Nation of Islam were still given Arabic names, studied Arabic, viewed Mecca as their original home, and were forbidden to wear African clothing.[132] The Nation always identified more strongly with Islamic countries in particular than with sub-Saharan African countries in general. In the 1970s, when the Nation needed financial assistance it turned to the Arab-Islamic countries of Libya and the United Arab Emirates, for example.[133] Pan-Africanists of the 1950s were aware that the Nation was an Asiatic organization and not a Pan-Africanist one. They criticized Elijah Muhammad for his "lack of understanding that the so-called Negroes are Africans and not Muslim, Asiatic or Arabs."[134]

In a number of other respects, the Nation of Islam's teachings and practices ran counter to much of the black nationalism of the late 1960s. The Nation opposed the music, fashion, and food that came to define "soul" within the popular culture of Black Power.[135] The Nation of Islam believed that blacks wasted too much time singing and dancing. They favored conservative and modest dress for both men and women and explicitly prohibited African clothing and afros. The involvement in protest and electoral politics among civil rights and Black Power activists was not endorsed by the Nation.

In understanding the Nation of Islam, scholars need to remember that the organization began in 1930 and not 1950 or 1960. It was a continuation of the Moorish Science Temple of America. The Moorish Science Temple, which predated the Nation of Islam, was a heterodox Islamic organization. It defined its members as Asiatic, advocated economic black nationalism, and bore a number of other obvious similarities with the Nation of Islam. Karl Evanzz presents evidence that Fard Muhammad and Elijah Muhammad were both members of the Moorish Science Temple.[136] At one time, Fard Muhammad claimed that he was the reincarnation of the founder of the Moorish Science Temple.[137] Instead of realizing the "Moorishness" of the Nation, scholars have tried to fit the Nation into the mold of civil rights and Black Power organizations. However, the Nation's relationship to those movements is complex. On a number of issues it moved against the agenda of both civil rights and Black Power and away from American blackness.[138]

We must remember that although racial identities are believed to be natural and essential, they are in fact socially situational. To say that members of the Nation of Islam saw themselves as Asiatics does not deny that they were seen and treated as black Americans by others. This is precisely why the organization has been misunderstood. All its statements and actions were interpreted as emanating from black people with black identities who were celebrating blackness. When it is examined from a social constructionist perspective, however, one sees that the Nation of Islam was not celebrating being black but being Asiatic. Asiatic was the way that believers defined themselves and it had a significant impact on their behavior and cultural life. As Elijah Muhammad stated, "There is no such thing as a race of Negroes."[139]

3

Achieving Blackness during the Black Power Era

In 1940, W. E. B. Du Bois insightfully defined a black person as "a person who must ride 'Jim Crow' in Georgia."[1] The expression "riding Jim Crow" meant being confined to blacks-only spaces. In a broader sense, it suggested a variety of Jim Crow policies which maintained and made visible blacks' subordination to whites. Du Bois consciously did not define a black person by skin color because he was intimately aware that "within the Negro group especially there were people of all colors."[2] His definition also alludes to the experience of Homer A. Plessy. Although Plessy was seven-eighths "white" and looked 100 percent "white," he was not allowed to ride in a whites-only train car in Louisiana. Civil rights activists arranged to have Plessy arrested for violating a Jim Crow law in order to pose a legal challenge to Jim Crow. They thought that having a "white" person excluded from a whites-only train car would strengthen their case. In the 1896 *Plessy v. Ferguson* decision, however, the U.S. Supreme Court determined that the fact that Plessy looked "white" did not at all exempt him from blackness. Plessy was black and therefore required to ride Jim Crow in Louisiana. In this decision, the Court made explicit the fact that blackness is a social, not a biological, fact.[3] One could appear to be 100 percent "white" physically and yet socially be 100 percent black.

Du Bois's definition of a black person as someone who must ride Jim Crow also highlights the very important fact that race structures social life. Different racial groups are subject to different opportunities and constraints. In 1940, blacks were subject to Jim Crow policies. They were not allowed their full rights as citizens. They were blocked from entry into certain occupations. In their interactions with whites, blacks were often required to show deference to whites. In many aspects of social life, blacks faced constraints where whites had opportunities. While Jim Crow policies were stronger and more developed in the

47

South, they were not completely absent from other parts of the country.[4] The racial structures of a society are an important dimension to the meaning of race.

Racial structures present opportunities and constraints in the daily life of members of racial groups. These opportunities and constraints are constructed in part from the political and economic desires of powerful groups and in part from the beliefs and stereotypes about races. They also change over time and place. These changes in racial structures are one of the reasons that race is a sociohistorical phenomenon. The racial structures during the period of slavery differ from those of Jim Crow. Those of Jim Crow differ from those of today. The blackness of this era is not the blackness of previous ones.

Race can be understood as a social status or social position in society with accompanying roles or normative expectations. These normative expectations are the "dos" and "don'ts" of a social status. For example, a "do" for a black person in the South in 1940 was to ride in the blacks-only train car. These normative expectations, which are formally and informally enforced, define the social opportunities and constraints that accompany racial categorization.

Sociologists have long distinguished social statuses that can be *achieved* through individual effort from those that are *ascribed* or assigned by society. Unlike being a doctor which one *achieves* through study, passing examinations, and completing other requirements, one's race is *ascribed* by the social rules of categorization. That race is an ascribed social category is conventional sociological thinking.

Race, however, is also *achieved* by one's proper performance of the normative expectations for the racial category.[5] Failure to perform one's proper roles results in an individual being seen as deviant and as not truly occupying his or her social status. It is possible to be categorized as black but be seen as behaving in normatively or stereotypically white ways. In this way, one can be a "white" black person or a black person who "acts white."[6]

In the United States, black people have always "acted white" by defying the norms of blackness. In Jim Crow America, there were innumerable ways to "act white." By examining the lynchings of blacks during the Jim Crow era we can see some of the ways blacks "acted white." Despite the rhetoric of black men raping white women, most lynchings did not even involve allegations of rape. Among other things, blacks were lynched for acquiring wealth and property, working in "white" occupations, resisting white exploitation, and speaking to whites as equals. Additionally, black men were lynched for having platonic friendships with white women and for having consensual sexual relationships with them.[7] In engaging in all these activities, blacks were "acting white" by suggesting that they were equal to white people. Lynching was a means by which whites communicated and policed the norms of blackness.

Blacks also have norms for black people. These black norms for blackness have been informally enforced, whereas whites have had formal norms (i.e., laws) as well as informal ones. Blacks have developed many negative terms for "white" black people to shame them into behaving like "black" black people. Interestingly, blacks have developed many more disparaging terms for "white" black people than they have for whites.[8]

For example, during the Black Power era of the 1960s and 1970s, Black Power activists transformed "Negro" from a respectful term for a black person to mean a "white," and therefore deviant, black person. "Uncle Tom," which meant the same as "Negro," was also a popular phrase. Malcolm X popularized the term "house slave," which also meant "Uncle Tom."[9]

These terms cannot be dismissed as *merely* name-calling. Human beings are symbolic creatures. Shared beliefs, values, and other ideas—which can be called culture—shape much of our behavior. For these reasons, ideas about "correct" and "incorrect" blackness have been powerful social forces in black life. Because of the history of racism in American society, blacks have depended upon other blacks for friendship, love, and a variety of social needs. This support also means that blacks are subject to social control by other blacks to a considerable degree.

For example, one black college student at a predominantly white Midwestern university remembered how normative expectations during the Black Power era shaped his behavior:

> My freshman year it was not the thing to go to University Theater productions. And there was a group of us who were really into music and theater. And so freshman year I never went to a university Theater production—didn't go to [the annual variety show], didn't go to concerts

or anything. But sophomore year I started saying [to myself], "Well, wait a minute, I *know* I'm black. I went to a black high school, I lived in a black neighborhood all my life. I really can do this without risking my blackness."[10]

The campus norms of blackness kept this student who loved theater away from it for a year. It is possible that the desire to display the "correct" blackness kept other blacks away from the theater for even longer periods.

The same social dynamics were at play in a West Coast youth correctional institution during the Black Power era. A black youth, Larry Dillard, reported how he was coerced into not having even casual friendships with whites. When he first entered the institution, he was not aware that there was a strong norm for racial separation.

When I was coming down on the bus, man, I wasn't hip to the thing. Me and this cat named John, this honky—Italian or something—we used to get out and just run around the track. Just for the fun of it. And we were talking about what we were going to do to their track records and things.

Well, we got to camp. A brother came and told me, "Don't you go around talking to a honky, man." And me and him was sitting up having a cigarette and a bunch of brothers came over. Say, "You smoking behind that honky, man?" I said, "Yeah, it's his cigarette, you know. I ain't got none." They say, "Man, you don't smoke behind honkies. Wanna be a D.B. [dead brother], man?" And I didn't smoke behind the honkies. Nor eat behind the honky or nothing.[11]

Dillard quickly learned that if a black male had white friends in that institution, "No more brothers talk to you, you know. . . . You have to hang with the honkies. And the honkies don't want you." Dillard went from someone who could have casual friendships with whites to one who would often refer to them as "honkies" and who joked that he "would like to kill a white man."[12]

Even the parts of Louisiana that had managed to escape the "one-drop rule" for much of U.S. history felt the force of Black Power norms for blackness. Many Creole youth were forced out of their intermediate racial identification between black and white and made to act "Black." Virginia Dominguez reported:

Afros have "saved" many of the young light-skinned colored Creoles who choose now to identify themselves as black and disavow any connection with colored Creole society. . . . So keen was the criticism of Creoles by non-Creole blacks, especially in the early 1970's, that light-skinned teenage boys whose hair was straight began to put vinegar on their hair to make it kinky.[13]

From colleges to prisons, from North to South and East to West, many blacks felt extreme pressure to conform to the new Black Power norms of blackness.[14] Being of African descent alone did not make one authentically black by the definitions of Black Power advocates. One had to *achieve* blackness by one's actions.

Black Macho

1966 shall be remembered as the year we left our imposed status of Negroes and became *Black Men*.
—Floyd McKissick, civil rights activist turned Black Power activist

Many Black Power activists were very concerned with the norms of black masculinity. For them, black oppression was understood as the emasculation of black men by white men *and* by black women. Black liberation, therefore, would require the hypermasculinization of black men. To this end, they made black machismo the normative ideal. Black men who failed to meet this ideal were "Negroes." Being "Negro" could therefore convey not only a "white" blackness but also an emasculated or effeminate blackness.

The Nation of Islam was a powerful model for Black Power activists and the Nation's ideas about gender were very conservative. The Nation of Islam relegated women largely to the domestic sphere. Women's duties were to serve men and care for children. Men were responsible for protecting women. Women in the Nation were required to dress conservatively. Short skirts and other "provocative" dress were seen as white-inspired debauchery. Women were not to venture into the world outside the Nation without the permission of men. Abortion, Elijah Muhammad argued, was a white attempt at genocide. Abortion and homosexuality were both viewed as sins. Minus the ideas about whites, these ideas are basically traditional conservative American ideas about the roles of women and men in society. Black women, however, had historically been more active and involved outside the domestic sphere. The Nation's ideals were therefore for black men to have greater control and to place greater restrictions on black women than had been typical for blacks. Material social realities made many of these conservative ideals difficult to enforce. But what the Nation viewed as the ideals for true black womanhood were clear.[15]

The belief in male dominance is also clear in the pronouncements of the most famous Minister for the Nation of Islam, Malcolm X. Malcolm X's sexism and misogyny predate the Nation of Islam, but within the Nation his beliefs and his sense of gender norms could be presented as religious and political virtues. He stated:

> Every month, when I went to Chicago, I would find that some sister had written complaining to Mr. Muhammad that I talked so hard against women when I taught our special classes about the different natures of the two sexes. Now, Islam has very strict laws and teachings about women, the core of them being that the true nature of man is to be strong, and a woman's true nature is to be weak, and while a man must at all times respect his woman, at the same time he needs to understand that he must control her if he expects to get her respect.[16]

Malcolm X was not merely strongly sexist, as was the ideal for the Nation. He was also a misogynist. He stated:

> I wouldn't have considered it possible for me to love any woman. I'd had too much experience that women were only tricky, deceitful, untrustworthy flesh. I had seen too many men ruined, or at least tied down, or in some other way messed up by women. Women talked too much. To tell a woman not to talk too much was like telling Jesse James not to carry a gun, or telling a hen not to cackle. . . . And for anyone in any kind of a leadership position, such as I was, the worst thing in the world that he could have was the wrong woman.[17]

Malcolm X decided that he could trust his wife "seventy-five percent."[18] The model of male and female roles that the Nation in general, and Malcolm X in particular, posed for Black Power activists was far from equality.

The Nation of Islam and civil rights activists were enemies because of their very different goals for black people and because they were competing against each other for the hearts and minds of black America. The Nation argued that blacks should separate from whites as much as possible, while civil rights activists fought for racial integration between blacks and whites. Malcolm X also used gender ideals to distinguish the Nation of Islam from its rivals in the civil rights movement. Malcolm X criticized civil rights activists for pursuing what appeared to him to be a docile, subservient, and emasculating mode of political engagement. Adolph Reed provides a glimpse into this reasoning and Malcolm X's persuasiveness. Reed recalls his youthful encounter with civil rights activism:

> Both live and on television we regularly saw people—among them slightly older, more precious members of our social world—being attacked and dragged roughly off to jail, singing and passively resisting all the while. We were awed by the demonstrators. As urban, adolescent males, all engaged in swaggering vaguely toward adulthood, we thought them crazy to take what they did, admired them, and were quietly enraged and humiliated by the treatment they received. Meek acceptance of being beaten and limply carted off carried, in our view, a taint of cowardice, no matter how modified. And the gleeful taunts and physical abuse from white bystanders seemed to reinforce that opinion, even while stoking our empathy with the demonstrators and hatred for their victimizers. . . .
>
> This was the context in which I learned of Malcolm X. . . . I think the first reference was on television news, in a story raising the specter of dangerous "Black Muslims" and "black separatists."[19]

Malcolm X, better than anyone else, was able to exploit this "taint of cowardice" in civil rights activism. As Roy Wilkins of the NAACP observed, "With Malcolm, the only way you could judge things was whether you did the thing that was *manly*, no matter if it was suicidal or not."[20] Peter Goldman adds, "Malcolm assumed that what was middle-class was venal and that what was polite was cowardly."[21] Civil rights activism, in Malcolm's eyes, consisted of venal black leaders pursuing the wrong aims in an unmanly manner.

For Malcolm X, the unmanliness of black civil rights leaders was merely one example of the emasculation of black men. He argued, "I live in a society whose social system is based upon the castration of the

Black man, whose political system is based on castration of the Black man, whose economy is based upon the castration of the Black man."[22] For many Black Power activists, "castration" became the favorite metaphor for black oppression. This metaphor reveals how the oppression of black males was privileged over that of black females. According to this viewpoint, one of the ways that white men had "castrated" black men was by making black women relatively independent of black men. Daniel Patrick Moynihan's government report, *The Negro Family: A Case for National Action*, which presented the black family as a matriarchy was the scholarly articulation of this idea.[23]

With the sexist Nation of Islam as a model of black nationalism and emasculation as the metaphor for black oppression, Black Power became a macho movement. During the Black Power era, as Paula Giddings observes, it was often the case that the more "Black" the organization was, the more sexist it was.[24] Among the more extreme demands of Black Power activists was for black women to walk two (or more) steps behind their man, to acquiesce to male abuse, and to avoid using birth control so that they could have babies for the revolution.[25]

All these demands were placed in a "Black" perspective. Activists argued that in Africa men walked ahead of women to protect them from danger. As African people, blacks in America who are aware of their cultural roots should therefore continue this tradition. Black Power activists argued that black men were more oppressed than black women and that they were emasculated by racism. Black male violence against black women was a result of their frustration with American society. Black women who complained about black male abuse were therefore being unsympathetic to black men. Activists argued that birth control was a white attempt at genocide. Given that activists believed that there was a coming race war, black people also needed as many warriors as possible. Many of the leaders of prominent Black Power organizations were clearly sexist in their ideology and practices.[26]

It is important to remember, however, that most of these activists formed their ideas about the roles of men and women prior to the Second Wave of American feminism. For American society in general, female subordination to men was the norm. The ideals of American masculinity were difficult for black men to realize. Because of racial discrimination against blacks, black men had difficulty being as financially sovereign in the household as white men were. Greater proportions of black women worked compared to white women, and working black women tended to make more significant contributions to the family income than working white women.[27] Black men also failed to meet the social requirements for American manhood. They could not protect black women and children from exploitation and abuse by whites. They could not even insure that they were treated with respect by whites. They were often called "boy," and often treated as children who would be inclined to misbehave if whites were not vigilant. Racial norms required that all blacks exhibit great deference to whites. Any violation of these norms or even imagined violation of them could be severely punished. All blacks had to be deferential, but in a society where men were generally accorded more respect than women, the extreme deference of black men to white men and white women caused additional psychological pain. When blacks began to fight for their rights in American society, many were also fighting for their rights to practice traditional gender roles where men were dominant.[28]

We see these goals among civil rights activists as well. Aldon Morris conveys how the conservative ideas about women among the leaders of the civil rights organization, the Southern Christian Leadership Conference (SCLC), affected Ella Baker, "one of the most significant and unheralded leaders of the Civil Rights Movement":[29]

> Here was a woman [Ella Baker], twenty-five years older than most of the SCLC's leadership, who possessed a solid organizational background, entering an organization controlled by black ministers. During that era men in general, and many black ministers in particular, were condescending toward women and could not envision them as full-fledged leaders. This stance of the ministers was bound to generate friction with Baker, who was self-directed and did not feel that women should automatically defer to men.[30]

Morris concludes that in spite of Baker's age, experience, and knowledge "sexism and Baker's nonclergy status minimized her impact on the SCLC."[31] Andrew Young, a member of the SCLC, argued, "a system of oppression tends to produce strong women and weak men," just as Black Power activists did. Young felt that it was important for Martin Luther King, Jr., the head of the SCLC, "to be free of that strong matriarchal influence."[32] Homophobia was also a problem for the civil rights movement. Homophobia kept the important activism of Bayard Rustin, a black gay man, invisible. Rustin was important in organizing the

SCLC and the 1963 March on Washington. Despite his efficacy as an organizer, attacks on him because of his sexuality forced him out of activism between 1960 and 1963.[33]

While Black Power has drawn considerable criticism for its "black macho," the civil rights movement was not progressive on these issues either. Black Power, however, *was* a macho movement. Civil rights activists were activists who in addition to their commitment to civil rights may have been sexist and homophobic, but Black Power was *defined* in male-dominant and heterosexual terms. To be a Black Power activist generally required a homophobic, male-dominant gender ideology.

Maulana Karenga, an important Black Power activist, stated that relations between men and women should be based on "male supremacy." "Equality," he argued, "is false; it's the devil's concept" ("devil" was the Nation of Islam's term for a white person). He called for women to be submissive because a woman "can't be feminine without being submissive" and stated, "The role of the woman is to inspire her man, educate their children and participate in social development." "Male supremacy" was beyond question for him because, he argued, it was based on "tradition, acceptance, and reason."[34] Black Power activists attempted to put these ideas into practice with varying degrees of success.

Angela Davis recounts her experience working with members of US Organization ("US" as opposed to "them"):

> I was criticized very heavily, especially by male members of Karenga's organization, for doing "a man's job." Women should not play leadership roles, they insisted. A woman was supposed to "inspire" her man and educate his children. The irony of their complaint was that much of what I was doing had fallen to me by default. The arrangements for the publicity of the rally, for instance, had been in a man's hands, but because his work left much to be desired, I began to do it simply to make sure that it got done. It was also ironical that precisely those who criticized me most did the least to ensure the success of the rally.
>
> I became acquainted very early with the widespread presence of an unfortunate syndrome among some Black male activists—namely to confuse their political activity with an assertion of their maleness. They saw—and some continue to see—Black manhood as something separate from Black womanhood. These men view Black women as a threat to their attainment of manhood—especially those Black women who

take initiative and work to become leaders in their own right. The constant harangue by the US men was that I needed to redirect my energies and use them to give my man strength and inspiration so that he might more effectively contribute his talents to the struggle for Black liberation.[35]

In the Black Panther Party, a very similar dynamic occurred. Members of the Party at one time quoted Karenga's ideas on the role of women. The Party cultivated a very macho image and defined black liberation in terms of redeeming black manhood. But over time women, in numbers, dominated the organization. Women were more diligent and responsible in getting the day-to-day work done.[36]

In the construction of blackness among Black Power activists, blackness came to be gendered as masculine. Black men were more likely to be truly "Black" than women. Black women had two different and sometimes competing paths to this authentic black-nationalist blackness. They could be "feminine" and "inspiring" to their "Black" men and gain "Blackness" by association. Alternatively, they could display machismo just as men did to prove their "Blackness."

One difference between the Black Panther Party and US Organization was that while both organizations were committed to machismo, the Panthers allowed women to be macho also. US Organization insisted on women playing only feminine roles. Assata Shakur, a former member of the Black Panther Party, remembers, "a lot of us [women] adopted that kind of macho type style in order to survive in the Black Panther Party."[37] Some women Panthers were attracted to this black macho. Regina Jennings joined the Black Panthers because, in her view, "it was the only organization that faced White America forthrightly without begging or carrying signs for equality and justice."[38] Jennings concurred with Malcolm X and the young Adolph Reed that civil rights activism suggested cowardliness or effeminacy. Instead Jennings was attracted to the macho mystique of the Panthers, "the . . . leather jackets, berets, guns, and their talk—aggressive and direct."[39] Although Elaine Brown, a one-time leader of the Black Panthers, at first hoped to resist the machismo in the Panthers, her ability to lead the Panthers depended on it. When she took control of the Panthers, she stated, "I HAVE ALL THE GUNS AND ALL THE MONEY. I can withstand challenge from without and within."[40] She would also easily resort to violence to settle disputes and to maintain Party discipline.[41] Rather than transforming the macho image and ideals of the Black Panthers, women in the organization either embraced it or were transformed by it.

Within the ideology of Black Power, not only was the most authentic blackness male, but the most authentic maleness was "Black." In the ideological struggle with whiteness, white men were redefined as effeminate. "Negro" males—"white" black men—were consequently also seen as effeminate. Amiri Baraka expressed these ideas most strongly. In 1965 he wrote, "Most American white men are trained to be fags."[42] The unmanliness of civil rights activists—"Negroes"—in the eyes of Black Power activists could then also be read as a sign of their "faggotry." Baraka's 1966 "Civil Rights Poem" presented the leader of the NAACP, Roy Wilkins, in these terms. In the poem, Baraka stated that Roy Wilkins was "an eternal faggot," and he threatened to beat Wilkins up if he saw him.[43]

Lesser-known activists shared these sentiments. In *Black News*, a Black Power newspaper, one could read of "sissified devils" and "pigs" (the Black Panther's term for the police) with a "faggot's cowardice."[44] Another *Black News* author wrote:

> It should be pointed out emphatically that the only real men in this society are black men. Physically hardened in the crucible of harsh slavery, the black man who confronts the white man on equal terms inspires fear in the latter. The honky with a gun quakes with terror at the sight of an angry black brother.[45]

For this author, it goes without saying that civil rights activism did not involve confronting whites on equal terms; civil rights activists did not inspire visible signs of fear in white people. Black Power activists did.

All the gender ideals of blackness as defined by Black Power activists are present in a short article by another *Black News* author, Sister Cheryl Azeza. In her statement, "My Sisters the Black Man is the New Man of Today," she reflected the social conservatism of many Black Power activists when she told black women to listen to black men "when the brother tells you not to wear a mini skirt, not to show your flesh and to have respect for yourself." Azeza also agreed that black men were the real men. She wrote:

> Have you ever asked yourself why the white woman finds our men more attractive than her own? The reason is that the white man is

becoming more faggoty and the Black man is asserting his masculinity. . . . The white man is in the unisex bag. Sometimes one cannot tell
which sex is which.

She went on to argue that black men were more oppressed in society:
"[The Black man] is in an exploitative and dehumanizing society and
that it has and always will be much harder for the Black man to make it
than for the Black woman." Azeza's remarks were not motivated merely
by a desire to celebrate black manhood. They were also animated by a
perceived white threat to black unity: the white woman. "If the alien
white woman is willing to listen to our men, makes them feel like they
are kings and feel that They [sic] are worth fighting for, then what is
wrong with us? I damn well know that our men are worth fighting
for."[46] According to Azeza, therefore, the price black women had to pay
for the black nationalist project was female subordination.

The Sources of Black Power Norms for Blackness

The New Integrationist

I
seek
integration
of
negroes
with
black
people.
　　　—Don L. Lee, 1968

Although today black Americans rather casually claim a "Black" or an
"African-American" identity, in the 1960s to call oneself "Black" or
"African" was to claim a particular politicized racial identity. Simply
being a person of African descent did not make one "Black." Black
Power activists believed that while they were "Black" most people of
African descent were "Negroes"—that is, black people who thought
and acted "white."[47] By the 1970s, in part due to the rising Pan-
Africanism among Black Power activists, "African" (often spelled "Afri-
kan") became the new term to indicate an authentic black identity.

As with the Asiatic racial identity of the Nation of Islam, for Black Power activists being "Negro" and "Black" were not determined by physical appearance. Within the Nation of Islam, a person of any appearance could be Asiatic. Unlike the Nation of Islam, however, Black Power activists accepted the dominant racial categories. Activists' determinations of who belonged in the black racial category matched the dominant society's. But for Black Power activists, it would be possible for one identical twin to be "Black" and for the other to be "Negro," although both twins looked the same. Their distinction between "Negroes" and "Blacks" stressed the performative aspects of race.

In the eyes of these activists, "Negroes" did not think and act like true black people. The presumption was that "Negroes" wanted to be white or were controlled by whites and therefore they were not truly black. They were "white" black people. One of the goals of Black Power was to coerce "Negroes" into being "Black." Don L. Lee's poem "The New Integrationist" expresses this ideal. In Lee's poem, the black-white integration of the civil rights movement is rejected in favor of the Black Power goal of unifying civil rights "Negroes" and Black Power "Blacks." This "new integration" would, no doubt, require civil rights activists, but not Black Power activists, to change their political goals. In Lee's view, "Black" people did not support black-white integration, though "Negroes" did.

The Black Power movement shows clearly that blackness can be conceptualized as something that one does or that one can fail to do. In other words, race is not only socially assigned by the rules of racial categorization, but it can also be achieved or not achieved by an individual's behavior.

As is often the case with innovation, the new ideas are greatly indebted to ideas that came before. The Black Power movement and its ideas about blackness did not arise spontaneously in the 1960s. Other movements and events led to its development. The most important factor in the emergence of the Black Power movement was the civil rights movement, which showed would-be activists the power of grassroots organizing and the possibilities for social change. The problems encountered by the civil rights movement also convinced activists that a different type of social movement was needed. Black Power activists defined their movement and their norms for blackness largely in opposition to what they perceived as the failures of the civil rights movement and the norms of blackness expressed by civil rights activists. It is not surprising that they turned to the Nation of Islam for ideas, since the Nation was already the chief critic of civil rights activists. Given that Black Power activists perceived the civil rights movement to be failing, the apparently successful independence movements in Africa and in other parts of the Third World in the 1950s and 1960s also became sources on which they built their movement. In the Third World it appeared that people of color had achieved complete liberation from European domination. Black Power activists believed that by importing ideas from the Third World, black Americans could also achieve liberation from white domination.

The Nation of Islam

The Nation of Islam's relationship to Black Power is a complicated one. The Nation was part of Black Power, but it also stands *apart* from Black Power. Although the Nation predates Black Power by about three decades, its teachings, delivered by Malcolm X, served as a catalyst for the emergence of Black Power.[48] The Nation inspired activists to black nationalist politics, but it limited its own political activism to rhetoric.

Like the Black Power movement generally, the Nation of Islam developed into a major social force in black America, in large part due to the civil rights movement. While Malcolm X was effective in building the membership of the organization, the Nation of Islam could not have become as large and as influential as it did without national media attention. The enormous media attention that Malcolm X and the Nation of Islam received helped to bring the teachings of Elijah Muhammad to many, many more black Americans than Malcolm X could have reached on his own.[49]

The Nation of Islam and especially Malcolm X became of interest to the mainstream media in the context of the news story that was the civil rights movement. Malcolm X was not only a critic but a dramatic counterpoint to Martin Luther King, Jr., and the civil rights movement. His no-toriety rested on his being the "angel of darkness," as one civil rights activist put it, always ready to launch a sensational, rhetorical attack on Martin Luther King, Jr., the "angel of light." He regularly called King and other civil rights leaders Uncle Toms. "Martin Luther King isn't preaching love," he stated, "he's preaching love the white man."[50] Without the civil rights movement to serve as its counterpoint, the

Nation of Islam would have continued more or less as it had in the first three decades of its existence. It would have gone down in history as merely one of many interesting but marginal alternative religious organizations among black Americans.[51] Instead, it helped to bring into existence a black countermovement to the civil rights movement, namely, Black Power.

Malcolm X and the Nation of Islam's attacks on the civil rights movement were powerful because they were witty and cutting, and also because they raised serious questions. It was reasonable, given the long history of racial oppression and the regular images of black civil rights activists being beaten by whites on television, to wonder whether whites were capable of treating blacks equally.[52] Could a gospel of love[53] really overthrow white supremacy? Peter Goldman summarizes Malcolm's critique well:

> King, [Malcolm] said, was a "chump, not a champ" for committing black women and children to be hosed and clubbed and bitten [by police dogs]; Kennedy was a fox who had talked prettily but had sent in troops only when white property was threatened, not when blacks were being brutalized in the streets, and had thereafter tried to buy peace with a bill permitting blacks to eat at white lunch counters. "Coffee with a cracker," Malcolm snorted. "That's *success*?"[54]

Over time, many civil rights activists grew tired of being hosed, clubbed, and bitten, and they grew skeptical about the prospects for achieving their more radical visions of success. They came to agree with Malcolm that the cost of "coffee with a cracker" was too high to pay. Again, Goldman summarizes the issues well:

> [the movement kids] came into the sixties as King's children, and came out Malcolm's. The process of disenchantment . . . came out of too many knocks on the head and nights in jail, and too many funerals; . . . out of the gathering suspicion that the Federal government saw the events not as a moral struggle but as a contention of interests to be balanced; . . . out of the great compromise at the 1964 Democratic Convention, when the necessity of re-electing Lyndon Johnson took precedence over the claims to justice of a little group of disfranchised black people from Mississippi; . . . out of the discovery that "integra-

tion" was a delusive hope for the black poor in the backwater South and the inner-city North, . . . and, anyway, the liberals talking integration weren't talking about integrating with *them*.[55]

The Student Nonviolent Coordinating Committee (SNCC) and the Congress of Racial Equality (CORE), two of the four major civil rights organizations, would undergo a painful transition from being civil rights organizations to Black Power organizations in the late 1960s. Despite having members who called for "Black Power" in 1966, it was not until 1968 that SNCC and CORE would fully embrace the black nationalism of Black Power.[56]

While SNCC and CORE were moving closer to black nationalism, Black Power had already begun in the North. In California in 1965, activists who saw themselves as following the teachings of Malcolm X formed US Organization.[57] One of the founding members of US Organization was a cousin of Malcolm X's who had been in the Nation of Islam for several years.[58] The leader of US Organization, Maulana Karenga, had explored joining the Nation of Islam before deciding to found his own organization.[59] Many of US Organization's practices echoed those of the Nation. Branches of US were called "temples,"[60] as were the branches of the Nation before the Nation became more orthodox and switched to "mosques."[61] Nation members chanted "all praise is due to Allah," US members chanted "all praise is due to Maulana."[62] The use of Kiswahili, African names, and neo-African rites is similar to the development and incorporation of Asiatic culture in the Nation of Islam. Overall, US Organization had a quasi-religious tenor around its black nationalism, just as the Nation of Islam had a heterodox Islam encapsulating its social and economic black nationalism.

Important parts of Maulana Karenga's teachings were restatements of the Nation's teachings. Karenga argued, following the Nation, that the practice of Christianity amounted to self-hate for blacks because Christianity was a white religion. He stated that blacks should see themselves as gods and reject "spookistic" religion.[63] Elijah Muhammad called Christianity the religion of a "Spook God."[64] The theology of the Nation of Islam speaks of Allah as well as a multiplicity of lesser gods—all of whom are material—not "spooks." Karenga's idea of blacks being gods comes from the Nation's idea that all black men were, in their true nature, a type of god.[65] As the Nation's catechism stated, "The Original Man is the Asiatic Black Man, . . . *God* of the Universe."[66] Karenga also argued against nonviolence and in favor of self-defense, as Malcolm X and the Nation of Islam did.[67] US Organization was one of the earliest of the major Black Power organizations and it bears the clear imprint of the Nation of Islam.

Another very important Black Power organization also emerged in California. In 1966, the Black Panther Party was founded in Oakland, California. Like US Organization, the Panthers followed the teachings of Malcolm X. One of its leaders, Eldridge Cleaver, was a member of both the Nation of Islam and the Organization of Afro-American Unity, Malcolm X's organization after he broke with the Nation.[68] Just as the Nation of Islam regularly published a list of statements in its newspaper supposedly documenting "What . . . the Muslims Want" and "What the Muslims Believe," the Black Panther Party's newspaper published the Panther's "What We Want Now!" and "What We Believe." The Nation's and the Panther's "Wants" both began with the statement: "We want freedom." Many of the other Panther "wants" also echo the Nation's. For example, the sixth Nation "want" stated, "We want an immediate end to the police brutality and mob attacks against the so-called Negro throughout the United States." The Panthers' seventh "want" stated, "We want an immediate end to *police brutality* and *murder* of black people."[69] In both organizations, there was a significant difference between the listed objectives and the actual focus of organizational energy and resources, though less so in the case of the Panthers.

The more substantive Nation influence on the Panthers was the critique of nonviolence and the revaluing of what the Panthers in their leftist jargon would call the lumpen—the unemployed and the criminal. Malcolm X ridiculed nonviolence and spoke passionately in favor of armed self-defense. The primary agenda of the Panthers at their founding was black self-defense against police brutality.[70] Just as the Nation had many former prisoners in its ranks, like Malcolm X himself, so too the Panthers recruited and celebrated their transformation of former criminals into Black Power activists.

The Nation of Islam had a broad influence on Black Power. SNCC and CORE activists were influenced by Malcolm X, and his criticisms of civil rights were a factor in their move from civil rights to Black Power.[71] Nearly every Black Power activist claimed Malcolm X as a hero.[72] Black Power activists reclaimed the word "Black," previously viewed as a supreme insult, as a name for black Americans. In calling themselves "Black," they were following a path laid by the Nation of Islam. The Nation argued that black Americans were only "so-called Negroes." The Nation saw the term "Negro" as having been created by whites to diminish blacks and to deny blacks their true identity.[73]

In black America in the 1960s and 1970s, things associated with the Nation of Islam as well as orthodox Islam became indicators of the new Black Power blackness. The Black Power activist Kasisi Jitu Weusi recounted an exchange he had with a black woman in 1973:

> "Wow!" a sister told me the other day, "The Black Movement has become so real pure, till I'm afraid to breathe. You can't smoke, you can't drink, no pork, no meat, certain kind of clothes, no cussing, what's going on?"
>
> The sister had just returned from a few years on the continent and a brief swing of Europe and was totally befuddled by what she saw among certain progressive Black circles in the northeast U.S. I tried to explain to her that we were going through an "Islamic" phase of struggle that demanded that we CLEAN-UP (at least externally) BUT we sure hope this cleanliness goes beyond just the booze, smoke, and pig. We hope that the clean-up establishes a new level of moral behavior among our folks.[74]

These ideas of self-restraint and dietary restrictions came from the Nation of Islam.[75] As Malcolm X once detailed,

> Any fornication was absolutely forbidden in the Nation of Islam. Any eating of the filthy pork, or other injurious or unhealthful foods; any use of tobacco, alcohol, or narcotics. No Muslim who followed Elijah Muhammad could dance, gamble, date, attend movies, or sports, or take long vacations from work. Muslims slept no more than health required. Any domestic quarreling, any discourtesy, especially to women, was not allowed. No lying or stealing, and no insubordination to civil authority, except on the grounds of religious obligation.[76]

The Nation's rationale for these rules was that "the white man *wants* black men to stay immoral, unclean and ignorant." Malcolm X preached,

"As long as we stay in these conditions we will keep on begging him [the white man] and he will control us."[77]

Many Black Power activists agreed that black liberation required healthy and moral black people, and they too adopted much of the Nation's code of behavior. Although pork is one of the favorite meats in traditional black American cuisine, "soul food," a number of Black Power activists began to shun pork and encouraged other blacks to do so also. Some activists followed Elijah Muhammad's dietary ideas even further and became vegetarians.[78] Since the Nation defined Christianity as a white religion, a number of Black Power activists turned to Islam—but not necessarily to the Nation of Islam. A number of blacks joined and started other Muslim groups during the Black Power era.[79] The Muslim greeting of "Asalaam Alaikum" along with the Kiswahili greeting of "Habari Gani" were both used at Black Power conferences. Some Black Power activists substituted the word "Allah" for "God" although they were not Muslims.[80] Arabic was as "Black" as Kiswahili.

APART FROM BLACK POWER

Although the Nation of Islam inspired many Black Power activists, a number of its practices also went against the grain of Black Power activism. Economically, the Nation advocated and practiced "Black Capitalism." However, most other Black Power activists called for socialism. "Cultural" black nationalists studied "African socialism," "revolutionary" black nationalists quoted Marxist theorists, and even Martin Luther King, Jr., wrote that capitalism permitted "necessities to be taken from the many to give luxuries to the few."[81]

In the Nation of Islam, "Black Capitalism" mainly consisted of encouraging members and sympathizers to give whatever they could to projects that would benefit the Nation of Islam. These Nation-owned organizations would then work to benefit black communities. For example, the Nation solicited donations for the founding of a bank, which was expected to invest in ventures that would develop black communities. It is not clear whether these ventures ever benefited anyone other than the Nation's leadership. The more successful aspect of the Nation's economic nationalism focused on encouraging members to sell small goods (e.g., the Nation's newspaper, bean pies, etc.) and to start small businesses.[82]

Aside from the Nation, few Black Power activists embraced capitalism. The black nationalist CORE was one of the few "Black Capitalist" organizations. But even in CORE's case we can see that anticapitalism was strong in Black Power. Ironically, CORE's "Black Capitalism" required an alliance with white corporate leaders, and it was imposed by the leadership on the rest of the organization. Not surprisingly, many CORE members rebelled. The head of Brooklyn CORE, Robert Carson, protested, "There cannot be any negotiation with industry and capitalism since capitalism is what put us [black people] in the situation we're in. We feel capitalism should be destroyed." The conflict over "Black Capitalism," among other things, led the East Coast chapters of CORE to secede from the national organization.[83] Like the CORE secessionists, many Black Power activists believed that capitalism was incompatible with black liberation.

The Nation of Islam also stood apart on the issue of political activism. Although Black Power activists viewed Malcolm X as a hero, relatively few of them became members of his organizations. Those who wished to be *politically* active, as opposed to focusing on religion and economic black nationalism, did not stay in the Nation of Islam when Malcolm X was one of its leaders, nor did they join Malcolm's Organization of Afro-American Unity when he broke with the Nation. Malcolm X and the Nation of Islam helped to catalyze the Black Power movement, but for many Black Power activists Malcolm X's strength lay in criticizing civil rights and not in building Black Power.[84]

Malcolm X became the historic figure that he was as a member of the Nation of Islam. His fame did not begin or even peak in the last year of his life when he broke from the Nation. During his last year, his influence declined considerably.[85] As a spokesperson for the Nation, he primarily restated Elijah Muhammad's teachings. As Malcolm X stated in his autobiography, "Anyone who has listened to me will have to agree that I believed in Elijah Muhammad and represented him one hundred percent." "I *loved* the Nation, and Mr. Muhammad. I *lived for* the Nation and for Mr. Muhammad," he added.[86] Malcolm presented the Nation of Islam's teachings with perhaps more charisma than any other Minister, but it was always, essentially, the Nation's teachings.

If so many political activists claimed Malcolm X, the Minister of the Nation of Islam, as their inspiration to political activism, why did they not join and stay in the Nation? Malcolm X was keenly aware of the major problem with the Nation: it was essentially an apolitical organization. Elijah Muhammad believed that Allah—not activism—would bring about social change. He believed that justice would come to black Americans "only through [the] Divine and not through civil government."[87] Muhammad prophesied that Allah would destroy America. Therefore, he could argue:

> Allah is sufficient for all our needs. This is why I do not have to beg from our oppressors or march on their Capitol with my hat in my hand. For how can I on one hand preach the doom of the oppressive system and then with the other hand ask alms of the oppressor.[88]

The Nation also supposedly differed from civil rights activists on the issue of self-defense. Malcolm lectured, if you "put your hands on us thinking that we're going to turn the other cheek . . . *we'll put you to death just like that.*"[89] But when the police killed Ronald X Stokes, a member of the Nation, the Nation held a protest march and even invited the NAACP, a major civil rights organization.[90] After the Stokes affair, Malcolm said to confidants, "We spout *our* militant revolutionary rhetoric and we preach Armageddon, but when our own brothers are brutalized or killed, we do nothing."[91] Malcolm X wanted the Nation to be a politically activist organization, but he was forced to keep these desires to himself.[92] People who joined the Nation of Islam assuming that they would be in battle with whites were very disappointed. Walter D. Abilla found that the recruits who were interested in fighting racism were more likely to end up leaving the organization.[93]

When Malcolm X broke with the Nation to form Muslim Mosque Inc. and the Organization of Afro-American Unity, few of those who would later claim him as a martyr flocked to his organizations. The Organization of Afro-American Unity, the political organization, had only a few dozen core activists, although twenty-two thousand people came to view the body of the slain Malcolm X.[94] It is likely that the violent feud between the Nation and Malcolm kept many away who did not wish to be harmed or killed. It is also possible that people were uninspired by the Organization for Afro-American Unity because during his last year it was not clear what Malcolm's new beliefs were. He seemed to change them with each speech.[95] Thus, although nearly all Black Power activists claim Malcolm X as a political hero, most of them did not join his organizations; they built their own.

African Independence Movements

The name of Malcolm X's Organization of Afro-American Unity was inspired by the Organization of African Unity. Like other activists at the time, Malcolm X was excited by the newly independent African nations. While the civil rights movement was taking place in the United States, African nations were achieving their independence from European colonizers. The parallels between African independence and black Americans' fight for freedom were obvious. The independence of African nations convinced black Americans that it was possible to win their civil rights struggle. However, the civil rights movement was not able to achieve its more radical economic goals, and even its legal successes had a more limited impact than expected.[96] As activists turned away from the political strategy of civil rights to that of Black Power, they also began to turn their identities away from America and toward Africa. If blacks were not allowed the full rights of American citizens, then maybe blacks were not American. These activists came to believe that black Americans, like Africans, were a colonized people. What was necessary, therefore, was not a struggle to become integrated into American society but one to be free from colonial domination. The writings of leaders of the newly independent African nations served as inspiration for the black American struggle against what was called internal colonialism. These writings put forward socialist, nationalist, and Pan-African ideas which would be incorporated into the meaning of Black Power.[97]

In 1954, Richard Wright published a book entitled *Black Power* about his reactions to his travels in Ghana (then the British colony of the Gold Coast) and about his hopes for Ghanaian independence from Britain.[98] In 1957, Ghana did become independent. Ghana was the first to do so in sub-Saharan Africa, but it was part of the end of European colonialism across the globe. From 1945 to 1965, most of the Third World achieved its independence from Europe.[99] For many black Americans, what Africans and the rest of the Third World achieved was an example of what black Americans could achieve. Martin Luther King, Jr., wrote:

> Consciously or unconsciously, [the American Negro] has been caught up by the *Zeitgeist*, and with his black brothers of Africa and his brown and yellow brothers of Asia, South America and the Caribbean, the United States Negro is moving with a sense of great urgency toward the

promised land of racial justice. If one recognizes this vital urge that has engulfed the Negro community, one should readily understand why public demonstrations are taking place.[100]

He added:

Witnessing the drama of Negro progress elsewhere in the world, . . . it was natural that by 1963 Negroes would rise with resolution and demand a share of governing power, and living conditions measured by American standards rather than by the standards of colonial impoverishment.[101]

The fact that Africans and other nonwhite people had, apparently, ended their racial subordination to whites suggested that the civil rights struggle would also be victorious.

Africa was also an inspiration for those who rejected civil rights. John Henrik Clarke, the black nationalist historian, felt that he had witnessed the birth of a new era of black nationalism in the United States in February 1961. On February 15 of that year, black Americans rioted in the United Nations to protest the murder of Patrice Lumumba, the first prime minister of the Congo. For the rioters, Clarke wrote, "Lumumba became Emmett Till and all of the other black victims of the lynch law and the mob. The plight of the Africans still fighting to throw off the [yoke] of colonialism and the plight of Afro-Americans . . . became one and the same." Clarke used the UN protest as the beginning of a discussion of seven of the more notable black nationalist groups in the United States at the time. These were only the more notable groups. At the time, in Harlem alone there were more than two dozen black nationalist organizations.[102]

From Clarke's discussion of "The New Afro-American Nationalism" we can see that many of the ideals of Black Power were already present in 1961. The protest showed that black nationalists at that time were interested in the political development of contemporary Africa. They were also interested in African culture. The priest of the Yoruba Temple of New Oyo in Harlem declared:

We must Africanize everything! Our names, our hats, our clothes, our clubs, our churches, our religion, our schools, home furnishings, businesses, holidays, games, arts, social functions, political parties, our manners and customs, etc., etc.

. . . It is distinctly unnatural and degrading, even ridiculous, for persons of African descent to have and keep European customs and habits forced upon them during their enslavement.[103]

Through his New Alajo Party, the priest also issued the political demand for the United States to provide reparations to blacks. Additionally, Clarke makes the claim for an indigenous African socialism that one would hear repeated in later years. Clarke stated:

The new Afro-American nationalists, like the African nationalists, are gravitating toward a form of African Socialism. This new African Socialism will be nothing more than a rehash and an updating of the old communal Socialism that existed in Africa for more than a thousand years before the European Karl Marx was born.[104]

He also argued that black nationalists "feel that the Afro-American constitutes what is tantamount to an exploited colony within a sovereign nation."[105] For Clarke, the concern for Africa made these black American nationalists Pan-Africanists who were striving for "the unification of all people of African descent the world over."[106] At the height of Black Power, all these ideas would be core principles of the movement: political and cultural Pan-Africanism, socialism, and the idea that black Americans constituted an internal colony within the United States.

For Maulana Karenga, the leader of US Organization, the re-Africanization of black Americans was also crucial. Karenga believed that blacks in America did not truly have a culture of their own. He therefore set out to provide black Americans with a culture. To this end, Karenga propagated the use of Kiswahili and the adoption of "neo-African" practices. The most popular of these was Kwanzaa, but it was only one of many.[107]

Karenga's Pan-Africanism was not narrowly cultural; it was also political. Karenga's thinking was shaped by the political ideas of African leaders from the newly independent countries. Under their influence Karenga came to see all aspects of a society as an integrated whole. For example, the political could not be seen as separate and independent from the religious. The religious could not be seen as separate and independent from the economic. Jomo Kenyatta, the Kenyan national-ist, Pan-Africanist, and the first prime minister of Kenya,[108] argued that in African culture all the parts of social life "are the parts of an inte-grated culture" where "no single part is detachable" and each part "is fully understandable only in relation to the whole."[109] Karenga imbibed similar ideas from the writings of the first president for Senegal, Léo-pold Senghor. Senghor argued that cultural independence would be the basis for building political, economic, and social independence. The cul-tural was therefore linked to the political and the economic. Karenga's socialist leanings also followed the ideas of Senghor, Julius Nyerere (the first president of Tanzania), and Kwame Nkrumah (the first prime min-ister of Ghana). It was Senghor who argued that Africans are communal and "had already achieved socialism before the coming of the Euro-pean."[110] Many Black Power activists incorporated these African lead-ers' ideas into their political theories.

Franz Fanon, the Martiniquean radical who argued for the necessity of violent struggle for the oppressed, was also a staple in Black Power circles. Fanon was particularly important for the Black Panther Party. Fanon's argument, of course, fit well with Black Power's rejection of nonviolence as a strategy. For many, to be a Black Power activist meant being anti-American, and among the many things America stood for was capitalism. As a result, Marx, Lenin, and Mao were also important influences on Black Power activists.[111]

It is not possible to determine definitively when a social movement that encompassed a large number of changing and unspecified organi-zations began, or to identify all the constituent elements that led to its formation. The mere existence of black nationalist organizations and activism did not bring about the Black Power movement. The Nation of Islam and dozens of other black nationalist organizations had been around for decades prior to Black Power. What made the Black Power movement a movement was the heightened levels of support for the ide-ology of black nationalism and the rapid increase in black nationalist activism. The membership of the Nation of Islam began to increase rapidly in the 1950s, and peaked in the 1960s.[112] John Henrik Clarke felt that he saw a new black nationalism in 1961. In the latter part of the 1960s, important new black nationalist organizations came into being. All these increases in black nationalist activity were concurrent with the development of the civil rights movement.

An exact date for the origin of Black Power is not important. It is important to realize that black nationalism in the 1960s did not begin when Stokely Carmichael of SNCC uttered the phrase "Black Power" in 1966. Even the term "Black Power" had been used before. Adam Clayton Powell, Jr., used it before Carmichael.[113] Richard Wright used it before Powell. Carmichael was merely articulating ideas and feelings that had been growing in popularity among black Americans for at least a few years.

The Black Power movement took its form and ideology from the Nation of Islam and from Third World independence movements. It turned to these movements in part as a means of turning away from the civil rights movement. Its understanding of blackness called for racial separation, not integration. It called for an aggressive and macho way of relating to whites, as opposed to an interaction based on a "passive," nonviolent ethic of love. For many, it called for embracing socialism and rejecting America. For some, it called for rejecting "soul food," smoking, and drinking. These ideas helped distinguish those who were "Black" from those who were "Negro."

4

The Racial Structures of Black Power

The 1960s and 1970s were turbulent times for America. Many Americans believed that society was being turned upside down. For young people immersed in activist circles, these feelings were even more palpable. Much of the Third World had recently waged successful independence struggles against European colonialism, and people of color in the United States increasingly came to see themselves as part of the Third World. A number of prominent American political leaders were assassinated: John F. Kennedy, Malcolm X, Martin Luther King, Jr., and Robert F. Kennedy. The racist violence around the civil rights movement and the riots that burned out the core of many of America's major cities made the prospect of a racial war very real. To appreciate the ideology and practices of the black nationalists of the Black Power era, we must keep this context in mind. They lived at a time when it was easy to believe that a revolution was imminent, if not already occurring.[1]

The analysis of the Black Power movement is typically based on a political analysis of its goals and efficacy rather than an examination of its attempt to modify and construct racial structures. While many scholars would agree that Black Power activists attempted to impose new norms for blackness, they are divided over how committed Black Power activists were to transforming the larger political and economic racial structures that constrained black life in the United States. Many civil rights movement scholars argue that Black Power activists had no significant political and economic structural concerns. Many Black Power movement scholars argue that while "revolutionary" black nationalists had larger structural concerns, "cultural" black nationalists did not. This chapter will demonstrate that Black Power activists—both "revolutionary" *and* "cultural"—were seriously committed to changing the political and economic racial structures which constrained black life.

In the civil rights perspective on the Black Power movement, Black Power was responsible for the decline of civil rights. Black Power activists supposedly did not attack organizations and institutions which denied blacks political and economic opportunities. This perspective on Black Power is illustrated by the scholar Norman Kelley. According to Kelley, "the cry of Black Power was also a retreat from the kind of pivotal organizing work [such as] voter registration, freedom schools, [and] political mobilization" of civil rights activists. Kelley argues that Black Power "moved away from problem-solving in favor of 'symbolic' or 'expressive' politics" in which "flamboyant rhetorical skills replaced organizing and programs."[2] Kelley's views are not uncommon among civil rights scholars.[3]

Black Power activists often did not continue the strategies of civil rights activists because they were not trying to achieve what Civil Rights activists were. Many civil rights scholars fail to recognize that Black Power was a different movement with different goals, and that Black Power therefore requires different criteria for assessment. It makes no sense to fault activists for pursuing the wrong means to achieve racial *integration* when they were actually trying to achieve racial *separation*. Black Power was not a phase of the civil rights movement. It was in part a movement *against* the ideals of the civil rights movement.

Much of the analysis of the Black Power movement has focused on the "revolutionary" black nationalist wing best exemplified by the Black Panther Party. There is a growing and increasingly narrow literature on the Black Panther Party. While this literature does not have the same flaws as the civil rights literature, it still distorts the Black Power movement. The Black Panther Party was certainly an important part of Black Power—but it was only a part.

Both those who loved the Black Panther Party and those who hated it have reduced the black militancy of the 1960s to the Party, argues Nikhil Pal Singh. He writes, "the Black Panthers are the privileged signifier of Black militancy writ large," but "the more complex history and significance of Black radical traditions in the United States (and the Panthers' place within them) is left unwritten and unexplored."[4] We can gain a more complete understanding of the Black Power movement by appreciating the significance and place of the "cultural" black nationalist wing within it.

The Black Panthers were literally at war with US Organization ("US" as opposed to "them"), the seminal organization for "cultural" black nationalism. Despite the animosity between these organizations, scholars have treated the Panthers' characterizations of US Organization and of "cultural" nationalism as objective facts. For example, many scholars truly believe that "US" stands for "United Slaves," a term of slander created by the Panthers.[5] Also, despite the fact that "cultural" nationalists described themselves as socialists, wrote about the relationship of "cultural" nationalism to socialism, and established small-scale cooperative ventures, a number of scholars repeat the Panthers' claim that "cultural" nationalists espoused capitalism.[6] The increasing literature on the civil rights movement and the Black Panther Party has done little to improve the understanding of the "cultural" nationalism of Black Power, and there is little awareness of the great influence that "cultural" nationalism had on the Black Power movement as a whole.[7] This chapter will illustrate the meaning and significance of the "cultural" nationalism of Black Power.

Clarifying Terms: "Cultural" and "Revolutionary" Black Nationalism

One goal of this chapter is to put an end to the long-standing idea that there were clear ideological divisions between the "cultural" and "revolutionary" black nationalists of the Black Power era. I hope that in the future scholars will see both groups as merely Black Power black nationalists and not as "cultural" or "revolutionary" nationalists. Before we can get to that point, we have to distinguish the "cultural" from the "revolutionary" nationalists, so that we can see that they are similar. Unfortunately, the only way to do this is with some slightly cumbersome terminology.

Maulana Karenga, the founder of US Organization and the main developer of the "cultural" black nationalism of Black Power, uses the term "black cultural nationalism" to refer to the black nationalism he espoused.[8] This term suggests that he was advocating a type of "cultural nationalism." For scholars of nationalism generally, "cultural nationalism" refers to the assertion, celebration, and rejuvenation of cultural difference in intellectual and artistic movements.[9] But Karenga's "black cultural nationalism" extended beyond black cultural pride and included political nationalism—the struggle for black political autonomy. For this reason, Karenga's term "black cultural nationalism" is misleading. From the perspective of the comparative scholarship on nationalism, his black nationalism was simultaneously political and cultural. For analytic clarity, it is better to use the term "'cultural' black nationalism" to distinguish it from a real cultural nationalism like Afrocentrism which is discussed in chapters 5 and 6.

The Black Panther Party is often labeled a "revolutionary black nationalist" organization, but in fact it was not revolutionary. The leaders of the Party initially called for a UN plebiscite to determine black people's national destiny. The Party was later involved in electoral politics. These are not revolutionary acts. Manning Marable calls them radical reformers.[10] The Panthers also were simultaneously political and cultural nationalists. Despite the frequent portrayals of US Organization and the Black Panther Party as representing opposite poles of black nationalism, they were both quite similar and both in the mainstream of Black Power. Like the Panthers, US Organization also considered itself to be a revolutionary organization.[11]

The ideological differences between "cultural" and "revolutionary" black nationalists during the Black Power era have been exaggerated.[12] In general, "cultural" nationalists saw class as very important, but race as more so. They felt that white leftists were just as bad as white capitalists. "Revolutionary" nationalists were more likely than "cultural" nationalists to be open to coalitions with white leftists.[13] Although this "cultural" nationalist viewpoint has been misinterpreted to mean that they did not see class as important, "cultural" nationalists often called themselves "African socialists."[14] "Cultural" nationalists had a class analysis; it was just secondary to their race analysis. "Cultural" nationalists also tended to value cultural nationalism and African culture more than "revolutionary" nationalists did.[15]

While these general differences existed, they have been exaggerated and have obscured the many similarities between "cultural" and "revolutionary" nationalists. The racial separatism of the "revolutionary" nationalist Dodge Revolutionary Union Movement (DRUM), for example, bears a great deal of similarity with the position of "cultural" nationalists on race. DRUM rejected the "pseudo-democracy of the UAW [United Auto Workers union]" a presumably left-leaning organization. DRUM stated, "[the] honkey has been the historic enemy, betrayer, and exploiter of black people" and "we support everything the enemy opposes and oppose everything the honkey supports."[16] This "revolutionary" nationalist position on whites bore considerable similarity to the "cultural" nationalist position.

The West Coast Panthers did not concern themselves too much with African culture, but East Coast Panthers did. Scholars studying Panthers in New York found them to be more rooted in African culture than those on the West Coast. The former Black Panther Mumia Abu-Jamal reports that the New York chapter of the Party had a number of Muslims, Yorubas, and practitioners of the African-based Latin American religion, Santería.[17] These religious and cultural practices could fit well within "cultural" nationalism.

There were more similarities than differences between "cultural" and "revolutionary" nationalists of the Black Power era. The Freedom Library Day School in Philadelphia, for example, was a "cultural" nationalist organization because it subscribed to the teachings of Maulana Karenga.[18] This same school has been charac]terized as training students in "revolutionary nationalism" by William L. Van Deburg, based on his more limited examination of their ideology.[19]

The words "cultural" and "revolutionary" are therefore not truly descriptive of the type of nationalism these and other Black Power organizations espoused. For this reason, keeping them in quotation marks will draw attention to this fact. For example, both US Organization and the Black Panther Party were broadly focused black nationalist organizations, but one had a "cultural" *reputation* and the other a "revolutionary" one. As a shorthand, the word "black" in "black nationalism" will often be omitted since the discussion will focus primarily on black nationalism. US Organization, therefore, will be referred to as a "cultural" black nationalist or "cultural" nationalist organization. The Black Panther Party will be referred to as a "revolutionary" black nationalist or "revolutionary" nationalist organization.

Since the organizations that defined themselves as "cultural" black nationalist during the Black Power era are grossly understudied—no doubt due to misunderstandings about what they stood for—this chapter will dedicate as much space as possible to the ideology and practices of the "cultural" nationalism of Black Power. A "cultural" nationalist organization will be defined as an organization which accepts and attempts to follow Maulana Karenga's principles of blackness called the Nguzo Saba.

The Meaning of Black Power

> . . . the surrounding streets [were] full of our brainwashed black broth-
> ers and sisters, drinking, cursing, fighting, dancing, carousing, and using
> dope—the very things that Mr. Muhammad taught were helping the
> black man to stay under the heel of the white man here in America.
>
> —Malcolm X

> The "Negro" has more records than books and is dancing his life away.
>
> —Maulana Karenga

There is no one meaning of the Black Power movement. For different
groups, Black Power meant different things and impacted their lives in
different ways. For Black Power *activists*, the black popular culture of
the Black Power era—the movies, the music, the fashion, as well as the
"drinking, cursing, fighting, dancing, carousing, and using dope"—
more often than not went against their vision of black empowerment.
The activists on whom this chapter focuses saw the images of blacks
in the popular media as one of the many devices that enslaved black
minds.

The movies *Superfly* and *Shaft*, as well as many others like them,
were prime examples of white brainwashing, according to many Black
Power activists. These activists agreed that these films were more about
"blaxploitation"—black exploitation—than black liberation. The editor
of the "cultural" black nationalist *Black News* newspaper, for example,
thought that the black filmmaker, Gordon Parks, Jr., had enacted a
"most savage crime against Black Humanity" by making the movie
Superfly. According to Williams, *Superfly* was counterrevolutionary because it valorized using and dealing drugs. Since drugs harm black
people and since one cannot be a revolutionary and on drugs, in his
view the movie was clearly working against the aims of Black Power.[20]
Another activist argued:

> Today, though many of us talk about nation building, Black youths
> continue to be misguided in directions which make this sound ludi-
> crous. Can you imagine a nation being built from Superflys, Slaugh-
> ters and Shafts? These Black super dudes may be beating the man
> on the screen, but in reality they are only caricatures of a fantasy
> invented by those who oppress us. We must begin to help a young

brother understand that being a mack [a pimp] is not synonymous with being Black. And that Issac Hayes (Black Moses) can only lead him to the record store to be shafted.[21]

The Black Panther Party also criticized black popular culture. The Panthers' Ministry of Information stated:

Music today is tied up in stimulations, the blues makes you sad while rhythm makes you happy and you end up dancing to keep from crying, dancing while pigs [the police] are ripping off brothers and sisters in the streets of Babylon, and across the globe. . . .

We like the beat of James Brown, we say the Temptations sound great, but if we try to relate what they are saying to our conditions we'd end up in a ball of confusion. If we run around saying, "It's my thing and I can do what I want to do," we would never be free or singing "Cloud 9" to help the Mafia launch a new era of drugs.[22]

For activists, the black movies, music, and fashion of the 1970s did not capture the essence of what Black Power meant to them. Recently, the famous Black Power activist Angela Davis has lamented the iconographic status of her image from the 1970s. She is distressed that in the popular culture "I am remembered as a hairdo. It is humiliating because it reduces a politics of liberation to a politics of fashion."[23]

Being in opposition to black popular culture meant being in opposition to the lifestyles of most of black America. Maulana Karenga argued, "Black people don't have a culture, they have elements of a culture."[24] By this he meant, "Blacks have a popular culture rather than a national culture." For Karenga, black popular culture could not bring about positive social change because it was suffused with "lumpenism"—"hustler values" such as "quick money at any cost, heavy sex, conning, getting over." Black popular culture did not engender the values and practices that he thought would bring about a black nation.[25] While the Black Panthers were not as extreme in their views of what constituted a revolutionary lifestyle, they too saw a significant difference between average black Americans and black revolutionaries.[26]

It is important to distinguish the beliefs and actions of Black Power activists from the general black popular culture of the Black Power era. The activists were very critical of the popular culture. Yet some recent scholarship reduces the Black Power movement to the black popular culture of the time.[27] "Cultural" nationalists objected to much of black popular culture. What they meant by "cultural" nationalism was not *Shaft*.

This distinction has been missed by many analysts. William L. Van Deburg's *New Day in Babylon*, for example, is a very useful reference for the popular culture of the time. He also covers Black Power activists and provides an excellent overview of Black Power activism among athletes. However, his understanding of the meaning of Black Power as a whole is flawed. He begins his study with the intention of placing the Black Power movement in what he calls the "culture-and-community" perspective[28] and then rests his analysis heavily on black popular culture. Three times as much space is devoted to popular culture as to activists. Given that he begins with a bias toward "culture-and-community" and a heavy focus on popular culture, it is not surprising that he concludes, "The Black Power movement was not exclusively cultural, but it was essentially cultural."[29]

For some people, Black Power was the black popular culture of the 1970s. For Angela Davis and many other Black Power activists, though, there was a clear difference between the struggle for black liberation and black fashion. A good project for future research would be to examine the way activists and their ideas were reflected and distorted by the popular culture. But to conduct this analysis we have to be able to distinguish the activists from the popular culture.

The Black Power Conferences

> The fact was that they [the civil rights movement and Malcolm X] were going in opposite directions; they could not have walked together without him surrendering to them or them to him on all the questions that then seemed central—nonviolence, integration, even the meaning of blackness.   —Peter Goldman, *The Death and Life of Malcolm X*

In the civil rights perspective on Black Power, Black Power is often presented as a phase of civil rights—the phase when the civil rights movement lost its way and fell apart. In this narrative, the concept of Black Power is often described as having no real meaning. For Harvard Sitkoff and many others, "Black Power remained more an angry slogan than a clear program."[30] The first error in this analysis is the assumption that social movements are guided by a clear program rather than, as Adolph Reed states, an "ambiguous, yet global, vision" and the dialectic of struggle.[31]

For example, in the struggle that arose around Rosa Parks's arrest in Montgomery, Alabama, no one knew that they were part of the beginning of "the civil rights movement." There was no civil rights program. Among the initial demands was a compromise with Jim Crow laws, not their overthrow, as later developed. The "civil rights" activists at first called for "passengers to be seated on a first-come first-served basis—Negroes seating from the back of the bus toward the front while whites seated from the front toward the back."[32] The result would have been a softer and more flexible segregation but segregation nonetheless. Eventually the Montgomery struggle evolved into a struggle for "freedom"—a term indicating an ambiguous, yet global, vision and open to as many different interpretations as "Black Power."

In the popular civil rights narrative, the civil rights movement is defined backward from the legislative victories, thereby producing a history with a clear program that ends in success. But as Charles Payne has argued, for local people, the movement was about freedom, not just [the legislative victories of] civil rights. He explains, "At the very least, their conception of freedom would have included decent jobs, housing, and education."[33] It was because of the failure to realize these broader economic goals that many activists in the late 1960s and the 1970s became disillusioned with civil rights.[34] A number of them then turned to the strategies and goals of Black Power. For scholars who have defined the "program" of the civil rights movement as being only about legislation, however, there were no failures or disappointments in civil rights—it was a "textbook case of political success."[35]

The second error in the civil rights perspective on Black Power is the idea that Black Power was a part of civil rights. The assessment of Black Power in the civil rights perspective tends to rely heavily on the Student Nonviolent Coordinating Committee (SNCC) and CORE, two of the four main civil rights organizations.[36] When SNCC and CORE became Black Power organizations, they declined and disintegrated.[37] For scholars who examine Black Power through civil rights, the trajectory of these organizations becomes the trajectory of Black Power. But SNCC and CORE were never central to Black Power. Although SNCC member Carmichael's use of the phrase "Black Power" is the most famous (because of civil rights scholarship), Black Power did not begin in SNCC. If we must simplify history and identify a "father" for Black Power, it would have to be Malcolm X, not Carmichael. While SNCC and CORE did become Black Power organizations, their decline did not correspond to the decline of Black Power.

A good place to begin to grasp the meaning of Black Power for activists is with the Black Power conferences. Every year from 1966 to 1970, Black Power activists convened a national Black Power conference to discuss the goals of Black Power and to attempt to implement these goals and coordinate their activities.[38] All these conferences were organized in accordance with Maulana Karenga's idea of "unity without uniformity." They attracted black activists from a wide range of organizations, including civil rights organizations, who were interested in new approaches to black liberation. At these conferences, Black Power activists worked hard to be ecumenical and they largely achieved it among blacks. Whites were not invited.

U.S. Representative Adam Clayton Powell convened the first Black Power Conference in 1966. Notably, Powell had used the term "Black Power" before it was popularized by Stokely Carmichael of SNCC. For Powell, Black Power referred to black people exercising their "God-given rights," as opposed to man-made civil rights, to "build black institutions of splendid achievement."[39] He rejected the previous twenty-five years of the black struggle for integration and civil rights. He believed that "during those years, our leaders . . . drugged us with the LSD of integration."[40]

> Instead of telling us to seek audacious power—more black power—instead of leading us in the pursuit of excellence, our leaders led us in the sterile chase of integration as an end in itself in the debasing notion that a few white skins sprinkled amongst us would somehow elevate the genetics of our development.
>
> As a result, ours was an integration of intellectual mediocrity, economic inferiority and political subservience.[41]

For Powell, "Black Power" meant that black people should have black pride and should be in political and economic control of their organizations and communities. The conference attendees unanimously agreed with Powell when they defined "Black Power" as the "effective control and self-determination by men of color in their own areas. Power is total control of the economic, political, educational, and social life of our community from the top to the bottom."[42]

Leslie Campbell (Kasisi Jitu Weusi), a political and educational activist, came to a similar understanding of the meaning of Black Power after the 1967 Conference. He stated:

> With the convening of the [1967 Black Power] conference, the nightmare of integration ended for most black Americans. The thought that black Americans could successfully intermingle and intersperse themselves into white American society, sometime in the near future, has officially died and was buried at this conference.
>
> The dream that was born of this convention was the idea of black nationhood (here in North America) and self-determination for black people. The ideas and resolutions adopted by the conference all project toward that day when the black population of North America can say proudly, 'I don't want to be part of yours, I have my own.' If black power has one common meaning it most certainly means that black people have a right to and must rule and control their destinies here in America.[43]

For Campbell, like Powell, the meaning of Black Power was that black people should build their own organizations or take control of the organizations that served them. Both Powell and Campbell make clear that Black Power is not simply a new strategy within the civil rights movement but a rejection of the goals of that movement.

These ideas were restated at subsequent Black Power conferences. The activists at the 1968 Conference stated, "Black control is Black nationalism; control and chosen by Blacks for the benefit of Blacks. Separation has always been a fact. The difference now is that Blacks want to control and humanize it."[44] In the 1970 Black Power Conference, known as the Congress of African Peoples, the "Four Ends of Black Power" were defined as self-determination, self-sufficiency, self-respect, and self-defense for black Americans.[45] This conception of Black Power was only a slight expansion of Maulana Karenga's 1967 definition of Black Power as self-determination, self-respect, and self-defense.[46] The two hundred fifty organizations attending the 1970 Congress of African Peoples formally adopted this understanding of Black Power as part of the Conference.[47] This basic conception of Black Power was present from the first Black Power conference in 1966.[48]

One potential source of confusion for scholars studying the Black Power movement was the fact that by 1970 many Black Power activists began defining themselves as Pan-Africanists. The historian Manning Marable, for example, believes Pan-Africanism was a shift away from Black Power.[49] Again, if we turn to the Black Power conferences, we can understand what "Pan-Africanism" meant. The 1970 Congress of African Peoples defined Pan-Africanism as "the global expression of Black Nationalism," in other words, as the global expression of Black Power.[50] They argued that the "*Four Ends of Black Power* [are] not only . . . priorities of Africans on the American continent, or in the Western Hemisphere, but . . . major priorities for Africans all over the world."[51] Pan-Africanists argued, "all Black people are Africans, and that as Africans, [Black people] are bound together Racially, Historically, Culturally, Politically, and Emotionally."[52] Pan-Africanism, therefore, was not an opposing ideology to Black Power; rather it was the extension of Black Power to address black people globally.

Pan-Africanist ideals were present from the second Black Power Conference which had representatives from Nigeria and Bermuda. All subsequent Black Power conferences also had representatives from outside the United States and discussion of black political struggles elsewhere in the world. Although the organizers of the third Black Power Conference hoped that the fourth one would be held in Tanzania, that did not happen. It was still held outside the United States but in the more accessible Bermuda. C. L. R. James, the renowned socialist and Pan-Africanist scholar, chaired the political workshop at the Bermuda Conference. Pan-Africanism manifested itself at the fifth conference, in Amiri Baraka's call for a worldwide black political party. Baraka and his Committee for a Unified Newark would work on the first step to building this party: building a black political party in the United States. Black Power Conference attendees also displayed their Pan-Africanism through their African names and African garb.[53]

Although many scholars present Black Power activism as part of the civil rights movement, it is clear from the Black Power conferences that Black Power was not civil rights. Black Power was in part a rejection of many of the ideals of civil rights. Black Power activists rejected nonviolence in favor of self-defense. They rejected racial integration for racial separation. They rejected the pursuit of civil rights in American society for the pursuit of black self-determination. More and more activists came to see themselves not as Americans, but as Africans who were living as a colonized people in the United States.[54]

Black Power activists were interested in black people taking control of the organizations and institutions that affected them. In other words, Black Power advocated the ideas of black nationalism. Prior to the Black Power conferences, Malcolm X stated that black nationalism "means that the Black man should control the politics of his own community and control the politicians of his own community," and that "black nationalism . . . means that the Black man should have a hand in controlling the economy of the so-called Negro community."[55] Their global, heroic vision was black nationalism—for the United States and across the globe.

While in the popular civil rights narrative, all civil rights activism is interpreted as being directed toward specific legislation,[56] Black Power activism cannot be reduced in this way. Activists chose a tremendous range of targets on which to exert black control. Wherever black people were and whatever they were interested in became an arena in which they tried to give concrete expression to the ideas of Black Power: political activists worked to elect the first black mayors of many of America's major cities and to build independent black political parties; black artists formed a Black Arts movement; the Black Panthers and others decided to try to control the police in black communities; blacks in unions formed a radical black union movement; black educators agitated for community control of black children's education; blacks in Congress took the unprecedented move of forming the race-based Congressional Black Caucus; Pan-Africanists raised money for African liberation struggles; and so on.[57]

While the civil rights movement can largely be studied by focusing on four organizations (the SCLC, the NAACP, SNCC, and CORE), the Black Power movement is organizationally more complex. Activism in a multiplicity of arenas yielded a multiplicity of organizations. An analysis of national black organizations from a 1972 directory revealed that a disproportionate number were established during the Black Power era. Despite having organizations dating from as early as the late nineteenth century in the directory, at least 21 percent were founded between 1966 and 1972.[58] These organizations addressed political, economic, and cultural concerns and were said to be "technical support groups for the black liberation movement."[59] Other scholars have acknowledged the "organizational proliferation" of the Black Power era.[60] Given this proliferation of new organizations, we cannot argue that Black Power activists were not committed to organizing. The multiplicity of Black power organizations should not be seen as "confusion" but rather as evidence of the strength of the vision that was Black Power.

Both civil rights and Black Power activists were concerned with the racial structures that constrained black life in America. Civil rights activists hoped to remove obstacles so that blacks could participate fully and equally in American society. Black Power activists, after seeing white resistance to civil rights activists, decided to address structural inequality by removing blacks from white political and economic control as much as possible. The two movements were moving in opposite directions. Civil rights activists sought to participate more fully within American society and therefore interact more with whites; Black Power activists sought to interact less with whites and withdraw, at least to a degree, from American society.

Black Power was not civil rights. While many civil rights activists could focus their activism toward the U.S. government, Black Power activists were ambivalent about their relationship with the government and about the possibilities of the government being an agent of social change. Instead of organizing protests to appeal to a general white audience who would then pressure elected officials, Black Power activists built organizations that would achieve black autonomy. While Black Power activists did have angry, aggressive, and macho rhetoric, it is clear from the Black Power conferences that they were also concerned with the political and economic racial structures affecting black life. They concluded that black political and economic control over black life—Black Power—rather than the "LSD of integration," was the correct approach to achieving "freedom."

The Politics of "Cultural" Black Nationalism

The "cultural" black nationalism of Black Power has been misunderstood almost from the moment of its first articulation. This confusion is due in part to the fact that it is possible to define "culture" in several very different ways. Rather than defining "culture" narrowly to refer to the arts or values or traditions and customs, the "cultural" nationalists of the Black Power era defined "culture" broadly, as anthropologists do. Early cultural anthropological studies viewed all aspects of a society as "culture." The political and economic systems of a society, for example, were considered part of the "culture" of that society.[61] Many scholars, however, have come to understand the "cultural" nationalism of Black

Power along the lines of a narrow definition of "culture." For this reason, the "cultural" nationalism of Black Power is often represented as being apolitical. But in fact "cultural" nationalists were concerned with the same political issues as the "revolutionary" black nationalists of Black Power.

Because they believe that "cultural" black nationalism is about the arts, scholars often emphasize the black nationalist poetry of the Black Power era in discussions of what they call "cultural nationalism."[62] In these discussions, all Black Power poetry becomes an example of the "cultural" nationalism of Black Power. The problem with labeling any poetry written by someone advocating black nationalism "cultural" nationalism is that it arbitrarily privileges form over content. For example, during the Black Power era, the poet Nikki Giovanni was inspired by Malcolm X and the Black Panther Party and she expressed their ideas in her poetry.[63] She asked, "Can we learn to kill WHITE for BLACK" and asserted that "the barrel of a gun is the best / voting machine."[64] If we call the ideas spoken by Malcolm X or the Panthers political, we should also call them political when they are expressed in poetry.

Just as Black Power poetry is automatically placed under the "cultural nationalist" label, Black Power poets are defined as "cultural" nationalists because they write black nationalist poetry.[65] It is true that a number of prominent black nationalist poets were "cultural" nationalists, but that is not because they wrote poetry. They were "cultural" nationalists because they followed the teachings of Maulana Karenga, who developed the "cultural" nationalism of the Black Power era. Karenga practiced "cultural" nationalism for more than a decade before he published any poetry.[66] For Karenga, the arts were just one part of the broad meaning of the word "culture" and thus of "cultural" black nationalism. One could be a "cultural" nationalist without being a poet or artist of any sort.

Another reason for the misunderstanding of "cultural" nationalism is that many scholars have accepted the Black Panther Party's characterization of it. The Black Panther Party and Maulana Karenga's "cultural" nationalist US Organization were engaged in a violent conflict with each other. Surely, under these circumstances, we should be skeptical about how they might characterize each other.[67] The Panthers argued that Karenga's "cultural" nationalism was defined by a focus on the arts and African traditions which they saw as procapitalist and reactionary. Huey Newton, one of the founders of the Black Panther Party, stated:

Cultural nationalism . . . is basically the problem of having the wrong political perspective. It seems to be a reaction instead of responding to political oppression. The cultural nationalists are concerned with returning to the old African culture and thereby regaining their identity and freedom. In other words, they feel that the African culture will automatically bring political freedom. Many times cultural nationalists fall into line as reactionary nationalists.[68]

Another member of the Black Panther Party wrote in the Party's newspaper: "Cultural nationalism can be summed up in James Brown's words—'I'm Black and I'm Proud.'"[69] She added:

Those who believe in the "I'm Black and Proud" theory—believe that there is dignity inherent in wearing naturals; that a buba makes a slave a man; and that a common language; Swahili; makes all of us brothers. These people usually want a culture rooted in African culture; a culture which ignores the colonization and brutalization that were part and parcel; for example; of the formation and emergence of the Swahili language. In other words cultural nationalism ignores the political and concrete, and concentrates on a myth and fantasy.[70]

Many scholars have accepted the Black Panther Party's characterization of "cultural" nationalism as a reactionary focus on symbols of African culture.[71]

We can understand what Maulana Karenga meant by "cultural nationalism" and why he thought it would be useful for black liberation by examining the writings of the African nationalist leaders who influenced him. His name "Karenga" was taken from a book by Jomo Kenyatta, the Kenyan nationalist, Pan-Africanist, and the first prime minister of Kenya.[72] Kenyatta used the term "Kareng'a" to describe the nationalist schools of the Gikuyu[73] ethnic group in Kenya. Kenyatta celebrated these schools for being free from European influence and he defined "Kareng'a" as "a pure-blooded Gikuyu, a nationalist."[74] Maulana Karenga has translated "Karenga" to mean "keeper of tradition."[75] (Karenga translated the Kiswahili "maulana" to mean "master teacher" and "highest of high priests.")[76]

In *Facing Mount Kenya*, an anthropological study of his ethnic group, the Gikuyu, Jomo Kenyatta stated, "We cannot too strongly emphasize that the various sides of Gikuyu life"—the political, economic, educational, familial and religious—"are . . . parts of an integrated culture. No single part is detachable; each has its context and is fully understandable only in relation to the whole."[77] He explained:

> When the European comes to the Gikuyu country and robs the people of their land, he is taking away not only their livelihood, but the material symbol that holds family and tribe together. In doing this he gives one blow which cuts away the foundations from the whole of Gikuyu life, social, moral, and economic.[78]

For Kenyatta, all of Gikuyu social life was so tightly integrated that economic change would also change the tribal structure, the family structure, the educational system, religious practices, and sexual norms.

Léopold Senghor, the first president of Senegal, also influenced Maulana Karenga. Senghor argued that cultural independence would be the basis for building political, economic, and social independence. It was Senghor who argued that Africans are communal and "had already achieved socialism before the coming of the European."[79] Maulana Karenga's ideas about the meaning and importance of culture in nationalist movements came from African leaders who had successfully built black nations. In choosing to follow these leaders, he was not attempting to avoid the political, but hoping to succeed *politically* as these leaders had done.

Maulana Karenga noted that many people misunderstood the meaning of the word "culture" in his "cultural" nationalism:

> The problem with most people who do not understand cultural nationalism is that they see cultural nationalism in terms of a narrow definition of culture which deals with the arts. Whereas we of US, which is a Revolutionary Party with a correct revolutionary ideology, see culture as a total value system and institutions to maintain and develop that value system.[80]

Karenga specified "seven basic areas of culture: a. Mythology; b. History; c. Social Organization; d. Economic Organization; e. Political Organization; f. Creative Motif; g. Ethos."[81] "Cultural" nationalism addressed four areas: "1) religious nationalism, 2) political nationalism, 3) artistic nationalism, and even what may be called 4) 'atavism'—a return to the past because one cannot deal with the present and refuses to face the future."[82] In his ideology, Karenga explicitly defined politics as a subset of culture.

Maulana Karenga used the Nguzo Saba, the seven principles of his "African value system," as a device to encapsulate his ideology of "cultural" nationalism called Kawaida. Since he advocated the use of Kiswahili as a means of enabling black people to connect with their African heritage, the seven principles were presented in Kiswahili. These principles were:

Umoja—Unity
To strive for and maintain unity in the family, community, nation and race.

Kujichagulia—Self-determination
To define ourselves, name ourselves, create ourselves, and speak for ourselves.

Ujima—Collective Work and Responsibility
To build and maintain our community together and make our brothers' and sisters' problems our problems and to solve them together.

Ujamaa—Cooperative Economics
To build and maintain our own stores, shops, and other businesses and to profit from them together.

Nia—Purpose
To make as our collective vocation the building and developing of our community in order to restore our people to their traditional greatness.

Kuumba—Creativity
To do always as much as we can, in the way we can, in order to leave our community more beautiful and beneficial than we inherited it.

Imani—Faith
To believe with all our hearts in our parents, our teachers, our leader, our people, and the righteousness and victory of our struggle.[83]

The Nguzo Saba is also central to the ritual of Kwanzaa that Karenga created. While the Kiswahili of the Nguzo Saba and the principles of

Faith and Creativity are part of cultural nationalism as defined by scholars of nationalism generally, the other principles are part of political nationalism. The ideal of national Unity is clearly a political goal. Collective Work and Cooperative Economics are consciously socialist political and economic principles which would be placed under political nationalism. The ideal of Purpose taps into the socialist political nationalist principle of "collective vocation [in] the building and developing of our community" and the cultural nationalist ideal of "restor[ing] our people to their traditional greatness." Self-Determination also has both a political and a cultural nationalist tenor. The political and economic concerns in Karenga's ideology are obvious. Karenga's "cultural" nationalism was an Africa-oriented black nationalism that Black Power advocates would call Pan-Africanism.[84] As such, it was not radically different from most of the other black nationalist ideologies of the Black Power era.

The violent conflict between the Black Panther Party and US Organization convinced many scholars that these were fundamentally different types of Black Power organizations. The common view is that the Panthers are revolutionary and political, and US Organization is not revolutionary, not political, and only concerned about rebuilding African customs and values.[85] Maulana Karenga's activities propagating the use of Kiswahili and his founding of Kwanzaa lent support to this interpretation. However, the conflict between the Black Panther Party and US Organization stemmed from their similarities, not their differences.

There are many similarities between the two organizations. The leaders of both organizations began their political education in black history in the Afro-American Association,[86] and decided to form activist organizations that went beyond merely studying black history. The leaders of both organizations saw themselves as continuing the political project of Malcolm X.[87] The Black Panther Party's first major concern was with policing the police. US Organization for a time cooperated with the Black Panther Party in this activity.[88] Both organizations were members of the Los Angeles Black Congress, a Black Power confederation.[89] US Organization joined the Black Panther Party in speaking out against the Vietnam War,[90] and Maulana Karenga demanded the release from prison of Huey Newton, one of the founders of the Black Panther Party.[91] The Panthers also supported Karenga's ideas on gender before the groups came into conflict.[92] The two organizations thus had an early history of working together and supporting each other on a variety of issues.

Part of the "revolutionary" mystique of the Black Panther Party was their prominent display of guns. The US Organization also had an armed paramilitary wing, but US believed that their preparations for violent struggle should not be publicized. US Organization hoped to finance its revolutionary struggle from the spoils of robberies, and indeed several of its members were arrested for armed robbery. Scholars are generally not aware of the paramilitary aspect of US, while the Panthers, on the other hand, tend to be defined by their guns.[93]

If we were to accept the idea that poetry is a major indicator of "cultural" nationalism, it could be argued that the Black Panthers were stronger "cultural" nationalists than the members of US Organization. Poetry was a constant feature of the Black Panther newspaper. At night, Panthers in Oakland read their poetry out loud to each other. They also shared poetry written by published authors, including poems by the "cultural" nationalist Haki Madhubuti. The Panthers also had a musical group and sponsored community dances. Elaine Brown, who would become the leader of the Black Panthers, wrote songs for the struggle. Their belief that revolutionary art should be revolutionary propaganda echoed the ideas of "cultural" nationalists. Like "cultural" nationalists, they were interested in educating black youth and formed black nationalist schools. While the West Coast Panthers downplayed the importance of Africa, the East Coast Panthers were very interested in West African-based religions. Any careful examination of the Panthers and US Organization or other "cultural" nationalists reveals considerable overlap in the ideology and activism of these supposedly contrasting wings of Black Power.[94]

The conflict between the Black Panther Party and the US Organization was not a conflict between "revolutionary" nationalism and "cultural" nationalism. This point is illustrated by the fact that the Panthers did not have conflicts with "cultural" nationalist organizations in other parts of the United States.[95] "Cultural" nationalists outside Southern California expressed their support for the Panthers. Other "cultural" nationalists also concurred with the Panthers' critique of "reactionary nationalism."[96] The conflict between the Panthers and US Organization was really about two very similar, powerful, and aggressive organizations both attempting to control black nationalist activities in Southern

California. The first violent conflict between US Organization and the Panthers occurred as they were both attempting to gain influence over the UCLA Black Student Union. If US Organization consisted of only people studying Kiswahili and African customs, they would have been easily dominated by the Panthers, as other black nationalist organizations in Southern California were.[97] Instead both organizations had armed members, which led to the killings. It is from the vitriol spewed by these conflicts that the caricature of "cultural" nationalism came about.

Another leading "cultural" nationalist of the Black Power era, and a disciple of Maulana Karenga, was Amiri Baraka. Scholars classify Baraka as a cultural—meaning "artistic"—nationalist because of his involvement in the Black Arts movement.[98] But Baraka and the members of his Committee for a Unified Newark (CFUN) were grassroots organizers who were an important factor in the election of Newark's first black mayor, Kenneth Gibson. CFUN members were also the organizers of the international Congress of African Peoples and Baraka was the coordinator of the workshop on political liberation. This workshop issued a call for the formation of an independent black political party. Toward that end Baraka and CFUN organized the first National Black Political Convention in Gary, Indiana, which aimed to have all black elected officials agree to a national black political agenda. For "many black scholars and activists, the Gary Convention represented the culmination of the entire legacy of black struggles," writes Manning Marable. If the Gary Convention was the political high point of a "Second Black Reconstruction," to paraphrase Marable, it was Baraka and CFUN—"cultural" nationalists—who made it happen.[99]

It is clear that Baraka's understanding of "cultural" nationalism was not limited to the arts. In addition to CFUN's deep involvement in politics at the local and national levels, it was also an umbrella organization for black nationalist activity in several arenas. CFUN had a drama group, an independent school, two newspapers, a publishing house, a book and clothing store (Nyumba ya Ujamaa), a grocery store (Duka Ujamaa), a cafeteria (Chakula Ujamaa), a communications school, a political activist school, and an urban planning committee.[100] All these activities were geared toward practicing and propagating black nationalism. Each venture was controlled by blacks and, more importantly, by black nationalists, but not by whites. Baraka's writings, for example, could be published by CFUN's Jihad Productions instead of a white-controlled publishing house. All the activities disseminated the ideals of "cultural" black nationalism, whether directly or indirectly.

Other "cultural" black nationalists also indicated their concern with building black nationalist-controlled organizations or "institution building," as they called it. While Haki Madhubuti was a poet, he was also one of the leaders of the Institute for Positive Education in Chicago. The Institute was an umbrella organization for an independent black school, a magazine, a typesetting operation, and the Ujamaa Food Cooperative. Madhubuti supported the African Liberation Day Support Committee, which raised funds for African independence movements. He also founded his own publishing house, Third World Press.[101]

We again see the importance of institution building at the Ahidiana umbrella organization in New Orleans led by the poet and "cultural" nationalist, Kalamu ya Salaam. Members of Ahidiana organized demonstrations against apartheid in South Africa and against police brutality in New Orleans. Ahidiana also ran an independent school, a poetry and music ensemble, a publishing house, and a food cooperative.[102]

One could be a prominent "cultural" nationalist leader without being a poet. Kasisi Jitu Weusi was not a poet, but he was the head of an umbrella organization in Brooklyn, New York, called East. East had an independent school, a newspaper (*Black News*), a day care center, a catering service, and a food cooperative.[103] For Weusi, Pan-Africanism was of practical value in his community organizing work. In Brooklyn in the 1970s there were increasing numbers of black immigrants from a variety of Caribbean countries. Weusi believed that the ideology of Pan-Africanism could unify blacks with these various national identities into a political force in Brooklyn.[104] Activists in East also saw an international perspective as necessary for addressing "white capital." They argued, "in every country where Black people live, they [are] at the bottom of the socio-economic ladder . . . [and are] being exploited and cruelly used by white capital; capitalism is a system with international ramifications, thus the problem of black people becomes international in scope and any strategy for black liberation must, in order to be effective, involve international co-ordination."[105]

The conflicts "cultural" nationalists had with the Black Panther Party and later with black Marxists led to the accusation that "cultural" nationalists were either ignoring class or being procapitalist. Both positions are false. "Cultural" nationalism advocated Ujamaa—cooperative economics. All the "cultural" nationalist umbrella organizations discussed above had at least a food cooperative. Many had other cooperative ventures as well.

"Cultural" nationalists were anticapitalist. Karenga argued, "Capitalism is an individual concept. Blacks can only reach a stage of economic force through a co-operative economic system."[106] Like "revolutionary" nationalists, "cultural" nationalists were generally distrustful of middle-class blacks because middle-class blacks had succeeded in what they saw as a white system. Middle-class blacks needed to prove that they were not "Negroes" but "Blacks"—Black Power advocates.[107]

The conflict "cultural" nationalists had with other black leftists was over whether class was more important than race and whether alliances with whites were desirable. For "cultural" nationalists, race came first. However, there was a class critique within their race analysis. In their view, capitalism was reflective of individualistic, competitive, and exploitative white values.[108] As presented clearly in the Nguzo Saba—the Seven Principles of Blackness—collectivism was seen as a black value. Their views of whites made political strategies predicated on having white allies anathema.

CFUN, the Institute for Positive Education, Ahidiana, and East were all linked to each other and to Maulana Karenga and US Organization.[109] Haki Madhubuti provides a neat summary of the ideology behind all these organizations:

we're Pan-Afrikanists, Black Nationalists, and African Socialists (UJAMAA); all three areas are connecting and embody knowledge of the present and past, presenting a workable plan for tomorrow for all Afrikans wherever they are. To say we are Pan-Afrikanists is not visionary thinking or theorizing. We believe in one Afrika and the oneness of Afrikan people. As Black Nationalists we believe we must nationalize our thoughts and actions, must establish a national-international Black thought—international Black movement—can a Black in Zimbabwe think and act in concert with a Black on the West side of Chicago? Can the blood in the Caribbean feel the weight of crackers breeding their corruption among us as we feel it in New York City? As Afrikan Socialists, we must go back to the original Afrikan communalism—the basis of all humane governmental systems, the willingness to share and work together, UJAMAA (cooperative economics) and UJIMA (collective work and responsibility).[110]

A range of political activity emerged from this ideology: from community protests against police brutality, to electoral politics, to raising funds for African liberation struggles, to secretly stockpiling funds and weapons for a revolutionary struggle. Again we see the arbitrariness of the "revolutionary" and "cultural" black nationalist distinction by noting that the "revolutionary" Black Panther Party engaged in no political activity that the "cultural" nationalists did not engage in as well.[111]

"Cultural" nationalist organizations worked to have black people build or take control of organizations that served blacks. These organizations and their leaders not only embodied the ideals and practices of Black Power through their writings and their leadership of the Black Power conferences, but they were crucial to defining the meaning of Black Power for thousands of other activists across the country. "Cultural" nationalists were the mainstream of Black Power.

Pan-African Education

> The revolution being fought now is a revolution to win the minds of our people. If we fail to win this we cannot wage the violent one.
> —Maulana Karenga, US Organization, 1967

> We understand clearly that those who can control the mind can control the body. What we have is an educational system which is completely controlled by the power structure.
> —Huey P. Newton, Black Panther Party, 1971

Black Power activists strove to take control of organizations and institutions. Every social activity became an arena for Black Power activism. Education was an especially important arena because it was believed to be the key to the minds of the next black generation. If black children were allowed to be educated by whites, they would likely become "Negroes." But if they had a black nationalist education, they would become "Blacks" and continue the struggle to build a black nation. Although the focus here will be on the educational activities of "cultural" nationalists, "revolutionary" nationalists like the Black Panther Party were also involved in educating black youth, and they used the same rationale as the "cultural" nationalists for doing so.[112]

Although segregated schools were outlawed by the *Brown v. Board of Education* decision in 1954, by 1970 most black children still attended segregated and inferior schools.[113] In this arena, it appeared to many blacks that civil rights had failed. They were frustrated by the failure of American society to desegregate schools, and by the failure of American schools to properly educate their children. Black educators who were inspired by Black Power made education their arena for Black Power activism. Some educators brought black nationalism informally or formally into the public school system. Others formed private black nationalist schools.

Among these were the private black nationalist schools and educational organizations that joined together to form the Council of Independent Black Institutions (CIBI). A number of prominent "cultural" nationalists (e.g., Amiri Baraka, Haki Madhubuti, and Kasisi Jitu Weusi) had a CIBI school as part of their confederation of organizations.[114] By examining CIBI, we can gain another vantage point on the meaning of Black Power, "cultural" nationalism, and Pan-Africanism. While CIBI, like a number of other Black Power organizations and institutions, still exists today, the following discussion of the organization focuses on what CIBI *was* in the 1970s.

The Council of Independent Black Institutions

The Council of Independent Black Institutions came into being over a three-year period from 1970 to 1972. The idea for establishing what the activists imagined would become a national black school system was set in motion at the California Association for Afro-American Education conference at Nairobi College (in East Palo Alto, California) in August 1970. This meeting was attended by established Black Power activists and educators from more than twenty already functioning black private schools.[115] At the Nairobi College conference, the activists refined their model of black nationalist education and began to develop an organizational structure for black private schools nationally. These activities were continued at the Education Workshop of the Congress of African Peoples in September 1970 and the African-American Teachers Convention in April 1972. CIBI was founded in June 1972.[116]

Many of the ideas that would be incorporated into the philosophy of CIBI were already in place at the California Association for Afro-American Education conference. The keynote speaker, James Lee of Malcolm

X Liberation University, set the tone for the conference. Lee argued that black activists needed to recognize "that traditional solutions to the 'Black Problem' (e.g., integration) have not been functionally appropriate."[117] The American educational system had failed to produce black people who could be of use to black communities, and black Americans needed revolutionary education. Because "racism is a pervasive phenomenon within and throughout American social institutions," black Americans needed to build "an independent society through the development of independent social institutions—which by necessity involves the acquisition of land and power through struggle, revolution, and if necessary, war."[118]

The activists at the Nairobi Conference incorporated the basic ideas of Black Power into their understanding of black nationalist education. They defined the "Independent Black Institution" as follows:

> The ideology of the Independent Black Institution must include but is not necessarily limited to six fundamental concepts: (1) the concept of *communalism*, (2) the concept of *decolonization*, (3) the concept of the *African Personality*, (4) the concept of *humanism*, (5) the concept of *harmony* between the individual and his environment, (6) the concept of *nation-building*.[119]

These concepts blended political and cultural nationalist ideas. Decolonization and nation-building directly referred to the political nationalist ideals of black control of organizations and institutions that served blacks. The activists defined "decolonization" and "nation-building" as follows:

> *Decolonization* emphasizes the acquisition of ownership and control by African people of the political, economic, social, and educational institutions which are rightfully their own.
>
> *Nation-building* is an evolutionary process involving the utilization of human and material resources for community development, service, ownership, and control—survival.[120]

They reaffirmed the political nationalist goals of Black Power and rejected the civil rights pursuit of integration.

The CIBI activists felt that black liberation also required a wide range of social values that would root black Americans in Africa as opposed to America. The other four concepts of "Independent Black Institutions" represented these cultural nationalist African values:

> *Communalism* represents the antithesis of competitive individualism, that is, a set of human relationships based upon cooperativeness, cohesiveness, and concern for African peoples transcending self.
>
> Though as yet fully undefined, the *African Personality* as embodied in the New African Man is representative of a set of attitudes, values, and behaviors which are necessary for the development, maintenance, and perpetuation of African peoples throughout the world. The concept of the African Personality includes but is not limited to respect for ancestors and the African heritage, identification with Africa and African people throughout the world, concern for the unification of all African people, positive self-identification, and faith and trust in Black people.
>
> *Humanism* is in essence an attitudinal and behavioral perspective which stresses *distinctively* human rather than material profit concerns.
>
> *Harmony* between the individual and his environment suggests a functional relationship between man and his natural surroundings and stresses functional congruency between man and his environment.[121]

All these concepts were understood to distinguish the true nature of black or African people from the nature of white or European people. The activists believed that Europeans are competitive individualists and Africans are communal. Europeans value material profit over people; Africans value human concerns over profit. Europeans exploit people and the environment; Africans live harmoniously with people and the environment. Africans are rooted in their African heritage, Europeans in their European heritage.[122]

These values implied a political and economic orientation to being truly African. Africans are anticapitalist because they are communalists and humanists. A CIBI activist at the first meeting wrote, "Do you remember when you, I, we, us had communalism / Do you remember when the crackers made it communism."[123] Africans are also environmentalists because they value harmony with nature.

CIBI was a Black Power "cultural" black nationalist organization because it adopted the Nguzo Saba, Maulana Karenga's Seven Principles of Blackness. The statement of purpose for Independent Black Institutions read:

Since the present European value system has proven detrimental to our people we must present an alternative value system. This value system is embodied in the Nguzo Saba (Seven Principles of Blackness).[124]

CIBI was founded with ten schools and one educational consulting firm serving as full-time members. At its first work meeting, another school and two more educational organizations joined the confederation.[125] A year later, CIBI consisted of nineteen schools and two educational organizations.[126] By the end of the 1970s, CIBI had thirty schools.[127] We should realize that the CIBI represented only a portion of the independent black schools in existence at the time. For example, in 1970, one organization assembled a list of sixty-two independent black schools.[128] While CIBI is a significant organization in itself, it also serves as a window into a larger national movement of independent black education during the Black Power era.[129] We must now examine how the ideology of Pan-Africanism was implemented in independent black schools.

EDUCATION IN THE COUNCIL OF INDEPENDENT BLACK INSTITUTIONS

Black nationalist private schools differed in ideology and practice. Even within CIBI one finds variation. This study will not attempt to map these variations; rather, the focus will be on illustrating how the "cultural" nationalism or Pan-Africanism of Black Power shaped educational practice. This approach means that non-Pan-African practices will be ignored. As a result, the more strongly Pan-African schools will receive more attention. The overall goal is to show how the racial ideology shaped the racial structure (i.e., the establishment of black nationalist schools and the practice of education in black nationalist schools), not to document all practices.

CIBI activists believed that their political and educational aims could best be achieved by what they saw as an African communal ethos in their schools. When they selected teachers, many CIBI activists valued ideological commitment more than educational credentials and experience.[130] In the Afrikan Free School in Newark, which was part of Amiri Baraka's community organization, the Committee for a Unified Newark, the entire school staff had to be part of the larger community organization.[131] Communalism also meant that teachers were required to think of the students as their children, and the children had to think of the teachers as parents. Female teachers were referred to by the Kiswahili term for mother, "Mama," and male teachers by the term for father, "Baba." The students also referred to each other as "Ndugu" (brother) and "Ndada" (sister). The activists argued that this family orientation ensured that the students received the love they needed and that education was viewed as part of the collective work and responsibility of the community (Ujima).[132]

African and African American history were an integral part of education at CIBI schools. For example, at Umoja Sasa Shule ("Unity Now School") in Columbus, Ohio, one of the texts children used was a book entitled *Chaka of East Afrika*. This text introduced students to the life of a boy in Tanzania. Other texts used in the Umoja Sasa School, such as *Color Us Black, Think Black*, and *Billy's Surprise* introduced children to other aspects of African and African American life. *Billy's Surprise* taught students the names of African countries and stated that Africa was "the home of [Billy's] great, great, grandparents." Among the lessons of *Think Black* is that "Methodone is slavery."[133]

At Uhuru Sasa Shule ("Freedom Now School"), students began learning to read *The Weusi Alfabeti* ("The Black Alphabet"). *The Weusi Alfabeti* begins:

A is for Africa, B is for Black, C is for Culture, And that's where it's at." It continues, "D is for Defend, E is for Equality, F is for Freedom, We're going to get it, Just you wait and see. . . . L is for some Land, We'd better get some as fast as we can. . . . N is for our Nation, O is for organize and then we will nationalize, . . . X is for negro who's blind, deaf and dumb.

The *Weusi Alfabeti* is illustrated with pictures, drawings, and writings on Pan-African themes. There are drawings and photographs of armed African revolutionaries, pictures of black students, and writings on Malcolm X and the Nguzo Saba. High-school students at Uhuru Sasa read materials such as the "Rejection of European Rule with a Demand for Independence" by Patrice Lumumba, the assassinated leader of the Congo, *The Mis-Education of the Negro* by Carter G. Woodson, the "Nature of the Mau Mau Movement" by Waruhiu Itote, *Malcolm X on Afro-American History* by El Hajj Malik Shabazz (Malcolm X), "Ragtime Roots of Jazz" by James Weldon Johnson, and "How to Be a Good Political Organizer" by the SNCC activist, James Forman.[134]

The history provided in many of the schools was geared toward educating the students about black political struggles in the United States, Africa, and in the rest of the African diaspora. At Uhuru Sasa, they learned about political organizing from James Forman of SNCC, and about the violent resistance of the Kenyan Mau Mau to British domination. At Umoja Sasa, students learned to avoid drug addiction by learning that "Methodone is slavery." The antidrug use message was even stronger at Uhuru Sasa where high school students read antidrug use cartoons, poetry, and short stories.[135]

At the Afrikan Free School, the students' political consciousness was developed from their first days at school. As part of their orientation to the school, students were taken on walks through the neighborhood and were encouraged to reflect upon the problems of the community. The children walked to bars, welfare offices, department stores, and other centers of community activity. Teachers discussed who owned the stores and who shopped in them. The inconsistency between white ownership and black consumers was used to lead students to advocate black control of businesses serving black communities. After discussing this and other problems, students were encouraged to think about what they could do to solve them.[136]

For many CIBI educators, education was explicitly meant to create activists. As Kasisi Jitu Weusi, the headmaster of Uhuru Sasa Shule, stated, his school aimed to "develop a new personality, an African personality," and his graduates were to be "conscious political beings" who would organize and "take over all aspects of the community."[137] One of the first lessons Uhuru Sasa students learned was "O is for organize and then we will nationalize." "Cultural" nationalist education consisted of much more than "I'm Black and I'm Proud."

The politics of Pan-African education is also revealed by the fact that in 1973, seven of the twenty-one CIBI schools had prison programs.[138] The students at Umoja Sasa celebrated Kwanzaa with MPINGO, a black nationalist organization at the London, Ohio, Correctional Institution.[139] The Director of that school encouraged former convicts to become teachers in the school. He believed that reformed former convicts had greater insight into the political domination of black Americans than more traditionally successful blacks.[140] At Nairobi College, black men entered the college as part of their parole. By 1972, Nairobi College had enrolled fifteen men on parole and was proud of the fact that none had returned to prison.[141]

CIBI schools were small and poorly funded, and could have easily justified focusing on only the three Rs. If as "cultural" nationalists, they were truly focused on artistic nationalism, they could have directed their resources toward the arts. Instead, CIBI schools stressed scientific and vocational education. CIBI activists believed that it was important for their students to have these skills so that blacks, and not whites, would provide such skills for black communities. Weusi Shule ("Black School") and other schools taught woodworking.[142] The Afrikan Free School taught sewing, pottery making, typing, and auto mechanics.[143] Nairobi College required that their students learn one technical skill to graduate. The college also had a work study program that allowed students to work in community organizations for credit.[144] CIBI had annual science fairs that focused on how science could benefit black people.[145]

Uhuru Sasa's curriculum makes it clear that "cultural" black nationalism was not seen as antithetical to violent, revolutionary struggle. The illustration accompanying "D is for Defend" in the *Weusi Alfabeti* depicts a uniformed black male soldier with a shoulder patch containing an outline of Africa. "M is for our Men," is accompanied by a photo of a group of armed black male soldiers who are probably from an African army.[146] As students learned the alphabet, they also learned about black men engaging in violent struggle.

Although Uhuru Sasa was not the only school to incorporate martial arts, it was the most thorough.[147] In addition to the self-defense and disciplinary benefits of martial arts, students were taught that they might someday use their martial arts skills in a revolutionary struggle. They read an except from Sam Greenlee's *The Spook Who Sat by the Door* which depicted black guerillas at war with the U.S. government. In the excerpt, the leader of the guerilla army uses his martial arts skills to kill a black police officer. The reading question, "Why was it necessary, and why will it be necessary to kill people like [the black police officer]?" accompanies the excerpt.[148] Students also learned first aid for treating gunshot wounds.[149] The educators at Uhuru Sasa believed, just as James Lee of Malcolm X Liberation University did, that black liberation would require "struggle, revolution, and if necessary, war."[150]

Maulana Karenga taught that males and females complemented each other and were not equals. For Karenga, this meant that women should generally not be in leadership roles and should be restricted to domestic activity. He argued that it was the duty of women to inspire their

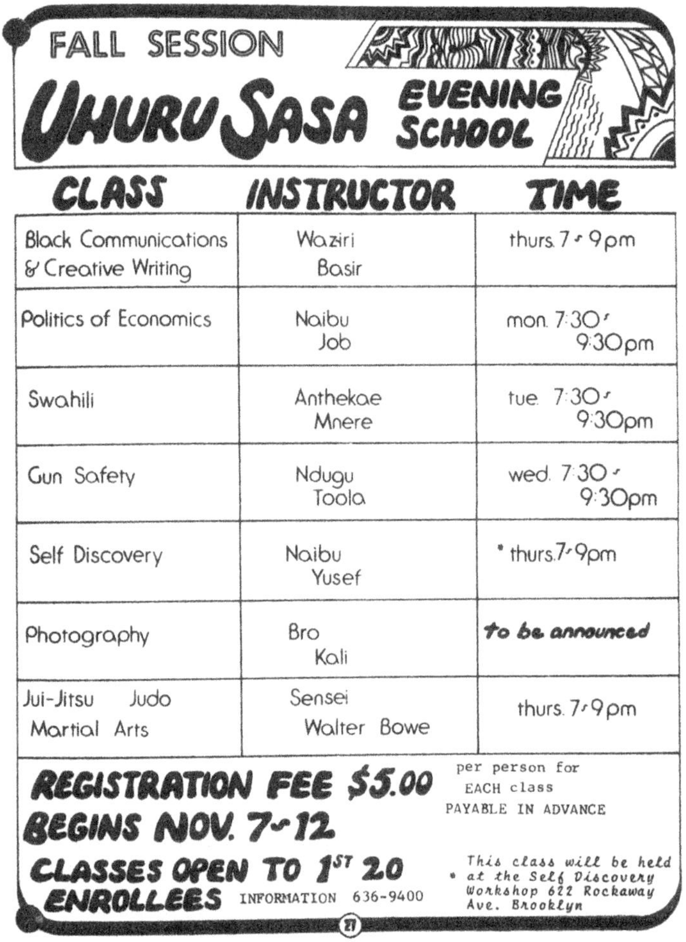

FALL SESSION

UHURU SASA EVENING SCHOOL

CLASS	INSTRUCTOR	TIME
Black Communications & Creative Writing	Waziri Basir	thurs 7 - 9 pm
Politics of Economics	Naibu Job	mon. 7:30 - 9:30pm
Swahili	Anthekae Mnere	tue. 7:30 - 9:30pm
Gun Safety	Ndugu Toola	wed. 7:30 - 9:30pm
Self Discovery	Naibu Yusef	* thurs.7-9pm
Photography	Bro Kali	*to be announced*
Jui-Jitsu Judo Martial Arts	Sensei Walter Bowe	thurs. 7-9 pm

REGISTRATION FEE $5.00
per person for EACH class
PAYABLE IN ADVANCE

BEGINS NOV. 7-12

CLASSES OPEN TO 1ST 20
ENROLLEES
INFORMATION 636-9400

This class will be held
* at the Self Discovery
Workshop 622 Rockaway
Ave. Brooklyn

Fig. 4.1. For the educators at Uhuru Sasa Shule (Freedom Now School), "cultural" nationalism was not solely about the arts or solely about re-creating African traditions. They did not see the study of Swahili as being incompatible with or in opposition to the study of the "Politics of Economics." They did not see the practice of "Black Communications" as incompatible with or in opposition to training in the martial arts and in the use of firearms for a coming revolutionary struggle. For "cultural" nationalists, being a black nationalist meant being a cultural *and* political nationalist. Only in the rhetoric of the opponents of "cultural" nationalists was "cultural" nationalism simply about "I'm Black and I'm Proud." (Advertisement from *Black News*, 22 October 1973)

men.[151] Many schools ignored this precept, but some conveyed the idea of "complementarity" in both subtle and overt ways. The Afrikan Free School and the Uhuru Sasa School, for example, segregated male and female students, although for the most part the same material was presented to both.[152] Gendered educational differences often arose around the issue of vocational education. For example, at the Martin Luther King, Jr. Community School in Atlanta, Georgia, the instructors stated, "the young men are exposed to carpentry and electronics, etc., while the young ladies delight in measuring, sewing, mixing, baking, etc."[153] Umoja Sasa had camping and "survival hikes" for fathers and their sons in the school.[154] At New Concepts in Chicago and other schools, boys were required to stand at "attention" with their arms folded across their chests; girls stood or sat in "submission" with their arms making an "X" across their chests by having each hand lie flat just below the opposite shoulder.[155]

By forming schools for black students that were under black control and by aspiring to build a national black school system, CIBI activists showed that they were serious about creating new educational structures. All CIBI schools claimed ideological independence from whites. In 1973, thirteen of twenty-one CIBI members' schools could claim complete financial independence from whites or the U.S. government. Black self-sufficiency was clearly the ideal.[156] As noted earlier, these schools were in many cases just one part of the black organization-building agenda of activists. The Afrikan Free School was part of Amiri Baraka's complex of community organizations known as the Committee for a Unified Newark.[157] New Concepts was part of Haki Madhubuti's complex of community organizations known as the Institute of Positive Education.[158] Uhuru Sasa Shule was part of Kasisi Jitu Weusi's complex known as East.[159] For these reasons, we have to take seriously the understanding of Black Power as being about blacks having control of the organizations that served them.

The activists in CIBI also used the schools to convey the ideology of Black Power and "cultural" nationalism to the wider community through the students. Many schools began the day with a Pan-African pledge. At New Concepts the students recited the general CIBI pledge:

We are Afrikan people struggling for national liberation. We are preparing leaders and workers to bring about positive change for our people. We stress the development of our bodies, minds, souls and consciousness. Our commitment is to self-determination, self-defense and self-respect for our race.[160]

Teachers and students in CIBI schools understood Pan-Africanism politically. The Africa that CIBI students and teachers were encouraged to think about was contemporary Africa, struggling against apartheid and imperialism, not simply a romanticized Africa in the distant past. They studied the writings of recent African independence leaders, many of whom were socialists, such as Kwame Nkrumah, Julius Nyerere, Jomo Kenyatta, Patrice Lumumba, and other modern Third World leaders.[161] CIBI educators and students also participated in the African Liberation Support Committee that raised money for and publicized the causes of African liberation movements.[162] CIBI activists hoped that through their schools and other community activities they would achieve Black Power: self-determination, self-defense, and self-respect for black Americans and blacks across the globe.

From "Black" to "Afrikan"

By the 1970s, "cultural" black nationalists increasingly called themselves "Afrikans," not "Blacks." The move from "Black" to "Afrikan" was motivated by the growing international perspective of activists and by their increasing alienation from America. "Afrikan" was also a useful term because by the early 1970s more and more "Negroes" were calling themselves "Blacks." As a term, "Black" was losing its power to distinguish the more committed Black Power activists from the general black population. The success of Black Power meant that more people adopted the symbols of Black Power without accepting its political and economic message. The blaxploitation movies employed the "black macho" style but without Black Power's leftist critique of American society. As Angela Davis has suggested, the politics of fashion obscured the politics of liberation.

In an attempt to counteract this depoliticization of their movement, activists repeatedly insisted that Black Power meant more than just racial pride. While cultural pride and positive racial identities were necessary, they insisted that Black Power was about power. Black nationalist educators argued, "Blackness must change its emphasis from that which is seen, such as Afros and dashikis, to that which is necessary, such as living and working with Black people to achieve our goal of liberation."[163] The editors of *Black News* told blacks, "Just to be Black is not enough. . . . What are you going to do when the Man comes to your home and you only have a dashiki. . . . Beat him with it . . . or butt him with your Afro?"[164] At the 1970 Congress of African Peoples Jesse Jackson emphasized that Black Power meant "Black economic and political organization," "nationalism," and "Pan-Africanism."[165] Nationalism, he clarified, is not about "going home just saying" the Kiswahili greetings "'Habari gani' and 'yebo.'" "I'm talking 'bout go back home now and organize your economic unit."[166] It must be noted that these points were made by "cultural" nationalists or at "cultural" nationalist-sponsored events.

Some scholars state that the Black Power movement was about black people developing racial pride, and they see this as a positive statement about the movement.[167] During the Black Power era, activists could easily have perceived this statement as an insult. It was precisely by saying that "cultural" nationalists were only interested in saying "I'm Black and Proud" that the Black Panthers disparaged US Organization. It was because activists took political and economic change seriously that they viewed "I'm Black and Proud" as an insult.

Activists in the "cultural" nationalist CIBI viewed nationalists who were just concerned with narrow cultural identity issues as reactionary, just as the Black Panthers did. The CIBI activist Frank Satterwhite argued,

> It is imperative, however, that every IBI [independent black institution] realistically assess whether or not it is actually making contributions to nation-building. . . . It is not enough, for example, for a school to teach students that Black is beautiful if these students ultimately are trained to serve the interests of the oppressor—by definition this school is *not* fulfilling its responsibilities for nation-building. That an institution is Black, therefore, *does not automatically* qualify it to deal with independence and nation-building.[168]

John Churchville, another CIBI activist, made a point of telling the participants at the first CIBI meeting that they should avoid teaching from a "reactionary base."[169] Churchville believed that nationalists who were only interested in narrow cultural issues would become allies of the white ruling class.[170] Pan-Africanists viewed blacks who were not anti-capitalist as being interested in economically exploiting other blacks.[171]

Black Power activists, including "cultural" black nationalists or Pan-Africanists, were concerned about the political and economic racial structures that affected black life. Many of the "cultural" nationalists who made up CIBI envisioned a day when blacks would be completely independent from whites and therefore no longer subject to white racial inequality. They saw their schools as merely one step in the process of the struggle for national liberation. For activists, therefore, the meaning of the Black Power movement lay in its name. It was about Power.

5

The Racial Ideology of Afrocentrism

"Was Cleopatra Black?" read the cover of *Newsweek* in September 1991. In this article and several others, *Newsweek* documented a cultural movement called Afrocentrism that began in the 1980s and continued throughout the 1990s among black Americans. Afrocentrists argued that black Americans were culturally African and that ancient Egypt should be seen as part of black Americans' cultural heritage. In the 1990s, not only was there an increasing amount of academic scholarship espousing Afrocentric ideas, but these ideas increasingly found their way into school curricula. One researcher estimated that in 1993 there were less than twenty Afrocentric public schools, but by 1999 there were more than four hundred. The influence of Afrocentrism was not limited to academics. In the 1980s and 1990s, black American music, fashion, and film were all impacted by the new Afrocentic black nationalism. The nationalism of the times culminated in 1995 in the largest ever rally of blacks, the Million Man March, led by Minister Louis Farrakhan, the leader of the Nation of Islam. This Afrocentric era, which lasted from about 1988 to 1998, was a major period in the history of black nationalism in America.[1]

Although the Afrocentric era is over, Afrocentrism is still with us. Effective social movements do not completely disappear when they end, because to some degree they transform the status quo. What was once new and controversial becomes normal and accepted. By the late 1970s, the use of the term "Black" ceased to be radical, as it had been in the early 1960s, because Black Power had in a small way transformed the popular culture. By 1988, when Jesse Jackson advocated for "African American," "Black" even seemed backward to some. Just as the Black Power era transformed "Negroes" into "Blacks," the Afrocentric era transformed "Blacks" into "African Americans." Some of the elements of the Afrocentric era have begun to fade, but others have had the ultimate success of simply being seen as normal. Both the fading and the normalcy of elements of a movement indicate the end of an era.

Like all black nationalisms, Afrocentrism is dependent upon the race concept. It is impossible to have a black nationalism that does not reify blackness. Afrocentric scholars, however, sound like and often claim to be social constructionists regarding race. Their claim can seem convincing if one understands race to be biological pseudoscience, since their discourse is explicitly about culture, not biology. Afrocentrists claim cultural continuity between ancient Egyptians and black Americans while asserting black and white American cultural difference. If one believes that racial ideologies require explicit references to biology, then Afrocentrism is not a racial ideology. But if race is defined by ideas about a heritable essential difference, biological *as well as* cultural discourses can be racial discourses. The idea that ancient Egyptians and black Americans have basically the same culture is an essentialist idea. "Culture" in Afrocentric discourse is an essence; it is unaffected by social and historical change. Afrocentrism is clearly a racial discourse since it depends on an essentialist idea of blackness. Afrocentrism is an example of ideas of cultural difference being used to construct racial difference.

Two Afrocentisms

The term "Afrocentric" is used in at least two ways: (1) to refer to a perspective that makes Africa in general and the ancient Nile Valley civilizations of Egypt and Nubia in particular central to black Americans; and (2) to refer to items about black Americans in general, and particularly to items expressing black pride.[2] In popular discourse, a black person who only watched dance performance groups that had a majority of black performers, like the Alvin Ailey American Dance Theater, might be called Afrocentric. That person's interest in dance is Afrocentric in that it is "black-centered." But for "Africa-centered" Afrocentric scholars, such as Molefi Kete Asante, Ailey's group and similar ones are not "Africa-centered" because they draw on ballet, a European dance tradition.[3] This chapter will examine the scholarly "Africa-centered" Afrocentrism. The following chapter will examine the looser and more varied conceptions of Afrocentrism as they applied to late-twentieth-century popular black nationalism.

Afrocentric black nationalism drew symbolically on the black nationalism of the Black Power era, but it was also significantly different from Black Power. Chapter 4 shows that the black nationalism of the Black Power era was not narrowly cultural. Even the "cultural" black nationalists or Pan-Africanists of the Black Power era were not solely concerned about the arts, or values, or cultural traditions. Their goal was ultimately black political and economic independence from whites. While the Black Power era was *not* "essentially cultural,"[4] the Afrocentric era was. In the Black Power era, artistic, intellectual, and symbolic activism followed or complemented political mobilizations. In the Afrocentric era, artistic, intellectual, and symbolic activism existed without concurrent political mobilization. The political referent of many Afrocentric cultural nationalists of the 1980s and 1990s was in the past—either the Black Power movement of the 1960s and 1970s or ancient Egypt.

The Afrocentric Academy

Melville J. Herskovits, a white, Jewish anthropologist, wrote one of the seminal statements of Afrocentrism. His 1941 publication, *The Myth of the Negro Past*, provides a long list of West African cultural retentions among blacks in the Americas and suggests that blacks in the United States are culturally West African. "To give the Negro an appreciation of his [African] past," Herskovits argues, "is to endow him with the confidence in his own position in this country." Herskovits also believed that when all Americans were aware of the retention of African culture among blacks, it would "contribute to a lessening of interracial tensions."[5] The goals of *The Myth of the Negro Past* were the goals of the Afrocentric racial project. Afrocentrists argued that the social standing and self-esteem of black Americans would improve through their knowledge of African culture.

As an intellectual movement, Afrocentrism did not begin with the 1941 publication of *The Myth of the Negro Past*. It was not until the black nationalism of the Black Power era in the 1960s and 1970s that black activists became interested in the book's Pan-Africanist potential. Pan-Africanist scholars during the Black Power era saw in *The Myth of the Negro Past* (and in other seminal works by other authors) a scholarly basis to affirm the Pan-Africanist position. *The Myth of the Negro Past* argued that West African cultural practices remained strong in the

United States and culturally validated the Pan-Africanist position. The scholarly Afrocentrism of the 1980s and 1990s was a revival of the cultural ideas of the Pan-Africanism of the Black Power era minus the more structural and political ones.

The development and dynamism of Afrocentric thought can be seen in the work of the Afrocentric psychologist Wade W. Nobles. Nobles began developing an African foundation for Black Psychology in the 1970s. In 1972, he argued, "Black Americans derive their most fundamental self-definition from several cultural and philosophical premises which we share with most West African 'tribes.'"[6] Nobles's idea of a West African cultural unity that formed the basis for black American culture came explicitly from Herskovits. By the mid-1980s, he had revised his views and argued that "ancient Egyptian thought" was the basis for "the development of African (Black) Psychology"[7]—not the West African thought of the Herskovitsian model. Like many other Afrocentrists, Nobles had discovered the Senegalese scholar Cheikh Anta Diop, who claimed a cultural unity for all of Africa, not just West Africa, as Herskovits did. Diop also argued that ancient Egypt should be seen as the birthplace of African civilization. Just as Eurocentrists might argue that ancient Greece and Rome are the birthplace of Western civilization, Afrocentrists argue that ancient Egypt is the birthplace of a Pan-African civilization.[8] Following Diop, Nobles's African basis of African (Black) Psychology moved from West Africa to ancient Egypt.

The same transformation can be found in the work of Molefi Kete Asante. In 1975, based in part on the work of Herskovits, Asante argued that there is a "continuity and a relationship between West African languages and African American English." He stated, "Despite claims that Herskovits' work . . . exaggerated differences between black and non-black, his primary thesis is essentially sound." By the 1980s, Asante too had moved the source of black American culture east and thousands of years back in time to ancient Egypt. He argued, "The centerpiece of Afrocentric theory was a reconnection, in our minds, of Egypt to Africa," and "the late Senegalese activist scientist, Cheikh Anta Diop, is the most prominent figure in this movement for the anteriority of Egypt." Other Afrocentric scholars have also been influenced by Herskovits.[9]

Whether the connection to Africa stresses West Africa or ancient Egypt, in either case there is a clear connection to Africa. Without this connection, there is no Afrocentrism for the academic Afrocentrists.

Academic Afrocentrists reject education for black children that begins black American history with American slavery. To do so, they argue, denies the African cultural continuity of black Americans and omits much of the greatness of black people. Asa G. Hilliard III and other organizers of a 1989 national conference on Afrocentric education argued, "There is no significant history of Africans in most academic disciplines before the slave trade. In the total school experience of most Americans, virtually no attention is paid to the major part of the history of African people." "There is no presentation of the cultural unity among Africans and the descendents of Africans in the African Diaspora," they add, and no presentation of the "deep structural cultural unity that can be found among many African populations all over the world."[10]

For academic Afrocentrists, black people throughout the world are part of a Pan-African culture that is distinct from European culture. As Asante states:

> We have one African Cultural System manifested in diversities. . . . We respond to the same rhythms of the universe, the same cosmological sensibilities, the same general historical reality as the African descended people. . . . In this way, we know that Yoruba, Asante, Wolof, Ewe, Nuba, and African-Americans possess values and beliefs derived from their own particular histories yet conforming to the African Cultural System.[11]

Asante also states, "Africans in the Americas are . . . Africans" and "African American culture and history represent developments in African culture and history."[12] For Afrocentric scholars, black Americans are culturally African.

Theories of Cultural Difference

A number of Afrocentrists, following Cheikh Anta Diop's "Two Cradle Theory," understood the cultural differences between Africans on the one hand, and Europeans and Asians on the other, as emerging from environmental differences between Eurasia and Africa.[13] Jacob Carruthers, an Afrocentric historian, summarizes Diop's major points about the two cultural cradles:

> In his major works Diop insists that "the history of humanity will remain confused as long as we fail to distinguish between the two early

cradles (the African and Eurasian cultural matrixes) in which nature fashioned the instincts, temperament, habits, and ethical concepts of the two sub-divisions before they met each other after a long separation dating back to prehistoric times." What Diop means is that there are two fundamental patterns of culture which developed independently of each other. Attempts to formulate a universal social science have for the most part denied the reality upon which Diop bases his theory.[14]

"Culture" in Afrocentric theory is quite durable. Once a "culture" has developed in response to prehistoric environmental conditions, it ceases to be responsive to new ones. Thus, black Americans born and raised in the United States, who have many ancestors who were born and raised in the United States, are still said to have a "culture" based in response to the ancient African-Southern cradle. Therefore Afrocentrists argue that we cannot have a single social science for two fundamentally different cultural groups.

Other Afrocentrists present what can be called three or six "cradle" theories. Molefi Asante claims that the worldview of black people is "personalism," that of Asians "spiritualism," and that of whites "materialism."[15] Edwin Nichols and Asa G. Hilliard provided a six-"cradle" theory for the multicultural education program in the Portland, Oregon, public schools. They argue that humankind is divided into six geocultural groups: Africans, American Indians, Asians, Europeans, Hispanics, and Pacific Islanders. Nichols states, "Millennia ago human beings were grouped together in specific environments which impacted their view of the world. World views and archetypes of geocultural groups impact the group's behaviors."[16] These cradle theories present each cultural group, with the exception of Hispanics, as having a unique culture that developed independently of all other cultural groups in response to ancient environmental conditions. This theoretical framework views cultural groups as being fundamentally different.

What exactly is this African culture that all black people possess? Jacob Carruthers presents "an inventory of the basic cultural features of the [Eurasian and African] civilizations":

For Diop, the Eurasian (Northern, Aryan) cradle is characterized by: a) hunting, b) nomadic land occupancy, c) patriarchal family, d) city-state as largest unity of governmental autonomy, e) xenophobia and provincialism, f) individualism, g) ideal of war, violence, crime and conquests, and h) pessimistic religious or metaphysical systems. In contrast, the African (Southern, Meridonal) cradle has these features: a) agricultural cultivation economy, b) sedentary land tenure, c) matrifocal family, d) countrywide governmental system, e) xenophilia and cosmopolitanism, f) collectivism, g) ideal of peace, justice and goodness, h) optimism in religious and metaphysical institutions.[17]

In Afrocentric thought, European culture is described by such negative terms as patriarchal, xenophobic, individualistic, violent, criminal, and pessimistic. African culture is the opposite of all these things.

Maulana Karenga, who became a leading Afrocentric scholar in the 1980s, uses the ancient Egyptian ethical system of Maat to indicate Afrocentric values. Karenga writes, "Ra created the universe through Maat, a term with multiple meanings, i.e., truth, justice, propriety, harmony, balance, order, reciprocity, righteousness, etc." He adds, "The [ancient Egyptians], thus, developed an ideal character type rooted in and reflective of Maat. . . . This ideal type was the geru, the self-mastered, i.e., calm, silent, controlled, modest, wise, gentle and socially active; and the geru Maat, who was truly the self-mastered."[18]

Kwame Kenyatta, the Afrocentric educator, provides a list contrasting Eurocentric values in teaching as he sees them with what he considers to be the black, and therefore Afrocentric, students' style of learning:

Eurocentric Style of Teaching	*Afrocentric Style of Learning*
Rules	Freedom
Standardization	Variation
Conformity	Creativity
Memory of Specific Facts	Memory of Essence
Regularity	Novelty
Rigid Order	Flexibility
Normality	Uniqueness
Differences Equal Defects	Sameness Equals Oppression
Precision	Approximate
Control	Experience
Mechanical	Humanistic
"Thing" Focused	"People" Focused
Constant	Evolving
Sign Oriented	Meaning Oriented
Duty	Loyalty[19]

It is highly debatable to say that people of African descent reject everything in the left column, and that people of European descent reject everything in the right. This point is revealed most clearly by the fact that Wade W. Nobles defines the valuing of differences and uniqueness as European traits while Kenyatta defines these very traits as African.[20]

For Wade W. Nobles, the social problems facing African Americans today are the result of a shift away from traditional, Afrocentric black family cultural values to drug-culture values. He contrasts the two cultural orientations as follows:

Black Family Cultural Orientation	*Drug Culture Orientation*
I. Cultural Themes	I. Cultural Themes
• sense of appropriateness	• anything is permissible
• sense of excellence	• trust no one
II. Cultural Value System	II. Cultural Value System
• mutual aid	• selfish
• adaptability	• materialistic
• natural goodness	• pathological liars
• inclusivity	• extremely violent
• unconditional love	• short fused
• respect (for elders)	• individualistic
• restraint	• manipulative
• responsibility	• immediate gratification
• reciprocity	• paranoid
• interdependence	• distrustful
• cooperativeness	• non–family oriented
	• not community-oriented
	• self worth—quantity[21]

Again one can raise the question about whether these black family values are peculiarly black or African. These Afrocentric family values would probably be supported by many non-black Americans.

According to Afrocentrists, however, blacks who are connected to their African culture are, among other things, calm, controlled, modest, humanistic, freedom loving, creative, loyal, respectful, and responsible. Europeans lack these things. Note that the drug-culture values of individualism, violence, and distrust (xenophobia) (and the fact that Nobles is referring to criminality) are European values in Afrocentric thought.

Molefi Kete Asante characterizes the European worldview as that of "materialism," another drug-culture value. Thus one can understand how many Afrocentrists see black social problems as the result of black Americans adopting "European" values.

Afrocentric Feminism?

While Black Power activists embraced a "black macho" that often subordinated women, Afrocentrists argue for equality among black men and women. They make this argument indirectly by denying that sexism exists, or has ever existed, among blacks. For example, John Henrik Clarke, the Afrocentric historian, writes:

> In Africa the woman's "place" was not only with her family. She often ruled nations with unquestionable authority. Many African women were great militarists, and on occasion led their armies in battle. The Africans had produced a civilization where men were secure enough to let women advance as far as their talent, royal lineage and prerogatives would take them.

Here Clarke is summarizing Diop's study of African matriarchies. According to Afrocentrists, one of the cultural commonalities among people of African descent is the "matrifocal family," to cite Carruthers (item "c" in his list). This means that male dominance, patriarchy, and sexism are not part of the African Cultural System. When Afrocentric scholars write about women, following Diop, they tend to write about the "Royal Women of Ancient Egypt," "Female Dieties and Queens of Ancient Kemet [Egypt]," and other African and black American female leaders.[22]

According to Afrocentrists, since sexism does not exist among blacks, a feminist movement is unnecessary. Afrocentrists view sexism as a Eurocentric tradition and feminism as an equally Eurocentric response. Valethia Watkins, an Afrocentric scholar, states:

> While feminism may be advantageous for European women and improve the condition of their lives in America, it could work ruin for us. The historical treatment of European women in the West, from ancient Greece to the present, does not mirror the African construction of gender and the treatment of African womanhood, from the time of Kemet (ancient Egypt) to the present.

Watkins rejects the very idea of a gender analysis for black people. She argues that for blacks gender cannot be separated from race and "African women and men share a mutual problem, a common foe, and a joint fate."[23]

When one ventures away from the strongly Diopian, "Africa-centered" scholars, one finds Afrocentrists who accept feminism. Even these scholars, though, find it difficult to address sexism in black communities. Patricia Hill Collins employed an Afrocentric framework in her 1990 *Black Feminist Thought*. Collins does not make sexism in black communities a major topic for discussion in her book. She even equivocates about whether or not it actually exists. When she does discuss black sexism, she presents it as an internalization of Eurocentric values. Thus, culturally authentic blacks are not sexist, which fits Diop's ideas.[24]

Melanin Theories and Other Afrocentric "Science"

As the Afrocentric scholar T. Owens Moore correctly notes, Diop "presented no argument that melanin had any influence on behavior."[25] Herskovits and Diop made cultural arguments, not biological ones. However, writers employing biological discourses about melanin to understand blacks—melanin theorists—have often melded Diopian and "Africa-centered" ideas with their "biological" theories. There has been enough intertwining of the biological and the cultural discourses that one can speak of an Afrocentric "science."

Frances Cress Welsing, a black nationalist psychiatrist, is the most popular of the melanin theorists. In her "Theory of Color-Confrontation," she explains white supremacy as the result of whiteness—which she understands as melanin deficiency—being "recessive," and non-whiteness being "dominant." Following this idea, if a white person mates with a nonwhite person, the resulting child will be nonwhite. Whites, therefore, fear "genetic" annihilation. They maintain themselves by an ethos of white supremacy. Her psychoanalytic training has led her to build an elaborate symbolic and psychosexual interpretive edifice of black and white behavior upon this foundation. Her creative psychosexual stories are the key to her popularity.[26]

There are enough melanin scholars and persons interested in the topic for there to have been an annual Melanin Conference since 1987.[27] For these scholars, there is little that cannot be explained by melanin. Central to the Afrocentric project is the celebration of blackness. This is the goal of Carol Barnes's *Melanin: The Chemical Key to Black Greatness*. Among Barnes's claims are that "melanin is a civilizing chemical and acts as a sedative to help keep the black human calm, relaxed, caring and civilized."[28] This sounds a lot like Maulana Karenga's geru, the calm, silent, controlled, modest, wise, gentle, and socially active person who embodies Maat.

Much of Afrocentrism has a New Age influence. Indeed, ancient Egypt has been an important site for New Age thought.[29] The New Age movement was another popular social movement which gained strength in the 1980s. New Age thought contains a host of alternative "scientific" theories that often emerge from the veneration of an old cultural tradition.[30] This New Age influence is especially pronounced in Afrocentric "science." Moore, for example, believes that "scientists in ancient Kemet [Egypt] created a body of knowledge to help humans master and harness invisible forces in nature"[31] such as electromagnetism. He attempts to explain this ability in modern scientific terms, stating:

> African people naturally have kinky or wiry hair. Non-African people have matted or animal-like hair. In other words, kinky or wire-like hair is an evolutionary advance since very few animals (sheep, buffalo, yak etc.) have hair similar to African people. Kinky or wire-like hair is constructed like an antenna to absorb more readily those naturally occurring electromagnetic waves in nature.[32]

Moore links this startling "fact" to melanin by noting that copper, which is a good conductor of electricity, has a molecular structure similar to that of melanin. In the Portland School District's *African-American Baseline Essay* for science, educators learn similar Afrocentric "facts." The author of the science essay informs Portland science teachers that "the ancient Egyptians were known the world over as the masters of 'magic' (psi): precognition, psychokinesis, remote viewing and other underdeveloped human capabilities."[33] One wonders how such a civilization could ever have declined.

Factual Problems

Many of the core cultural and historical claims of Afrocentrism are questionable. There have been a number of insightful critiques of Afrocentrism. Mary Lefkowitz's *Not Out of Africa* and Clarence Walker's *We Can't Go Home Again* are useful discussions of the problems in Afrocentric history. Kwame Anthony Appiah's *In My Father's House* presents a subtle and indirect philosophical critique of the assumptions and logic of Afrocentrism. Diane Ravitch's 1990 and 1991 exchange with Molefi Kete Asante in *American Scholar* and Craig L. Frisby's 1993 exchange with Janice Hale and another Afrocentric educator in *School Psychology Review* reveal the weaknesses of Afrocentrism's educational ideas. Bernard Ortiz de Montellano dissects Afrocentric "science" in a two-part article in *Skeptical Inquirer* (1991 and 1992). On every issue that Afrocentrists address it is possible to find scholarship that, many scholars would argue, is more empirically sound than theirs. The choice for educators is not between works that disparage blacks and Afrocentric celebrations. The twentieth century saw a rise in scholarship by blacks and nonblacks which dealt with Africans and black Americans seriously and respectfully without employing an Afrocentric framework.[34]

My summary of the ideas of the "Afrocentric Academy" reveals numerous factual problems. Among scholars, only Afrocentric scholars believe that there is a cultural unity to all of Africa and that black Americans are culturally African. I will show below that even Afrocentrists do not really believe that black Americans are culturally African. The Afrocentric values that blacks are supposed to have and that whites are supposed to lack amounts to baseless racial stereotyping. Afrocentrists' treatment of sexism in black communities is another example of delusion. It is not difficult to find sexism among black Americans and Africans. The natural scientific theories of Afrocentrists indicate a profound misunderstanding of science. The rate of errors and the impact of bias seem to be much greater among the leading Afrocentrists than among the leading mainstream scholars. The reader will have to sample both perspectives and decide for herself.

We should note that Afrocentrists also present information that is accurate and that they can make interesting, creative, and insightful points. Paul M. Sniderman and Thomas Piazza are wrong when they argue that Afrocentrism makes claims that "violate standard cannons of plausibility." They are also surprised that educated blacks are more likely to believe Afrocentric ideas than are uneducated blacks.[35] The simple fact that Sniderman and Piazza find people who believe Afrocentric claims is proof that these claims are plausible. Sniderman and

Piazza make the common scholarly error of assuming that what seems implausible to them—scholars with advanced, elite educations—will seem implausible to Americans without this background. This bias is probably part of the reason why scholars have generally paid more attention to racial ideologies drawing on scientific theories than to those drawing on religious and cultural ideas.

The claims that Sniderman and Piazza find implausible are: "The ancient Greek philosophers copied many ideas from black philosophers who lived in Egypt," and "African wise men who lived hundreds of years ago do not get enough credit for their contributions to modern science."[36] Those with a good knowledge of ancient history and an understanding of the scientific definition of the word "science," might find these claims implausible—but most people do not have such knowledge.

It is useful to consider the belief in Afrocentric ideas alongside the belief in alternative medicine. In both cases, popular beliefs can run counter to what those with an advanced, elite education see as the truth. "The people most likely to use unconventional medicine are well-educated, middle-income whites from 25 to 49 years old," states the *New York Times*.[37] In the 1990s, alternative medicine was recognized as having developed into a big business. For many medical experts most of these alternative medicines are "snake oil," yet, like Afrocentrism, they are more popular among the better educated.[38] Generally, what people believe is a product of social forces, not veracity. False ideas tend to be as believable as true ones.

Sniderman and Piazza are insightful in noting that Afrocentric claims might be literally false but true in a more allegorical way. Wilson Jeremiah Moses makes a similar point by saying that Afrocentrism can possess a "mythic truth."[39] People's responses to ideas about ancient Africans may really be a measure of their awareness of black contributions being ignored and denigrated in *American* history. Ultimately Afrocentrism teaches us more about American racial relations than about Africa.

Afrocentrism as a Racial Ideology

Although there are melanin theories in Afrocentric thought, the core of Afrocentrism is a cultural discourse. As the melanin theorist T. Owen Moore correctly notes, Diop "presented no argument that melanin had any influence on behavior."[40] Herskovits, Diop, and the leading academic Afrocentrists only discuss cultural continuities. The melanin theories in Afrocentrism are forced onto the cultural arguments. Logically and practically, it is easy to excise the melanin theories from Afrocentric thought. Therefore, an analysis of melanin theories is not truly an analysis of Afrocentrism.

Afrocentrism is explicitly a discourse about culture and identity. Afrocentrists have little or nothing to say about biological ideas of race other than to dismiss them. For example, Molefi Kete Asante writes that race "as a scientific term . . . lacks validity."[41] Jawanza Kunjufu, the Afrocentric educational consultant, states in his history textbook:

> Race is not a biological term; it's scientifically inaccurate to place five billion people into three groups—negroid, mongoloid, and caucasoid. Humans vary with the climate. To repeat: the birthplace of the human race—all of it—is in Africa. Race is a sociological term used by humans to categorize.[42]

Another Afrocentric scholar remarks, "All life is related . . . all things come together as one. . . . There is no superior race nor is there an inferior race. There is only one race—the human race."[43] In these statements, Afrocentrists sound like social constructionists. Afrocentrists not only reject biological notions of racial superiority and inferiority, but they see their work as an explicitly antiracist discourse.[44]

Afrocentric education is implemented in public schools in an explicitly antiracist framework. The mission statement for Philadelphia's Afrocentric Science Academy states, "Becoming aware of one's culture increases knowledge and encourages appreciation of other cultures."[45] In the Cooper B. Hatch Afrocentric Middle School in Camden, New Jersey, Afrocentric education is supposed to make students view foreigners as friends whom they have not yet met.[46] The philosophy of Portland Public Schools, a leader in Afrocentric education, states, "All geocultural groups have made and continue to make significant contributions to the world in which we live. No geocultural group is innately inferior or superior."[47]

Afrocentrism fails to explicitly meet the conventional sociological requirements for a racial discourse. The major Afrocentrists make no biological claims of racial superiority and inferiority. They only speak of culture and identity. Afrocentrism is, in fact, a racial discourse, but one which uses a racially essentialist idea of "culture." We can begin to see the essentialism in the Afrocentric discourse about "culture" and how race is fundamental to Afrocentric thought by examining the contradictions in the axioms of Afrocentrism.

Axiomatic Contradictions

There are revealing contradictions in Afrocentric thought. Afrocentrists say that black Americans *are* Africans culturally and they also condemn black Americans for *not* being Africans culturally. For example, Molefi Kete Asante argues that black Americans are part of an African Cultural System,[48] and that "Africans in the Americas are . . . Africans."[49] Asante also sees many Afrocentric deviations in black American behavior. He writes, "We have failed to be critical of the Alvin Aileys and Arthur Mitchells in dance," faulting the black American choreographers for incorporating American and European forms in their work. He also disapproves of black Americans for their "blond wigs, [their] fried, dyed and swept to the side hairstyles." This means that he disapproves of the majority of black women who artificially straighten their hair, and even of black women with "natural" hairstyles whose hair is blond or some other non-Afrocentric color. To meet Asante's standards of Afrocentrism, black Americans need to take African names, wear African clothing, and take part in African cultural practices.[50] He asks rhetorically:

> Suppose you met a European whose name was Osei Owusu who dressed in Kente cloth, and danced the Kete or Adua, what would you think if he told you that he did not like Africans or Africa? When you give yourself a European name, dress like a European, behave toward others as the European often has done, who is to say you are not European in mind no matter how hard you protest.[51]

Are black Americans culturally African or "European in mind"? Asante says both things while arguing that Afrocentric and Eurocentric cultures are fundamentally different.

Asa Hilliard does not provide us with a single answer to the question of black American cultural identity either. He criticizes school curricula for not presenting "the cultural unity among Africans and the descendents of Africans in the African Diaspora." He argues that there is a "deep structural cultural unity that can be found among many African populations all over the world."[52] Yet he also states the opposite. His writings also stress that black Americans have lost their African culture and identity. He states that blacks are "ignorant of our past, strangers of our people, [and] apes of our oppressors." He insists that blacks have to make the decision, "Whether to be African or not to be?"[53] He argues that black Americans are already culturally African *and* that blacks have to learn to be culturally African.

Afrocentrists know that black Americans are not African. The Afrocentric educational project is to *develop* African identities and Afrocentric culture among blacks because blacks lack these things. Cultural identity in Afrocentric thought is not simply based on observable cultural practices or beliefs. "Culture" in Afrocentric thought is a racially essentialist idea. Being an essence—a mystical and internal characteristic—it is believed to be there even when there is no external, observable evidence of it. In this way, Afrocentrists believe that black Americans are *essentially* African, even if black Americans are not aware of their African essence and even if they do not display any African cultural traits. In the same way, someone who has no observable "black" physical characteristics can be black by the racial essentialism of the one-drop rule. Because African culture is an essence in Afrocentric belief, it need not be observable.

We see this racial essentialism from another angle by examining another Afrocentric axiomatic contradiction. Afrocentrists argue that black American culture is Afrocentric because it is ultimately derived from ancient Egyptian culture. White American culture, they argue, is derived from ancient Greek and Roman cultures. However, they also argue that the ancient Greeks and Romans derived their culture from the ancient Egyptians. For example, Wise Intelligent of the 1990s Afrocentric rap group X-Clan argues, "Black people are the mothers and fathers of the highest forms of civilization ever built on this planet. . . . Plato, Socrates, and so forth, they learned from black masters of Egypt."[54] John Henrik Clarke writes, "Roman history is Greek as well as Roman, and both . . . Greek and . . . Roman history are Egyptian because the entire Mediterranean was civilized by Egypt; and Egypt in turn borrowed from other parts of Africa, especially Ethiopia."[55] He also makes the point even more plainly: "Egypt gave birth to what later would [become] known as 'Western Civilization.'"[56] If we proceed logically from the Afrocentric axiom that ancient Greek knowledge is really ancient Egyptian knowledge, there would be no need for Afrocentrism because the Western culture of America is already Afrocentric, and there would be no such thing as Eurocentrism.

Afrocentrists do not make this argument because Europeans are white. White people cannot have the same *essential* culture as blacks, no matter how culturally African they actually are; and blacks cannot be authentically or essentially European no matter how European they actually are. In Afrocentric thought and, importantly, in much non-Afrocentric thought, one's "true" culture is determined by one's racial or ethnic essence, not from one's actual cultural behavior. This way of thinking is common in American society. For example, an English-speaking American can see learning the Polish language that her grandparents spoke as learning about *her* culture. Although she speaks English, in a racial or ethnic frame she does not see English as her real culture. Rather than seeing our own culture as the culture we are living in and with, we view the culture of our ancestors as our real, authentic culture. Although we don't practice it, we see it as truer to ourselves than the culture we practice. It is not there, but *essentially* it is there.[57] In racialist thinking, the essence, or in other words, the belief in difference, trumps any facts on the ground.

Asa Hilliard writes, "There is no code of values and virtues anywhere on the planet, ancient or modern, that exceeds the MAATian system articulated in the Nile Valley thousands of years ago." He also believes that the ancient Egyptian writing system is "the most beautiful in the world."[58] He and other Afrocentrists think that ancient Egypt is the pinnacle of human civilization, yet they do not call for all humans to become Afrocentric, just black ones. Afrocentrists have claimed ancient Egypt as black cultural property. The Association for the Study of Classical African Civilizations, the organization to which most of the major Afrocentric scholars belong, states, "ancient Kemet (Egypt) belongs to the cultural and historical heritage of all African people in the world," and "all African people in the world must claim and own ancient Kemet (Egypt) without desiring, requesting or expecting prior authorization from others."[59] For Afrocentrists, "culture" defines race and race defines "culture."

"Cultural" Ideologies of Racial Difference

If we understand racial ideologies to be about constructions of essential difference, then clearly "culture" in Afrocentric discourse is a racial concept. The Afrocentric conception of "culture" is not social but transcendental. Afrocentric "culture" has been present over millennia and across vastly different sociohistorical and environmental contexts. Thus, Afrocentrists can argue that the ancient Egyptians and contemporary black Americans share an underlying African Cultural System. The African Cultural System is also fundamentally different from the cultural systems of all other groups, and is particularly antagonistic to "European culture." This conception of "culture" ideologically marks people of African descent as being fundamentally different from all other peoples.

Racial ideologies are never about describing reality; they are about constructing a social reality. The theories of racial difference and the related stereotypes about African values are developed to implement and enforce practices of racial difference. Afrocentrism also clearly has this normative aspect. By naturalizing an Afrocentric blackness, Afrocentrists justify the development of Afrocentric practices among blacks and justify the application of negative social sanctions to black deviance from Afrocentrism. We see the potential for Afrocentric social policing when Molefi Asante states: "We have failed to be critical of the Alvin Aileys and Arthur Mitchells in dance," and "we must now open the floodgates of protest against any non-Afrocentric stances taken by writers, authors, and other intellectuals or artists."[60]

Although Afrocentrists explicitly claim that Afrocentrism is in favor of racial equality, it can *potentially* be used for the production of racial inequality in two ways. The first is suggested in the preceding paragraph. Afrocentrism can potentially limit black Americans' freedom to pursue non-Afrocentric lifestyles. If these ideas are widely held, blacks would be pressured by blacks and nonblacks to conform to their presumed natural and authentic cultural orientation. Cultural stereotypes often function as prescription while pretending to be description.

Even if we accept the idea that each geocultural group is equal in an abstract way, the idea that they have fixed differences in their value orientations can produce racial inequality. For example, if people widely believe that the worldview of black people is "personalism," that of Asians "spiritualism," and that of whites "materialism," as Asante argues,[61] it is quite easy to imagine racial discrimination on this basis. "Personalism" is different from "spiritualism" which is different from "materialism." Because they are different, they can be differently valued. Occupations requiring one particular cultural orientation, for example, might be higher paying than those requiring a different cultural orientation. "Materialist" work might be more highly rewarded than "personalist" work. If this were the case, "personalist" blacks would be paid less than "materialist" whites. Even if "personalist" work were the most highly valued, we would still have cultural stereotypes serving a racial hierarchy. A truly antiracist discourse would not argue that blacks, whites, and Asians have an *essential* cultural orientation. Even if "materialist" work were more highly valued by society, no group would be stereotyped as being better suited to this work than any other group.

I am not saying that Afrocentrists participate in or advocate these types of unequal practices. Rather, the point is that essentialist "cultural" discourses, in the proper political or economic context, are perfectly amenable to developing a racial hierarchy. American slavery, for example, was justified on the basis of ideas of essential cultural difference. It was only after slavery had ended that more pseudoscientific biological racial ideologies were developed.[62]

Afrocentrism has already shown its potential for building and supporting racial structures. Afrocentrism led to the development of Afrocentric schools. In Milwaukee, Afrocentric educators were able to suspend a racial integration program for black teachers in Afrocentric schools so that the Afrocentric schools could have more black teachers.[63] Afrocentric schools depend upon racially segregated education.

Afrocentrism is meant to be antiracist and it contains a discourse of equality within it. But American political thought has made quite remarkable assertions of equality simultaneously with the practice of racial slavery. *Any* ideologies of essential difference—including explicitly "cultural" ideologies—in the proper social context can be used to develop social structures of racial inequality.

Afrocentrism is a racial ideology because it ideologically constructs a heritable essential difference among human populations. Within Afrocentric theory, people who are of the African Cultural System are presented as being fundamentally different from people outside this system. These differences are passed on to the descendents of people within this African Cultural System so that centuries later the descendents of Africans are said to be culturally African. Because these cultural differences are not influenced by social forces, they remain present in the same form over millennia. This African Cultural System contains stereotypes about the cultural and psychological characteristics of people of African descent. Consequently, Afrocentrism encourages prejudice and discrimination based on these stereotypes. Although Afrocentrism incorporates ideas of equality and antiracism, under the right conditions it could underlie a social structure of racial inequality.

At its core, Afrocentrism is a fairly conventional *U.S.* racial ideology. When American racists shout that blacks should "go back to Africa,"[64] they are indicating that they see black Americans as truly belonging to Africa, not America. In a similar fashion Afrocentrists see black Americans as belonging to Africa. Afrocentrism also adopts the American one-drop rule. Molefi Kete Asante sees the multiracial movement as an example of black self-hate:

> One cannot read magazines like *New People* and *Interrace* without getting the idea that self-hatred among some African Americans is at an all-time high. Both of these magazines, founded by interracial couples and appealing most to interracial families, see themselves as the vanguard to explode racial identity by claiming to be a third race in addition to African and European. Of course, in the context of a racist society the white parent wishes for his/her offspring the same privileges that he/she has enjoyed often at the expense of Africans. However, the offspring is considered by tradition, custom, appearance, and history to be black.[65]

Asa Hilliard sees the multiracial movement as an attempt to encourage blacks to deny their African identities. He writes, "The new census categories of 'mixed' and 'other' have already influenced some Africans to reframe their identities—identities based solely on their pigment, or 'race.'" Here Hilliard rejects "the fabricated European category of 'race,'"[66] but he is only rejecting strict *biological* conceptions of race based on appearance. He wishes to retain blackness as defined by the one-drop rule which is threatened by the multiracial movement. The one-drop rule for blackness is unique to U.S. racial ideology.[67] Afrocentrism therefore does not reject race. It embraces American racial ideology. Therefore, it is simply a particular variant of American racial ideology.

6

Conservative Black Nationalism in the Afrocentric Era

American politics shifted to the political right in the 1980s and 1990s. The black nationalism which emerged during this era was partially a response to this conservative politics, but interestingly it also absorbed some of the dominant conservative ideas. Conservatives tend to explain inequality as the result of cultural values and individual characteristics. Liberals tend to emphasize the social advantages and disadvantages of groups. Conservatives are likely to see poverty among blacks, for example, as stemming from blacks lacking a work ethic, whereas liberals are likely to see poverty as stemming from racial discrimination.

Afrocentrists believed the social problems facing blacks in the late twentieth century stemmed from a lack of the proper values. Although it is commonly believed that black nationalism represents a left-leaning position articulated by the black lower classes, Afrocentric nationalism was fairly conservative and its strongest advocates were among the black middle class. The Black Power movement was one of the roots of Afrocentrism, but Black Power's leftist critique of the political economy of capitalism was nonexistent in Afrocentric ideology. Instead of calling for "African socialism," Afrocentrists made conservative arguments about family values, cultural identity, and self-esteem which echoed the conservative politics of the era.

The Origins of the Afrocentric Era

From the late 1980s through the 1990s, there was a resurgence of black nationalism in America. Black nationalism rises when blacks are pessimistic about their prospects in American society.[1] The racial politics of President Ronald Reagan (1981–1989) and President George Bush's

(1989–1993) administrations did not inspire optimism. Reagan used false stereotypes about black Cadillac-driving "welfare queens" to attack welfare. Bush used the image of the black rapist in his campaign for president. Both administrations attacked affirmative action and were lax about the enforcement of antidiscrimination laws. Black communities were also plagued by the development of a crack cocaine economy. Blacks, along with the rest of America, became worried and fearful about the supposed growth of a black "underclass." Sporadic events of racist violence occurred throughout the 1980s, and more and more blacks felt that white Americans were racists. In 1981, 18 percent of blacks felt that more than half of whites shared the attitudes of the Ku Klux Klan. By 1986, the percentage of blacks with these views rose to 23 percent. By 1989, the percentage had increased to 29 percent. Other measures also showed increasing pessimism among blacks about racial relations. Many blacks felt that the country was moving back toward Jim Crow. The videotaped beating of Rodney King in 1991 and the 1992 acquittal of the police who beat him helped to increase black America's feelings of alienation from American society. This pessimism, worry, and alienation set the stage for a black nationalist resurgence.[2]

Pessimism, worry, and alienation can be produced by a realistic response to real situations as well as by other means. For example, media reports about crime can produce an increasing fear of crime while crime is actually decreasing. A 1996 *Chicago Tribune* poll indicated that "people believe the U.S. is in the grip of a crime wave, even though the statistics seem headed in the other direction." A majority of respondents based their opinions on news reports.[3] In a variety of ways false beliefs can shape perceptions and responses. The fear that one has from accurate information about increasing crime and the fear that one has from media distortions about crime are the same. The fear in each case is real.

The Afrocentric black nationalism of the 1980s and 1990s was a response both to real events and problems facing black America, and to media distortions. To understand the ideology and politics of the Afrocentric nationalism of the 1980s and 1990s one needs to explore some of the social issues that animated the movement. The supposed black community problems of "the underclass," "low self-esteem," and "failing schools" were three important issues of the 1980s and 1990s that shaped the ideological development of Afrocentric nationalism.[4]

Although the belief in these problems was widespread in American society, it was based on incorrect facts and erroneous analyses.

Afrocentrism and the "Underclass"

The image of the underclass—the largely black poor who are permanently dependent on welfare, crime, or drugs and who irresponsibly have too many children at too young an age—was widely disseminated in the 1980s and 1990s. Books like *Losing Ground* (1984) and *The Truly Disadvantaged* (1987) made poverty, welfare, and crime priorities for researchers *and* politicians. Among scholars, the underclass became an interdisciplinary subfield. However, this new interest did not begin in the academy. In 1977, *Time* magazine's cover read, "A Minority within a Minority: The Underclass." Other magazines were crucial to the development and dissemination of the idea that there was a new story regarding black urban poverty. In 1981, Ken Auletta published a three-part article on "The Underclass" in the *New Yorker* magazine. In 1986, Nicholas Lemann published a two-part article on the underclass in the *Atlantic Monthly*. Also in 1986, CBS aired *The Vanishing Black Family: Crisis in Black America*. The idea of the underclass was disseminated in all the media. The combination of scholarly research with popular anecdotes and images created a very convincing case that there was a new "crisis in black America."

The underclass argument often became a mere restatement of the "culture of poverty" argument. In this argument, poverty was seen as the result of the poor lacking the supposed cultural values of the middle class. For example, *Fortune* magazine stated, "'Underclass' describes a state of mind and a way of life. It is at least as much [a] cultural as an economic condition."[5] In the 1980s and 1990s, scholars and politicians increasingly discussed black urban poverty as the result of the cultural failings of the black poor and not the result of racial and class inequality in American society. The historian Michael B. Katz observed:

> Indeed, most . . . commentary on the underclass used imprecise definitions that stressed family and individual behavior and rested on implicitly moral concepts of class structure. For instance, . . . Nicholas Lemann revived the culture of poverty thesis to describe and explain the emergence of an isolated underclass. The rise in out-of-wedlock births —"by far the greatest contributor to the perpetuation of the misery of

ghetto life"—most accurately captured the distinction between the underclass and the rest of American society.[6]

There was a widespread belief that the problem of the underclass was a cultural one.

Afrocentrists also agreed that the culture of the black poor needed to be changed. Hannibal Tirus Afrik, an Afrocentric educator, argued, "One of the most compelling issues [for black communities] is a lack of socialization process for our young people," which results in youths "rebelling against traditional family authority structures." Afrik argued that these youth ran the risk of harming communities due to "the proliferation of drugs, the easy accessibility of guns and weapons and the increase in media sensationalism of sexuality." For Afrik, the underclass was the result of the lack of the proper socialization of black youth.[7]

Jawanza Kunjufu, an Afrocentric educational consultant, presents the cultural argument even more clearly in his book *Hip-Hop vs. Maat: A Psycho/Social Analysis of Values*. "Maat" is an ancient Egyptian value system celebrated by Afrocentrists. Kunjufu's culture of hip-hop is clearly the culture of the underclass. He describes hip-hop as a "male-centered culture [that] feels the need to show disregard for personal safety as a sign of membership. At-risk behavior could take on a variety of forms including substance abuse, promiscuity, academic failure, being a street player, and/or other characteristics."[8] His goal is "to move those people [from] the values of Hip-Hop and New Jack to the . . . values of MAAT and the Nguzo Saba."[9] Kunjufu also argues, "One of the most revolutionary things you can do is to keep your marriage intact and raise your children. I believe that is the *minimum*."[10] For Afrocentric educators, the problem of the underclass stemmed from blacks lacking the proper values, not from race and class inequality in American society. Afrocentrists hoped to use Afrocentrism to socialize black youth into the proper values.

Afrocentric school programs were a response to "[v]iolence, drugs, [and] early parenthood," as one educational researcher observed.[11] Because Afrocentrism was in part a response to the idea of the underclass, arguments for Afrocentric education typically rested not simply on the state of black education but also on a host of underclass images and statistics (on poverty, crime, homicide, and incarceration, among other things). In an essay supporting Afrocentric education, Michael D. Harris, an Afrocentric art educator, presents the expulsion rate, grades, and suspension rate of black students in Milwaukee public schools (Milwaukee was one of the pioneering sites for Afrocentric public education) followed by the national incarceration and homicide rates for black men.[12] Geneva Smitherman, the linguist who was involved in the development of Afrocentric education in Detroit, provides another example of the rationale:

> For some educators and scholars, the early 1980s marked the pivotal point where the reality of the Black male crisis could no longer be ignored. It was becoming painfully clear that young Black males experience negative social and educational problems, which have reached gigantic proportions today as we make our way to the Twenty-First Century. They were dropping out of school at alarming rates, and they were facing high rates of unemployment and incarceration.[13]

By moving so quickly from education to issues like unemployment and incarceration, advocates for Afrocentric education leave no space for racial discrimination as an explanatory variable. The implication is that if blacks, and black men in particular, were well educated they would be employed fully and well and not incarcerated. Therefore, blacks do not encounter discrimination in the labor market or in the criminal justice system. Afrocentrism is premised on the idea of racial bias, prejudice, and discrimination in "Eurocentric" curricula, yet when discussing American society in general racism recedes into the background. Arguments for Afrocentric education imply that racial discrimination is only clearly present in American society among those who oppose such an education.[14]

Both Harris and Smitherman emphasized problems confronting black males. Analyses of the underclass stressed the importance of having black men work and marry. Much of the crisis of the underclass was explained as a failure of black men to fulfill their responsibilities as the head of the household.[15] This emphasis on black men in the underclass discourse is part of the reason for the emphasis on black boys in Afrocentric education. In Detroit and Milwaukee, the Afrocentric schools were originally supposed to be schools for black males only.[16]

In endorsing a cultural solution to not only the problems in black education, but also the problems of crime, unemployment, and the like, Afrocentrists endorsed a mainstream and conservative perspective on black poverty. Mainstream observers of the underclass felt that the black poor needed cultural reform. Afrocentrists agreed that the black poor suffered from what amounts to a "culture of poverty." The difference between the Afrocentrists' and mainstream analysts' solution to the underclass was nominal. Afrocentrists called their cultural reform efforts "Afrocentrism" while mainstream reformers called it middle-class family values.

A CRITICAL CONTEXTUALIZATION OF THE "UNDERCLASS"

Although many people were convinced that there was a new phenomenon of a black underclass in the 1980s, when scholars looked more closely at the argument it became much less convincing. First it was not clear exactly what defined the underclass. To some the "underclass" of the 1980s looked remarkably like the "lower class" of previous decades. Despite the numerous studies and reports about the "underclass," there was little concrete evidence that there was a *new* crisis among the black lower class. In 1991, Christopher Jencks and Paul Peterson observed:

> Conventional wisdom tells us that the United States is witnessing a significant growth in the size of its urban underclass. Many believe that the percentage of the population persistently poor is large and rapidly increasing, that more and more unmarried teenage girls are bearing children, and that welfare rolls are exploding. It is frequently alleged that crime is on the increase, young people are dropping out of school in record numbers, and higher percentages of the population are withdrawing from the labor force. The poor are also said to be increasingly isolated in ghettos at the cores of our metropolitan areas.[17]

After looking carefully for evidence of these things, Jencks and Peterson concluded *"none of these propositions is true."*[18] The poverty rate for blacks had been roughly the same throughout the 1970s and 1980s. In the 1980s, "teenage girls were having fewer babies that at any time since 1940. Black teenagers were having more babies than white teenagers, but the gap was narrowing rather than widening."[19] There was no increase in the proportion of single mothers on welfare since 1974. Violent crime actually declined in the early 1980s before rising again. There was no new crisis that demanded that the black lower class be reclassified as an underclass.[20]

While there was little justification for labeling the black poor an underclass, there were real new problems in black communities in the 1980s. More black men dropped out of the legal labor force. This increase had begun in the 1970s, so it was not completely new. The crack cocaine economy developed and produced some of the increase in violent crime. More young black men killed other young black men. But black communities were still less violent in the 1980s than in the 1970s. While there are probably connections between these three issues, we cannot easily link them to the rest of the underclass story. Among blacks, poverty did not increase, teenage pregnancy did not increase, and reliance on welfare did not increase.[21]

The other fairly new development in the 1980s was the increase in female single-parent households. These households were headed by adults—not teens—and not restricted to black women. This apparent increase was driven by married women having fewer children, thus increasing the proportion of children whose mother was not married. It was also driven by increases in the number of children to unmarried women and by increasing rates of divorce. All these factors led to a greater proportion of American children being raised in homes without men.[22]

In the 1980s and 1990s, the idea of the underclass and the arguments around it were part of a shift in American political opinion to the political right. Liberals accepted conservative assumptions and therefore frequently came to conservative conclusions. Republican Vice President Dan Quayle, for example, provided the standard conservative position when he argued that the cause of "intergenerational poverty" was a "poverty of values." Quayle stated:

> Children need love and discipline. They need mothers and fathers. A welfare check is not a husband. The state is not a father. It is from parents that children learn how to behave in society.[23]

He added, "Marriage is probably the best anti-poverty program." On the importance of fathers, he stated, "When there are no mature, responsible men around to teach boys to be good men, gangs serve in their place." We find the same ideas in the film *Boyz N the Hood* by the black filmmaker John Singleton. One keen observer noted:

> *Boyz N the Hood* . . . is centered on the proposition that a poor black child's chances of escaping the ghetto are determined by how responsi-

bly he or she is raised. In one early scene, the film's hero lays the ground rules of his house for his son, explaining that it is his job to "teach you how to be responsible. Your friends across the street [raised by a single mother] have nobody to show them how to do that. And you're going to see how they end up, too." Sure enough, the heroic father with the strict guidelines raises a son who is accepted at Morehouse, while the reckless single mother finds both of her sons shot dead.[24]

In 1992, the liberal Democrat Bill Clinton promised to "end welfare as we know it" because he believed that it "undermine[d] the basic values of work, responsibility, and family trapping generation after generation in dependency." A broad cross section of American society, including Afrocentrists, accepted this conservative analysis of the underclass.[25]

Like others, Afrocentrists wished to solve the problem of the underclass. And like others they decided that values were the solution. They called their values black or African, but in fact they were the same values that everyone else had determined the underclass was lacking.

Afrocentrism and "Low Self-Esteem"

In the 1980s and 1990s, Afrocentric scholars and activists dedicated themselves to curing the supposedly low self-esteem of black students with Afrocentric curricula. Molefi Kete Asante argued, "What I want for blacks is the same self-esteem that white children automatically get when they walk into a class." Afrocentrists saw the low academic performance of black students as a direct result of black students lacking cultural pride and self-esteem. Repairing damaged black psyches was one of the most common justifications for Afrocentric education. For example, the Portland, Oregon, Afrocentric program promised to improve students' self-esteem. In the black middle-class suburb of Prince George's County, Maryland, a school board member claimed that the county's Afrocentric curriculum would "enhance self-esteem, motivate achievement, and help [students] to be law-abiding citizens." Donald Leake and Brenda Leake, the designers of Afrocentric education in Milwaukee, stated that one goal of their program was to produce "self-confident individuals" and "to vitiate the African-American students' feelings of inadequacy and impotence." The Afrocentric educators Kimberly R. Vann and Jawanza Kunjufu argue, "In textbooks, African-American history begins with American slavery, instead of with the genesis of civilization in Africa. Therefore, African-Americans are considered as descendants only of slaves, not of kings and queens." Vann and Kunjufu add, "If you have been constantly taught that your ancestors were well-educated, cultured innovators, how would you feel about the descendants of slaves? If you have been taught that your ancestors were illiterate, impoverished sharecroppers, how would you feel about yourself?" Kunjufu's curriculum is called Self-Esteem through Culture Leads to Academic Excellence.[26]

This renewed black American concern with self-esteem was part of a general rise in America's concern with self-esteem and pop psychology that began in the mid-1980s. (As a point of reference, we should note that Oprah Winfrey's talk show success began in the 1980s.) In books, magazines, and on television talk shows people from all walks of life shared with absolutely anyone their stories of psychological damage. In her 1992 anti–pop psychology book, *I'm Dysfunctional, You're Dysfunctional*, Wendy Kaminer observed, "On almost every [television talk show], someone is bound to get around to self-esteem; most forms of misconduct are said to be indicative of low self-esteem." In American popular culture, self-esteem became the universal problem solvent. Nearly all personal or social problems stemmed from having too little of it and nearly any personal or social problem could be solved by pouring more self-esteem on. "Self-esteem" became the "buzzword of the 1990s" for the average American and Afrocentrist alike. For this reason, the Afrocentric argument about low self-esteem among black students resonated powerfully with blacks and nonblacks.[27]

A CRITICAL CONTEXTUALIZATION OF THE IDEA OF BLACK SELF-HATE

From at least as early as the 1930s, scholars have argued that white domination has had psychological effects on black Americans. Given that in American society there are negative associations with blackness, negative stereotypes of black people, and that black people have been forced into the least prestigious and most despised social positions, it is plausible that these things would have detrimental psychological consequences for blacks. Black people may see themselves as negatively as many whites see blacks. As plausible as this argument is, it has not occurred. Blacks have managed to foster positive views of themselves and to hold themselves in amazingly high regard.

In 1935, W. E. B. Du Bois asked, "What did it mean to be a slave?"

His answer was that to fully understand slavery we have to go beyond the physical cruelty and beyond the "negation of human rights." For Du Bois, an important part of enslavement was psychological. He wrote:

> There was . . . a real meaning to slavery different from that we may apply to the laborer today. It was in part psychological, the enforced personal feeling of inferiority, the calling of another Master; the standing with hat in hand. It was the helplessness.[28]

In the 1954 *Brown v. Board of Education* decision, this idea was restated and popularized. The Supreme Court Justices argued:

> To separate them [black children] from others of similar age and qualifications solely because of their race generates a feeling of inferiority as to their status in the community that may affect their hearts and minds in a way unlikely ever to be undone.[29]

This type of reasoning led to the very popular idea that blacks suffer from self-hate. By "self-hate" I am referring to a number of related concepts and ideas that blacks have been psychologically damaged by racial oppression. The "inferiority complex" is one. The idea that blacks suffer from "low self-esteem" is another. Many arguments about inauthentic blackness draw on some version of the self-hate idea. For example, the "Uncle Tom" is said to be a self-hating Negro.[30]

Although the argument in the *Brown* decision was that *segregation* causes black self-hate, it is more common today to hear that *integration* causes black self-hate. Blacks' exposure to whites and participation in majority-white organizations are now seen as the cause of self-hate. The segregated communities during the Jim Crow era are now seen as communities which fostered black self-love. bell hooks, for example, argues that black self-hate is a post–civil rights problem. "Civil rights advocates," she writes, did not consider "whether or not it would be damaging to the self-esteem of black folks to interact with white folks . . . who had not unlearned white supremacist thinking and action." She "began thinking about the question of self-esteem precisely because of the extreme levels of self-doubt I was witnessing in the black students I encountered at the Ivy League schools where I taught."[31]

While hooks highlights the supposed self-esteem problems among black middle-class college students, Cornel West highlights the supposed self-esteem problems among the black lower class in the post–civil rights era. West prefers the term nihilism to self-hate but it is clear that he is referring to the same complex of ideas. He equates nihilism with "self-contempt and self-hatred," "personal worthlessness," and "self-loathing," among other things. Nihilism is West's way of talking about the cultural problems of the underclass. He argues:

> corporate market institutions have greatly contributed to undermining traditional morality . . .
>
> Like all Americans, African-Americans are influenced by the images of comfort, convenience, machismo, femininity, violence, and sexual stimulation that bombard consumers. These seductive images contribute to the predominance of the market-inspired way of life over all others and thereby edge out nonmarket values—love, care, service to others—handed down by preceding generations. The predominance of this way of life among those living in poverty-ridden conditions, with a limited capacity to ward off self-contempt and self-hatred, results in the possible triumph of the nihilistic threat in black America.[32]

For West, corporations in the post–civil rights era (he dates the problem of nihilism as beginning in the 1970s) have a disproportionate affect on "those living in poverty-ridden conditions."[33] West's poor are the underclass who lack the values of the nonpoor. They are nihilistic, lack a proper work ethic (because they are influenced by "images of comfort" and "convenience"),[34] and are deviant in their gender roles and sexuality (because of the images of machismo, femininity and sexual stimulation). Ultimately, for West, self-hate—nihilism—becomes part of the causal chain that explains the problems of the underclass.[35]

Black self-hate has become an extraordinarily powerful and flexible idea. In the 1950s, segregation was said to be the cause of black self-hate; today, integration is seen as the cause of black self-hate. Some scholars have discussed self-hate as a black middle-class problem,[36] while others see it as a problem among the black poor. Afrocentrists argue that Afrocentric education is a cure for black self-hate; one opponent of Afrocentric education has argued that Afrocentric education can cause black self-hate because it makes blacks hate the fact that they are American.[37] People are so convinced of the existence of black self-hate and of its explanatory power that few realize the contradictions within and among the many self-hate arguments.

Despite its popularity, *the idea of black self-hate is false.* For the past forty years, social scientists have looked closely at the issue of black self-hate. They have found that blacks have stronger racial identities[38] and greater levels of self-esteem than whites[39]—*the exact opposite of what the self-hate idea asserts.* Socialization within black families and black communities, the experience of being a minority and being discriminated against all contribute to these findings.[40] Black Americans have adapted culturally and psychologically to their subordinate status in ways that produce a strong collective black identity and that preserves their self-esteem. While other racial minorities also show racial identities about as strong as blacks, they have on average lower levels of self-esteem than whites.[41]

High black self-esteem may not be an absolute good. In the self-hate argument about self-esteem and academic achievement, low self-esteem is supposed to cause low academic achievement. However, Asian American students score lowest on self-esteem measures but have relatively high academic achievement. Black American students score high on self-esteem measures but have relatively low academic achievement. Some scholars now argue that the mechanisms that allow black students to have high self-esteem might actually work against their academic achievement. The issues around racial identity and self-esteem are much more complex than most people who casually propose self-hate arguments imagine.[42]

Afrocentrism and "Failing Schools"

The idea that American schools were failing black students academically was a powerful one in the 1980s and 1990s. Part of the explanation for the underclass was the idea that blacks were not being educated because of failing schools. Many Americans understand economic success or failure in terms of educational achievement. They believe that the more educated one is the more successful one becomes. The less educated one is the less successful one becomes. Poverty is therefore the result of having very little education. It is seen as an individual characteristic, not something produced by the structure of the economy. Thus the black underclass was explained as resulting from the failure of blacks to succeed educationally. Black students' failure to succeed educationally was seen as the result of failing schools.

For Afrocentrists, schools failed black students because they did not have Afrocentric curricula which engaged black students and improved their self-esteem. Afrocentric curricula would improve black students' self-esteem, which in turn would improve black students' academic performance (schools would therefore no longer be failing), which would lead blacks to well-paying jobs and prevent the formation of the underclass. All these ideas—the underclass, low self-esteem, and failing schools—fit together well to create the sense of a new crisis facing black America. For some, the solution to this new crisis was Afrocentrism.

A CRITICAL CONTEXTUALIZATION OF BLACK ACADEMIC ACHIEVEMENT IN THE 1980s

Black students have been denied access to educational resources equal to that of white students for all of American history. Black student academic achievement has been lower than white students for all of American history. While these general statements are true, the era of the 1980s was special in black American educational history. If ever there was a time to be optimistic about blacks and the American educational system, it was then. In *A Common Destiny: Blacks and American Society*, a report published in 1989 by the National Academy of Sciences, the panel of educational researchers concluded:

> substantial progress has been made toward the provision of high-quality, equal, and integrated education. Whether the baseline period is the 1940s, the 1950s, of even as recently as the mid-1960s, the amount, achievement outcomes, and intergroup context (integrated versus segregated) of black schooling have greatly improved.[43]

Black students made greater gains on white students in the 1980s than at probably any other time in American history. One of the best measures of academic achievement trends, the U.S. Department of Education's National Assessment of Educational Progress (NAEP) tests, showed dramatic gains for black high school seniors between 1980 and 1990 in reading, mathematics, and science. Even on the SAT, which tends to have a greater proportion of low-performing blacks than whites taking it, blacks improved absolutely and in relation to whites.[44] Had the NAEP trend in the 1980s continued, the average black high school graduate would be equal to the average white student in reading, math, and science ability today. It is even possible that black students would have surpassed whites in reading and math since the factors producing black gains in the 1980s did not affect whites. Unfortunately, the gains of the 1980s ended. There has been no significant convergence between black and white academic achievement since 1990. In other words, if the current trend continues, the achievement gap will never be reduced.[45]

Afrocentric educators, however, focused on the very real and persistent problems in the education of black students in the 1980s and 1990s and were oblivious to the improvements in black student achievement. They felt that black students were either not improving relative to whites or were getting worse. They felt that something new was needed to address the problems facing black students. An Afrocentric curriculum, they argued, was the solution.

It is not surprising that Afrocentrists would miss the improvements in black student achievement—nearly everyone did. The educational system was another public institution under attack by the Reagan and Bush administrations. In *The Manufactured Crisis*, David C. Berliner and Bruce J. Biddle excellently document, as their subtitle indicates, the "Myths, Fraud, and the Attack on America's Public Schools." They identify the Reagan administration's attack as beginning with the report *A Nation at Risk* (1983) sponsored by the Secretary of Education and endorsed by the president. The report widely condemned the educational system for producing "a rising tide of mediocrity." It declared, "If an unfriendly foreign power had attempted to impose on America the mediocre educational performance that exists today, we might well have viewed it as an act of war." These remarks are from the first page of the report. As Berliner and Biddle note:

> *Never* before had such trenchant rhetoric about education appeared from the White House. As a result, the press had a field day, tens of thousands of copies of *A Nation at Risk* were distributed, and many Americans thereafter read or heard, for the first time, that our public schools were "truly" failing.[46]

The only problem with *A Nation at Risk* was that much of what it claimed about American schools was wrong. The report stated, "Average achievement of high school students on most standardized tests is now lower than 26 years ago when Sputnik was launched." The Secretary of Education was later forced to admit that "today's children seem to know about as much math and about as much science and read about as well as their parents did at that age about 20 years ago." If the repeated reports during the Reagan and Bush years led one to believe that white Americans were doing worse educationally than in the past, it was also easy to believe that black Americans were doing even worse than whites. What really happened was that white students did about the same as in the past, and black students made significant gains.[47]

Afrocentrism and American Society

To fully understand Afrocentrism, we need to see that it is directed at all aspects of social life, not just education. "To go back to traditions is the first step forward," Afrocentrists argue.[48] They believe that they can produce greatness in black Americans by restoring the values of ancient African civilizations among black Americans. Afrocentrists see Afrocentrism as a way of addressing a variety of ills facing black communities and the black "underclass" in particular. For example, Molefi Kete Asante argues, "young African-American males who may be engaged in violent behavior are often off-center,"[49] by which he means they are not centered in African culture. He believes that "for a social worker to go into the homes of potential violent abusers and redecorate the walls with Afrocentric posters and messages is a small but powerful step."[50] Afrocentrists' targets are not only low educational achievement but also violence in black communities, problems in male-female relationships, personal psychological problems, poverty, and other social ills.[51]

Because black males performed worse than females academically and also were more likely to be subject to or involved in a variety of social problems (e.g., crime, unemployment, homicide), some Afrocentrists believed that black males had a greater need for the "cultural inoculation"[52] that Afrocentric education provided.[53] Some of the most publicized attempts to establish Afrocentric education were intended exclusively for black males. Although these schools were prevented from being exclusively male, in Detroit at least, they were still overwhelmingly so.[54] The central concern of the "underclass" discourse is also the black male.

The goal of Afrocentrism is not a transformation of white Americans, but primarily a transformation of blacks. Afrocentrists do hope to make revisions in the general historical record, but ultimately Afrocentrism does not require the complete obliteration of Eurocentrism. Valethia Watkins has "no quarrel with white women controlling and dominating the feminist movement. After all," she insists, "it is their movement."[55] Molefi Asante does not "[question] the validity of the Eurocentric tradition within its context."[56] White students can pursue Eurocentric studies; black students, Afrocentric studies. Since African and European cultures are fundamentally different, two social sciences are needed, according to Diop. The main purpose of Afrocentrism is to restore an African culture and identity to black Americans. It does not require a change in whites and other Americans.

Because Afrocentrism is narrowly focused on issues of culture and identity, Afrocentric blacks can participate fully in the political and economic institutions of the United States. Molefi Kete Asante argues that we should not see the "rejection of white values [as] a rejection of the United States."[57] He also states that a black American can "work for IBM and live in the suburbs and be Afrocentric."[58] The principal of the Afrocentric Malcolm X Academy in Detroit selected an African American male who is serving in the U.S. military as an example of the kind of success story that his school can produce.[59] Janice Hale, an Afrocentric educator, sees her curriculum as leading blacks to "upward mobility, career achievement, and financial independence in the American mainstream."[60] Although Afrocentrists insist that blacks are Africans culturally, no Afrocentric scholar, to my knowledge, has suggested that black Americans emigrate to Africa. They encourage black Americans to visit Africa while holding onto their American passports.

A Conservative Cultural Nationalism

The rise of Afrocentric nationalism in the 1980s and 1990s was the result of real negative events in American racial relations. In addition to administrations that did not fight for racial justice and various notable acts of violence against blacks, there were also false and inaccurate ideas that made black nationalism appealing to blacks. False ideas about the "underclass," "low self-esteem," and "failing schools" were popular in American culture at the time. Even non-Afrocentric reporters, school administrators, and others could be moved by the terms and images that Afrocentric activists used.

Afrocentric black nationalism was a true cultural nationalism. It was spurred by academics and stressed cultural identity over political economy. Afrocentric nationalists would wage a values offensive against the problems of the "underclass." They would argue for the study of Africa to rebuild blacks' "low self-esteem" and to repair "failing schools." Even if we disregard the errors and inaccuracies around the ideas of the "underclass," "low self-esteem," and "failing schools" and accept them as real problems, there is a liberal and conservative response to all these problems. Afrocentrism tends to the conservative position which attacks social problems by changing values, as opposed to the liberal position which attacks social problems by equalizing resources. For example, if the underclass is about the impoverishment of a segment of the black population then a liberal response would be to demand *more* welfare spending to lift people out of poverty. (Western European countries have lower poverty rates and lower percentages of people who remain in poverty for several years because they have a more generous welfare system than the United States.)[61] A conservative response would call for social policies that encourage self-help and the development of stronger work ethics that would keep one out of poverty. Afrocentrists want to change the cultural values of the black poor through Afrocentric curricula, not to redistribute the wealth in American society.

Self-esteem as a problem already puts one in the more conservative domain of individual characteristics as the explanation for one's achievement as opposed to the more liberal view that structural conditions explain achievement. However, if racial oppression causes low self-esteem, a liberal response is to work to end racial oppression. In 1989, for example, the black psychiatrist Alvin Poussaint said, "End poverty and discrimination and you'll solve a lot of identity problems."[62] Afrocentrists call for Afrocentric education to improve the self-esteem of black students, not a broad offensive against racial oppression.

If students are in failing schools, the liberal approach would be to call for more resources for failing schools to improve them, while one conservative response would be to try to change the values and attitudes of students to get them to work harder. To find a strong critique of funding inequalities between predominantly black and predominantly white schools in the 1980s and 1990s, one had to turn to the non-Afrocentric educational reformer Jonathan Kozol.[63] This issue was not a priority among Afrocentrists. In typical conservative fashion, they believed that Afrocentric curricula would change black students' attitudes and values toward education and thereby improve failing schools. In attempting to solve the "social problems" of the 1980s and 1990s, Afrocentrists consistently chose the conservative approach.

Popular Afrocentrism

The Afrocentric era was marked by not only Afrocentric ideas among intellectuals but also by "African-centered" and "black-centered" nationalism in black popular culture. The movement of Afrocentrism from colleges to primary and secondary education is not surprising. Of particular note was the growth of interest in and celebration of Africa and the Black Power movement in the rest of black popular culture. This popular Afrocentrism could be seen in the hairstyles, clothing, and music of the era. During the Afrocentric era, more black parents gave their children African or Muslim names (in the Black Power era Islam came to symbolize blackness, as described in chapter 3) than they had before. Collectively, many blacks began calling themselves "African American." The largest rally of black men in American history, the Million Man March, and the largest rally of black women in American history, the Million Woman March, occurred during this era. Both these events had strong black nationalist themes. Black nationalism during the Afrocentric era was not limited to the Afrocentrism of intellectuals.

Afrocentric Public Schools

There was a great deal of variation in the practices that fell under the heading of "Afrocentric education." Some schools were more "Africa-centered" and some were more "black-centered." Afrocentric programs in public schools ranged from programs that ran for a few hours a week and were merely affiliated with public schools to entire schools that were Afrocentric. There were schools that had one Afrocentric class. There were schools that had one Afrocentric grade. There were schools that had an Afrocentric school within a school. There was variation in the design, scope, and quality of the implementation of Afrocentric education.[64] A major reason for this variation was because in the early 1990s there was no clear model or definition of what Afrocentric education meant.[65] The following discussion will not attempt to document and survey all the variation in the practice of Afrocentric education, but it will provide some good examples of the translation of Afrocentric ideas into practice.

Afrocentric public schools revealed their Afrocentrism in the physical environment of the schools. The Afrocentric Malcolm X Academy in

Detroit flew the Pan-Africanist Red, Black, and Green flag of Marcus Garvey's Universal Negro Improvement Association alongside the American flag.[66] Not surprisingly, the Marcus Garvey Academy in Detroit also displayed the Red, Black, and Green colors on a sign with the school name.[67] In his *Guide to Implementing Afrikan-Centered Education* Kwame Kenyatta lists the Red, Black, and Green flag as a requirement for Afrocentric schools.[68]

In Milwaukee, murals and African and African-American art and artifacts decorated the school.[69] One observer in a classroom in Milwaukee's Dr. Martin Luther King Jr. Elementary School described what she saw in a second grade social studies classroom:

> There are three African dolls on the table next to me. They are dressed in brightly colored African clothing, head wraps twisted in different styles. Several drums sit next to various carved wooded animals. They all rest upon a piece of mud cloth which is draped over the table and comes to rest behind two African gourds. . . .
>
> . . . Opposite me there are five computers lined up against the wall. Above them are the numbers from one to ten in Swahili. Under these numbers a bulletin board is full of information on Dr. Martin Luther King, Jr. . . . On the opposite wall above the chalkboard are pictures of Famous Black Americans and Famous Africans. . . .
>
> The back wall and windows also hold pictures of Black Americans and Africans along with a large poster of Bill Clinton.[70]

The Afrocentric décor also included the African clothing worn by some teachers and sometimes by students.[71] Some Afrocentric schools also had the principles of the Nguzo Saba and the principles of the ancient Egyptian ethical teachings of Maat displayed on the walls of classrooms and in other parts of the school.[72]

As public schools, Afrocentric schools generally had to abide by the curriculum and other rules of the school district. The students in Afrocentric schools were given the same standardized tests as students attending other schools. Afrocentric education was therefore mixed into, and added to, the mainstream curriculum.[73]

It was not uncommon for Afrocentric schools to also impose additional requirements beyond the regular curriculum. Some schools had after-school and Saturday school requirements and a longer school year.

Some schools required students to learn Kiswahili in addition to the standard foreign language requirement. Some schools required students to perform community service.[74]

Afrocentric schools also acknowledged and celebrated different holidays from non-Afrocentric schools. The birthdays of famous black Americans were recognized. The Day of Atonement, started by Minister Louis Farrakhan of the Nation of Islam, might be acknowledged. Instead of Thanksgiving, there might be activities around a "unity feast." Instead of Halloween, there might be a celebration of "All Saints Day." Instead of (or in addition to) Christmas, Kwanzaa would be acknowledged and celebrated.[75]

Afrocentric schools imparted the values of Afrocentrism through school pledges and aphorisms. The school day often began with a school pledge that served to motivate and improve the self-esteem of the students. At the Martin Luther King Jr. School in Milwaukee, students recited the following:

> My heritage is one of greatness
> And I know that I can do more
> I must never, never do less
> Than those who have gone before[76]

At the Marcus Moziah Garvey Academy in Detroit, the school creed read:

> I will have faith in myself. I will succeed and most of all, I will reach my goals. I promise to accept responsibility for my duties and my own actions. I have self-respect and self-control. I can learn! I will learn!
>
> I will practice self-determination, as taught by the honorable Marcus Moziah Garvey. Expressed, I will define myself; I will speak for myself; I will name myself and I will create myself—so that others cannot define me; speak for me; name me or create for me. I am a Garveyite![77]

The students at the Garvey school also recited, "If it is to be, it is up to me."[78]

The ideal for "African-centered" education is for all subjects to begin in Africa. Science education might begin with a discussion of science and technology in ancient Egypt as well as a discussion of the technical achievement of the ancient Egyptian scientist and multidisciplinary scholar Imhotep. Mathematics instruction might explore ancient Egyptian multiplication techniques and other African ethnomathematics.[79] In studying Spanish, students begin by charting the African slave trade to establish the African diasporic connection between "English-speaking Africans and Spanish-speaking Africans."[80]

In all subject areas, teachers also highlighted heroic figures and heroic struggles. They might also discuss past and present examples of racial discrimination.[81] By highlighting heroic figures and heroic struggles, teachers hoped to provide positive role models and to develop the racial pride and self-esteem of their students.[82] Afrocentric schools also had Rites of Passage programs to provide adult role models for students and to address the duties of proper manhood and womanhood. Rites of Passage programs were also designed in the hope of improving students' self-esteem. The Detroit Malcolm X Academy even had a class designated solely for developing students' self-esteem. In addition to racial pride and self-esteem, Afrocentric schools stressed the values of discipline, respect for elders, and service to black communities.[83]

In some cities, Afrocentric education was disproportionately directed at black boys. In Detroit and Milwaukee, the programs were originally meant to be for black boys only. Only after legal challenges did the schools become coeducational. Even the coeducational schools, however, were disproportionately male. Their rationale was that on a number of statistics, black males have worse outcomes than black females. Therefore, the special attention and cultural "inoculation" provided by Afrocentric education was most needed by black males. While Afrocentric educators presume heterosexuality, their gendered education does not explicitly advocate male superiority over women.[84] Because Afrocentric theory identifies sexism as a Eurocentric value, there was ideological support for egalitarian practices between males and females in Afrocentric schools.[85]

The ideal instructors for Afrocentric education were black teachers because the teachers are supposed to serve as racial role models for the students. It was also assumed that there would be cultural compatibility between black students and black teachers. As public schools, however, Afrocentric schools typically had at least a few white teachers.[86]

Afrocentric teaching varies with the interpretation of Afrocentrism.

Fig. 6.1. These four boys have just graduated from the almost all-male, Afrocentric Paul Robeson Academy in Detroit in 1992. The only easily visible sign of Afrocentrism is the kente-print hat. What Afrocentric education meant could vary a great deal. The school uniform worn by the students, however, points to an important motivation for Afrocentric education: fear of being part of the "underclass." Afrocentric education was an attempt to culturally "inoculate" children, boys especially, against the social problems related to black impoverishment. Educators hoped that Afrocentric education would produce employed, law-abiding, and married black men. (Photo by Taro Yamasaki/Time Life Pictures/Getty Images, #50600735)

Some schools placed a great deal of emphasis on discipline. Other schools stressed creating a feeling of care and family bonding. One possible reason for the difference may be the age of the students. Black teachers might use black vernacular English although students were also expected to learn to speak and write standard American English. Teachers might be encouraged to have dynamic and energetic classrooms because Afrocentric theory postulates that this type of classroom fits the black student's learning style.[87]

Some Afrocentric schools required parental involvement in the schools and in their children's education. Given the special status of Afrocentric schools, in some cities parents had to apply and be selected to have their children receive Afrocentric schooling. These schools also required parents to work a specified number of hours in the school. Teachers were also expected to make a specified number of home visits.[88]

Afrocentrism was manifest in many aspects of Afrocentric schools. The décor might be Afrocentric. The curriculum might begin in Africa and might attempt to build black pride, Africanized identities, and self-esteem. Teachers might teach in an Afrocentric teaching style, however that was understood. Afrocentric educators hoped that these practices would create black students who excelled in school and later would become employed, law-abiding, married, and upstanding adults who were a benefit to black communities.[89]

From "Black" to "African American"

Afrocentric-era black nationalism extended beyond the classroom and into many aspects of popular life. An important aspect of this nationalism was the name black Americans called themselves. In 1988 black Americans began transforming themselves into "African Americans." "African American" as a replacement for "black American" arose at a planning meeting of black leaders attempting to develop a national black agenda. The term was proposed by Ramona Edelin, president of the National Urban Coalition, and endorsed by Rev. Jesse Jackson.[90] On December 19, Jackson announced at a press conference that blacks preferred to be called "African Americans." The members of the planning group argued that the term would provide blacks with, among other things, a "psychological lift" and "self-respect."[91] The name change to "African American" was therefore aimed at improving black self-esteem. "African American" had been in use on the margins of black America since the 1970s,[92] but with Jesse Jackson advocating for it, it quickly moved from margin to center.[93]

In the term "African American" one sees the influence of the Pan-Africanism of the Black Power era which linked black Americans to Africa. But it also went beyond that. Something new was occurring. Jackson argued:

> Just as we were called colored, but were not that, and then Negro, but [were] not that, to be called black is just as baseless. To be called African-Americans has cultural integrity. It puts us in our proper historical context. Every ethnic group in this country has a reference to some land

base, some historical cultural base. African-Americans have hit that level of cultural maturity. There are Armenian-Americans and Jewish-Americans and Arab-Americans and Italian-Americans. And with a degree of accepted and reasonable pride, they connect their heritage to their mother country and where they are now.[94]

When Black Power activists called themselves "Black," it was an anti-white symbolic move. When they called themselves "Afrikan," it was an anti-American move. Pan-Africanists saw themselves as Africans who belonged to a future Pan-African nation, not to America. Jackson's argument in favor of "African American," however, simultaneously embraced whites and America. He was saying that black Americans followed a similar cultural pattern as we had seen among white Americans. In contrast, in 1973 the Pan-Africanist Haki Madhubuti (Don L. Lee) objected to "Afrikan American" because it suggested that blacks "enjoy all the rights and privileges of other Americans."[95] Many scholars agree with Madhubuti and argue that blacks have experienced a greater degree of discrimination than white immigrants. "African American" runs the risk of obscuring this fact.[96]

As a term, "African American" is quite different from the Black Power Pan-Africanist "Afrikan" and "Black." "Afrikan" and "Black" can be used as a global racial designation, but "African American" cannot. Any black person, anywhere in the world, could be called an "Afrikan" or a "Black" by a Pan-Africanist, but the term "African American" applies only to blacks in the United States.[97] "African American" therefore encourages one to distinguish blacks in the United States from blacks elsewhere while also linking black Americans to Africa.

"African American" also emerged without prior usage of the term by a significant sector of black Americans. "Black" became the term used for blacks in the mainstream media in the 1970s because more and more blacks used the term in everyday conversations over the 1960s. The mainstream media *followed* the practices of the black public. In the 1990s, most blacks found out that they were "African American" *from* the mainstream media. There was no grassroots activist movement to which this symbolic move was connected. The decision for the name change was completely made by the decree of Jesse Jackson.[98] Like the term "African American," much of the black nationalism of the Afrocentric era referenced Africa but was not Pan-African in the 1970s sense.

Afrocentrisms in American Life

"Nigger, have you lost your mind."
"You must be crazy."
"You're not African."

—Responses to Kenneth M. Jones's dreadlocks in the
pre-Afrocentric era, early 1980s

The adoption of the label "African American" was only one of a variety of ways in which blacks signaled a new Afrocentric identity. Another popular Afrocentrism was the use of distinctive "black" names. Prior to the 1960s, there was considerable overlap in the names black and white Americans gave their children. The Black Power movement brought about the first rapid divergence in black and white names. In the Afrocentric era, even greater proportions of black children received distinctive names.[99] Over time, the many Afrocentric bookstores carried

Fig. 6.2. In the Afrocentric era, the Ghanaian kente cloth and kente patterns were assimilated into black American culture. Although there is no longer a "kente kraze" as there was in the late 1980s and early 1990s, it is still part of black American life. Kente stoles remain a common part of graduation ceremonies, for example. This photograph shows three kente-print umbrellas on sale at the African Festival of the Arts on the Southside of Chicago in 2004. The African Festival of the Arts, which defines "African" to include black Americans and the rest of the African diaspora, began in the Afrocentric era. (Photo by Robert Abbott Sengstacke © 2004. Reprinted by permission.)

Fig. 6.3. In the Afrocentric era, African and African-inspired clothing became accepted as formal wear for black Americans. Above we see Dr. Leonard Jeffries, an Afrocentric activist at the Million Man March, in his Afrocentric garb. Books like *Jumping the Broom: The African-American Wedding Planner* (1993, by Harriette Cole) with its Queen N'zinga braids, kente tuxedos, and wedding rings with ancient Egyptian symbols reflected and further popularized Afrocentric fashion. (Photo by Robert Abbott Seng-stacke © 1995. Reprinted by permission)

more than two dozen new books providing parents with African names for their child.[100] Many parents skipped the books and made up an "African" name of their own. Others chose unique black American name creations such as Latonya, Shaniqua, Kiara, and DeShawn.[101]

Even more common than distinctive names was kente cloth. The multicolored woven kente cloth has a long history as a sign of royalty and high status in Ghana. In the Afrocentric era, black Americans adopted it for a wide range of uses. Kente stoles were used in graduation ceremonies and by churches. While this maintained some of the revered nature of the symbol, its use was not limited to solemn occasions in the era. Every type of clothing could be found in kente. Many items used the kente pattern as a print instead of the actual cloth. Not only were there jackets, shorts, and caps with kente prints, but there

were also checkbooks, plates, and clocks in kente. Kente had truly conquered America, or maybe America had conquered kente when McDonald's restaurants in black communities began using kente print cups
and caps.[102]

Afrocentric fashion was not limited to kente. A variety of forms of
African art, artifacts, and aesthetic practices became popular and a wide
variety of typical American products were marketed with Afrocentric
touches. In 1996, *Emerge* magazine reported, "Afrocentricity has truly
woven itself into the cultural fabric of America. Dreadlocks, braids,
cowry shells, incense, mud cloth and essential oils have become the
norm for Black Americans from the nation's capital to Atlanta, Holly-
wood to Brooklyn."[103] The authors of *The Spirit of African Design*
(1996) implored blacks to go even further. They stated that it was possible "to integrate African art into every aspect of the home—furniture,
textiles, surfaces, windows and walls, beds and bathrooms, kitchens,
and even the garden."[104] Prior to the Afrocentric era, dreadlocked hair
usually indicated that a black person was a Rastafarian. It was a "crazy"
idea for a non-Rastafarian to have dreadlocks. In the Afrocentric era,
many elite black-owned hair salons without a Rastafarian clientele began to specialize in locked hair as well as African braiding styles.[105]

In 1997, the U.S. Postal Service issued its first Kwanzaa stamp. As
the historian Elizabeth Pleck has observed, the history of Kwanzaa is
full of ironies. Kwanzaa is the Pan-African celebration founded by
Maulana Karenga, the leader of US Organization ("US" as opposed to
"them"). In the 1960s and 1970s, US Organization secretly prepared
for a violent struggle against the U.S. government. However, the FBI
waged a secret counterinsurgency against US Organization. But in
1997—in the Afrocentric era—the radicalism of the 1960s and 1970s
was a thing of the past and Kwanzaa had no taint of the radical Pan-
Africanism of US Organization.[106]

Kwanzaa became increasingly popular in the Afrocentric era. In the
1960s, it began as a celebration limited to dedicated "cultural" nationalists, but by 1997 one out of seven blacks celebrated the holiday. Many
community groups and organizations held public Kwanzaa celebrations
and black middle-class families increasingly celebrated the event. Elizabeth Pleck writes:

> Born in part out of a critique of capitalism in the United States, the hol-
> iday owed much of its growing acceptance to refurbishing through con-

sumerism. Originating among a black nationalist scornful of black "matriarchy," Kwanzaa found its most eager enthusiasts among black women, who usually organized the feast in the home. Seen as an accessible ritual bound to appeal to the black masses, Kwanzaa was taken up mainly by the black middle class. . . . Created by an intellectual hostile to Christianity, Kwanzaa proved dynamic enough to be redefined as religious, secular, or both, and as fully compatible with Christianity. Stemming from a rejection of racial integration, the holiday-time Kwanzaa celebration at many public schools functioned as a sign of toleration for cultural difference. Seen as a ritual to develop a diasporic African identity, Kwanzaa became more appealing as it came to include many more elements of African American history and culture.[107]

Kwanzaa was transformed from a Pan-Africanist holiday that rejected capitalism, Christianity, integration, and American identities for blacks to an Afrocentric holiday that was compatible with all these things. Occasionally the holiday was even given an "Egyptocentric" history in black newspapers and described as an "authentic harvest festival, first celebrated by the ancient Egyptians."[108]

The growing interest in things African during the Afrocentric era led to increases in black Americans traveling to Africa. Goree Island in Senegal became a favorite destination for black Americans wishing to reflect on the African slave trade. The interest in visiting historic African slave trade sites was certainly helped by Haile Gerima's film *Sankofa*, which begins with a black American at an African slave-trading post. Gerima's *Sankofa* and Julie Dash's *Daughters of the Dust*, which focused on the African cultural survivals of the black South Carolina and Georgia sea island Gullah peoples, were two of the notable "African-centered" films of the era. There were also a number of new "black-centered" filmmakers during the Afrocentric era. Spike Lee ushered in a new era of black filmmaking. His *Malcolm X* spurred a Malcolm-mania. The "X" used in marketing and merchandising the 1992 film was ubiquitous in the early 1990s. Malcolm X's autobiography also found a new generation of readers.[109]

Another prominent arena for popular Afrocentrism was rap. Many of the leading rappers of the late 1980s and early 1990s used black nationalist themes and images in their work. As Jeffrey Louis Decker observed, black nationalist rappers drew their inspiration "primarily from the black power movements of the 1960s and the Afrocentric notion that the original site of African-American cultural heritage is ancient Egypt." Public Enemy was the most popular of the hip-hop nationalists. The group repeatedly referenced the Black Power movement. In an article in *Spin* magazine, Chuck D, the leader of Public Enemy, had the magazine restage a famous photograph of the Black Panther leader Huey Newton. In the original photograph, Newton sat on a wicker chair with a spear in one hand and an automatic rifle in the other. Chuck D restaged the photo with him as Newton. The rapper, KRS-One of Boogie Down Productions, restaged a photo of Malcolm X with a rifle looking out a window on his recording *By All Means Necessary*. This title is also a play on Malcolm X's call for black liberation "by any means necessary."[110]

References to the Nation of Islam and its teachings were common in hip-hop nationalism. Public Enemy and Ice Cube both explicitly voiced support for the Nation. Many rappers were members of the Five Percent Nation, an offshoot of the Nation of Islam that viewed Louis Farrakhan favorably. While much of the hip-hop nationalism evoked the Black Power era, groups also made "African-centered" references. Chuck D and his DJ Terminator X wore medallions with an outline of the African continent colored with red, black, and green stripes—the colors of the flag created by the famous black nationalist Marcus Garvey. The group X-Clan was one of the most "Africa-centered." Wise Intelligent of X-Clan strove to teach in his raps and videos that "Black people are the mothers and fathers of the highest forms of civilization ever built on this planet. . . . Plato, Socrates, and so forth, they learned from black masters of Egypt."[111]

While some blacks pondered the glories of ancient Egypt, others grounded their Pan-African sensibility in more immediate and contemporary activities. In the Afrocentric era, it became more common to see events and festivals that embraced black Americans, Africans, and the rest of the African diaspora. For example, in 1990 the *Chicago Tribune* began an annual African Festival of the Arts that defined "African" to include not only artists from the African continent but also black artists in the United States and the rest of the African diaspora. Although the DanceAfrica festival of dances originating in Africa, black America, and the rest of the African diaspora began in the 1970s, it was not until 1995 that the festival began touring nationally. In music, although the Jamaican reggae artist Bob Marley was an international success in the 1970s, he did not have much appeal for black Americans when he was alive. He was even probably more successful among whites. In 1988, his son Ziggy Marley's reggae tune, "Tumblin' Down," reached number 1 on the Billboard R&B Charts. Today, dance hall reggae is seamlessly part of black (and white) American popular music.

This popular Pan-Africanism which did not subordinate foreign blacks to black Americans was new in black American history. In the Black Power era, this type of Pan-African engagement was found only among black nationalist activists; in the Afrocentric era, it could be found in degrees among larger segments of the nonactivist black public. In earlier times, mutual cultural alienation would have prevented black Americans, black West Indians, and Africans from metaphorically and literally sharing a stage as equals. One factor in this embrace of the black diaspora was due to the fact that more black Americans were sec-ond- and third-generation West Indian and African (immigrant) Ameri-cans than before.[112]

Black, Gay, and Afrocentric

According to the Afrocentric psychologist Wade Nobles, homosexu-ality is a "self-destructive disorder."[113] Molefi Kete Asante once argued, "Homosexuality is a deviation from Afrocentric thought," and it "can-not be condoned or accepted as good for the national development of a strong people." He has since changed his position.[114] Not only are black homosexuals often viewed very negatively by other blacks, but they are often viewed as not being authentically black. Although Afrocentrism, like other black nationalisms, has been a comfortable space for black American homophobia, black gays and lesbians were also participants in popular Afrocentrism. Precisely because black gays and lesbians are likely to have their black authenticity questioned, they may choose to preemptively prove their blackness with Afrocentric symbols. Of course, black gays and lesbians are also drawn to Afrocentrism simply as black people.

Marlon Riggs's film *Black Is . . . Black Ain't* provides examples of gay Afrocentrism. The choir of the black gay and lesbian church de-picted in the film has kente stoles. The black lesbian, Barbara Smith, who is also wearing a kente stole in the film, rejects an Afrocentric chal-lenge to black homosexuality. She states, "We don't know for a fact that there was not lesbian and gay existence in Africa." "In fact," she adds, "anthropological research indicates that indeed there was. So, to be condemned on the basis of myths, that is really difficult for me." Although Smith confronts black homophobia she reinforces the idea that Africa is an appropriate site from which to determine black American norms. In making this defense, Smith legitimizes Afrocentrism.[115]

Afrocentric ideas were at least as popular among queer blacks as among straight blacks. Gay men participated in the popular Afrocentrism of the Million Man March. The National Black Lesbian and Gay Leadership Forum encouraged gay men to attend the Million Man March even though Minister Louis Farrakhan, who organized the march, supports the practice of capital punishment for homosexuality in Saudi Arabia.[116] A cursory glance at gay publications and organizations reveals evidence of popular Afrocentrism. In Chicago, for example, one can find Afrocentric symbolism in several black gay groups. The symbol of Brothers United in Support, a black, gay, HIV-positive support group, was the outline of Africa with red, black, and green stripes. Within this red, black, and green Africa were overlapping male symbols with a plus-sign at the center, symbolizing gay men and being HIV-positive respectively. A gay and bisexual discussion group adopted the Kiswahili and Nguzo Saba terms Imani Umoja ("Faith Unity"). Adodi Chicago was "a gathering for men of African Descent who love other men." The group reported, "Adodi is the plural of Ado, a Yoruba word that describes a man who loves another man. More than just a description of partners, in Africa, the Adodi of the tribe were revered as shamans, sages and leaders." Adodi Chicago also hosts Kwanzaa celebrations.[117]

Barbara Smith and Adodi Chicago's reasoning is that black homosexuality is legitimate because it was accepted in Africa, not because of any abstract principle of justice or equality. The reasoning of Smith, Adodi Chicago, and of Afrocentrism generally makes anything that a black person wishes to do that was not done in Africa potentially open to condemnation. By making the practices of African ancestors sacred, one closes off any critique of traditional African practices. If several African societies have long practiced female genital circumcision, for example, how can one criticize it and still be Afrocentric? I suspect that Smith and Adodi could find African societies where homosexuals were despised. What they are doing is typical of those wishing to have the past serve as a model for the present. They select from (and sometimes revise) history to serve their present purposes. This point applies to the Afrocentric project in general, and not only to gay Afrocentrism.

Fig. 6.4. Approximately one million black men rallied for "atonement and reconciliation" on 16 October 1995. This was the largest rally of black men in U.S. history.
(Photo by Robert Abbott Sengstacke © 1995. Reprinted by permission.)

Millions Marching

On 16 October 1995, approximately one million black men convened on the Washington Mall in a Million Man March for "atonement
and reconciliation" called by Minister Louis Farrakhan, the leader of
the Nation of Islam. The success of this march in terms of attendance
surprised everyone. It was followed by a number of other "Million"
marches, not all of them predominantly black and many of them not
even coming close to one million in attendance. The next most significant black march was the Million Woman March in Philadelphia in
1997 called by Philadelphia activists for "repentance, resurrection,
[and] restoration." The attendance at the Million Woman March was
also quite impressive, though it may have only reached approximately
500,000.[118]

Black nationalists with a wide variety of specific agendas spoke at
the Million Man and Million Woman marches. Of course, the Nation
of Islam was well represented at the Million Man March, since it was
initiated by the leader of that organization. Not only was Farrakhan
the keynote speaker, but there were nine other Nation speakers as
well. Maulana Karenga, Haki Madhubuti, and Jawanza Kunjufu spoke

as well as representatives from the National Black United Front, the Umoja Political Party of Washington, D.C., and other black nationalist organizations. In addition to the bona fide nationalists, there were also speakers who were on the integrationist end of the black political spectrum and some who fell somewhere in between. Also among the speakers were Rosa Parks, a representative from the union AFSME, members of the Congressional Black Caucus, Jesse Jackson, Joseph Lowery of the civil rights organization SCLC, Stevie Wonder, and a number of others who were comfortable with integrationist politics.[119]

The Million Woman March had an equally diverse range of speakers. The Nation of Islam not only provided security and an endorsement, it was represented among the speakers by Khadijah Farrakhan (Louis Farrakhan's wife) and Tynetta Muhammad (always presented at Nation of Islam events as the widow of Elijah Muhammad). Among the other speakers were the rapper and activist Sister Souljah, the actress Jada Pinkett, the head of the Congressional Black Caucus Rep. Maxine Waters, and the civil rights activist Dorothy Height. The organizers, Philadelphia community activists, Phile Chionesu, and Asia Coney also spoke. Rosa Parks and Coretta Scott King declined invitations because of previous commitments. For both marches, much of the black political spectrum was covered.[120]

Both marches also had a Pan-African sensibility. They both began with African drumming. They both had speakers from outside the United States. Many attendees were dressed in Afrocentric garb. The mission statement of the Million Man March called for "a sensible and moral [U.S.] foreign policy that provides for equal treatment of African, Caribbean and other Third World refugees and countries" and "that forgives foreign debt to former colonies." The South African activist, Winnie Madikizela-Mandela, was the keynote speaker of the Million Woman March.[121]

Although the Million Man and Million Woman marches were similar to the civil rights marches *and* the Black Power conferences, there were significant differences between these examples of popular Afrocentrism and the civil rights and Black Power activism of the 1960s and 1970s. Most importantly, the marches were attempts to *create* a more political social movement rather than being the *result* of a growing movement. Although the 1980s and 1990s saw the rise of black nationalism in the arts and in fashion, there was little political activism. The sociologist Michael O. West writes, "Despite the remarkable cultural renaissance, not a single organization emerged to mobilize or give *political* expression to the renewed discontent, unlike previous black nationalist moments."[122] West overstates his point, but he is correct that there was little political activism to match the massive amount of cultural activity.

During the Black Power era, Black Power in the popular culture was a response to the political activism of that time. Popular cultural activity during the Afrocentric era also largely referenced the political activism of the 1960s and 1970s. For example, Public Enemy adopted stylings of the Black Panther Party, Spike Lee marketed Malcolm X, and Afrocentrism in general focused and amplified the *cultural* Pan-Africanism of the Black Power era. The marches, therefore, attempted to proceed backward in relation to the activism of the 1960s and 1970s. In the 1960s and 1970s, years of political activism led to the March on Washington and the Black Power conferences. In the 1990s, the Million Marches were aimed at producing activism.

The 1963 March on Washington and the Black Power conferences were also better conceived. These events had a much clearer rationale to their form and a much clearer purpose than the million marches. Because civil rights activism was often oriented toward changing whites and Black Power activism was often oriented toward changing blacks, they often took different forms. The fact that the Million Man and Million Woman marches combined the protest march format of the civil rights movement and the ideological diversity of the Black Power conferences is one sign that they were not clear about their goals.

Civil rights activists strove for unity in protest events. They wanted to present a unified front before their opponents and the political elites. The 1963 March on Washington also had the clear political goal of putting pressure on Congress to pass civil rights legislation. The Black Power conferences were aimed at bringing more cohesion to the Black Power movement. At the 1970 Congress of African Peoples, black nationalists could encourage a degree of ideological diversity because they hoped to co-opt civil rights organizations and make them work for black nationalism. They hoped to change them from "Negro" to "Black" organizations. Amiri Baraka told the attendees plainly that as black nationalists they "must control everything in the community," including "politicians [and] celebrities." He pointed out, "There are more Black people involved with Roy Wilkins [of the NAACP] than are involved with the Congress of African People. There are more niggers who think like Whitney Young [of the National Urban League] than think like we do. We have to co-opt these people because they exist in our communities."[123] The workshops at the Black Power conferences also allowed activists with different perspectives to work together and discuss solutions to a particular problem. It was therefore possible for attendees to persuade each other and end the conference with more similar views than they had had before it.

The Million Man and Million Woman marches were poorly conceived. The reason for their ideological diversity was not that they hoped to co-opt the more integrationist activists, as the Black Power activists did in the 1970s, but because they did not have a clear political vision. It was nearly a year after Farrakhan issued the call for the Million Man March that he developed a committee to decide what the mission of the march was. Maulana Karenga and the rest of the committee drafted a broad statement that placed demands on black men *and* the U.S. government *and* corporations; but few people saw that statement. The speakers made calls for a variety of different types of activism, but there were too many speakers calling for too many different things.[124]

The clearest ideological moment was the pledge that Farrakhan had all the men present repeat. Although the pledge called for black men to develop themselves economically and to build businesses, the "family values" component was longer and more concrete. This part of the pledge called for black men to love each other, to "never raise my hand with a knife or a gun," to avoid abusing women and children, and to stay away from drugs.[125] Here we see that the Million Man March was a response to the black "underclass." In the Nation of Islam's flyer for the march, the reasons given for the march stated:

> Each day somewhere in this nation, the Black community witnesses and falls prey to an increased rate of crime and violence. The proliferation of drugs and violence in the Black community and the escalation of Black male fratricide has diminished the positive role and attributes of Black men, and instead has elevated ugly images of Black men as thieves, criminals and savages.[126]

Farrakhan believed that the black underclass was a serious problem and that the solution required black men to change their behavior. By "atonement and reconciliation" black men would solve the problems of the underclass. "Atonement and reconciliation" did not make demands on the U.S. government or on corporations. The underclass was therefore a cultural problem among black men, not a problem with political and economic roots.

The Million Woman March was also at least partially a march against the underclass. Again, there was a long list of speakers with different agendas, some political and some not, but most of them were not heard because of the poor sound system.[127] Again, most of the attendees were probably oblivious to the fact that there was an eclectic list of demands.[128] Phile Chionesu, one of the organizers, said the march was "a declaration of independence from ignorance, poverty and enslavement."[129] Asia Coney, the other main organizer, ignored the demands, and called on the marchers to do three things: (1) say hello to other black women when you pass them on the street, (2) remove vacant properties from your communities, and (3) nurture your children.[130] Sister Souljah was one of the few speakers to receive the crowd's attention. She talked about the sexual morality of black women. She told the women to reject the explicit raps of Lil' Kim and Foxy Brown and to behave and dress more conservatively.[131] Like the Man March, the most poignant moments of the Woman March were the "family values" moments.

Even if we were to accept the debatable view that gathering together, listening to speeches, and taking a pledge could solve the problems of the underclass, there was an additional problem: the majority of the black underclass missed the event. The attendees at both marches were overwhelmingly middle class. Their median household income was approximately twice that of the black median and approximately ten thousand dollars above the white median income. The women at the Million Woman March were three times more likely than black women generally to have a college diploma. The men at the Million Man March were twice as likely as black men generally to have a college diploma. The moral lessons of these million marches were therefore given to the blacks who were most likely already upholding middle-class standards of respectability.[132]

These marches could have been the beginning of a resurgence of a structurally oriented political nationalism, since the attendees at both of them seemed to be receptive to these types of goals and had the resources to finance a social movement. There were surveys of participants at both marches. A majority of the men attending the Million Man March said they would donate their money and time for independent black economic programs, to form a black political party, to boycott businesses that did not help black communities, and for a reparations movement. The women of the Million Woman March supported black radio stations and were connected to black organizations. A majority of them supported school voucher programs which could be used to support black nationalist schools. The attendees of both marches probably could have been harnessed for a structurally oriented political nationalist movement, had the leaders and organizers been more focused and concerned about developing these issues.[133]

However, the attendees of the marches were satisfied with cultural nationalism because they were as strongly culturally oriented as they were structurally oriented. Large majorities of the men also expressed strong support for improving the moral values of the black community and for atonement and reconciliation. Farrakhan's pledge spoke directly to these issues. Large majorities of the women believed that "Black women should focus on the family and less on politics" and that "in order for Blacks to progress, men must come to the forefront and women must take the role of supporter and nurturer." Therefore the women supported conservative gender roles and a "family values" position. Although the men and women of the million marches might have supported a political nationalist movement, they were satisfied with the cultural nationalism of the two events.[134]

The Million Man and Million Woman marches did inspire some blacks to become more politically active,[135] but for the most part it was political symbolism without the substance. The marches were poorly conceived, if social change were their goal. They incoherently adopted political forms from the 1960s and 1970s without appreciating the political logic of those forms and without comparable levels of political activism to make them meaningful. The attendees at the marches were supportive enough of symbolic politics that they did not demand more of the leadership. The major ideological messages about the underclass in these marches were conservative messages of debatable utility in addressing the problems of poverty. The leaders of the marches understood the solution to the problem of the underclass as largely dependent upon black behavior. Unlike civil rights and Black Power activists who considered political and economic change essential to improving the conditions of black Americans, these Afrocentric activists emphasized "family values." Moreover, this message was delivered to those who were already clearly committed to "family values."

A Conservative, Middle-Class, American Black Nationalism

Afrocentrists made culture key to explaining the social problems facing black Americans. Their focus on culture led them basically to endorse the culture of poverty argument about the black underclass. In endorsing the culture of poverty argument, Afrocentrists also endorsed the complementary idea of "immigrant cultural success." Since having a bad culture was assumed to lead to poverty, it followed that having a good culture that instills the value of hard work will lead to success. In the American narrative of "immigrant cultural success," immigrants with good cultures came to the United States and rose up from poverty through hard work. This idea of "immigrant cultural success" has been used by conservatives to argue that it is not discrimination which has kept blacks from advancing but their own bad cultural values.[136]

Asa Hilliard illustrates the "immigrant cultural success" argument in Afrocentrism well. He states: "I believe it can be demonstrated that a strong cultural identity is a prerequisite for the success of an ethnic group and the individuals within [it]."[137] Hilliard argues that we will not be able to solve the problems of "child abuse, substance abuse, teen pregnancy, Black-on-Black crime, school dropouts, school suspensions, the Black family crisis, and a host of others" until we recognize them as symptoms of a more fundamental problem of cultural identity:

> *Our problem is the disintegration of a sense of peoplehood.* Pure and simple, we have reached a point in our history where we have been socialized to see ourselves as individuals and cultural neuters. . . . As we become more and more isolated, alone, and culturally undefined, we lose the capacity to see group problems. Gradually the sense of belonging diminishes for so many of us, so there is hardly an "us" at all.
> . . . We readily admire the solidarity of the Asians, the Mormons, the Jews, and other groups that have accumulated wealth and power and that provide certain types of leadership in the United States and in the world. Yet we do not seem to appreciate the meaning of their group solidarity, even when it is a loose solidarity.[138]

Hilliard chooses Asians and Jews, two groups that conservatives have often singled out, to suggest that black Americans could improve themselves through hard work.[139] However, Hilliard stresses their cultural identity rather than a generic work ethic. Nonetheless, Afrocentrism, like the more mainstream version of the "immigrant cultural success" narrative, deemphasizes racial discrimination as an explanation for black social problems.

Afrocentrism is a black version of the American middle-class "ethnic" discourse of "immigrant success." Just as middle-class whites talk about how the cultural values of their immigrant ancestors pulled the family up from poverty,[140] Afrocentrism can be seen as attempting to create the same "ethnic" success by following the same logic. The African culture that Afrocentrists construct is the "ethnic" immigrant culture. Like all immigrant cultures in the "success" narrative, this culture values hard work, discipline, and the family.[141] Wade Nobles's "Afrocentric Values," for example, calls for the rejection of a "drug-culture orientation" and the embrace of "black family values" that include "excellence," "respect," "restraint," and "responsibility." Jawanza Kunjufu argues, "One of the most revolutionary things you can do is to keep your marriage intact and raise your children."[142] In the Afrocentric version of the "immigrant success" narrative, one values not only family but also the entire black race. It is assumed that if enough black Americans were to possess this African "ethnic" culture the success of black Americans would be assured, like the success of immigrant groups in the "success" narrative.

The "immigrant success" narrative is also present in popular Afrocentrism. The rationale for the term "African American" is explicitly based on the white "ethnic" model of identity. Jesse Jackson argued that blacks should model their identities on "Armenian-Americans and Jewish-Americans and Arab-Americans and Italian-Americans." Ramona Edelin, who proposed the name change to Jackson, felt that "the problems in our neighborhoods and cities of poverty, poor education, drug infestation, business development and freedom are *ours to solve*."[143] Again, we see that racial discrimination, a feature of a liberal analysis, is absent. The path to success for black Americans as defined by Afrocentric nationalists depends upon themselves, just as that of the immigrants in the "immigrant narrative" did. The million marches also stressed conservative "family values" as the solution to the black underclass. The argument from the Million Man March was that when black men atoned and accepted their responsibility as the head of black families the problems associated with the underclass would end. The Million Woman March had similar themes and a large majority of the women

Fig. 6.5. This attendee at the Million Man March carries a sign that states, "Whites Graduate from Penn. St., Blacks Graduate from State-Penn." The underclass ideology of the Afrocentric era led many black Americans to blame the culture of black Americans for black poverty. In the Million Man March, middle-class black men called on poor black men to change their values and behavior and become employed, law-abiding, and married men who respected black women. (Photo by Cynthia Johnson/Time Life Pictures/Getty Images, #50477343)

supported the idea that black men needed to lead and that black women needed to focus more on their families. Although Afrocentrism drew from and built upon the Pan-Africanism of the Black Power era, it was far to the right of that movement. Afrocentrism took the cultural ideas of Black Power, but not the radical structural ones.

Afrocentrism as a movement drew much of its strength from segments of the black middle class. The academics, intellectuals, and educators who produced Afrocentric scholarship and ran Afrocentric educational initiatives were all middle class. The black middle class was more likely to have the financial resources and the cultural knowledge to practice Afrocentrism best. They were likely to be most knowledgeable about authentic African names, authentic African textiles, and authentic African art. Kwanzaa's increased popularity was the result of the actions of black middle-class women. It was the black middle and upper class who could afford to take the expensive trips to Africa. And the black middle class was overrepresented at the Million Man and Million Woman marches. In the Afrocentric era, the black middle class showed that it is incorrect to think of black nationalism as only a lower-class phenomenon.

Afrocentrism was an *integrationist* black nationalism.[144] By being such a narrowly cultural black nationalism, Afrocentrism was compatible with a great deal of structural integration of black Americans. The goal of Afrocentrism was not to return blacks to Africa, or to establish a black nation in the United States, or even necessarily to have separate black institutions. The goal of Afrocentrism was to have black Americans function as respectable, middle-class Americans who also had African cultural identities. Thus, Afrocentrism could work within the mainstream American public education system; Afrocentric schools could have white teachers; Afrocentric schools could have U.S. corporate sponsors;[145] an Afrocentric classroom could have a picture of President Clinton; an Afrocentric success story could be a student who pursued a career in the U.S. military; and one could be Afrocentric and work for IBM. Afrocentrism did not jeopardize the material basis of the black middle class, but it did provide a cultural orientation that could sooth some of the insults on blackness in American society.[146]

While on the one hand Afrocentrism was focused on the historically common black middle-class goal of uplifting the black poor, it was also about competing with and challenging the cultural capital or "high culture" of the white elites. This was particularly the case for the academic

Afrocentrists. Black middle-class intellectuals attempted to prove that they were equal or superior to the white middle class by showing that they had equivalent or superior cultural capital. Ancient Egypt was important in Afrocentric thought not because it had a clear and obvious connection to black Americans, but because of Egypt's importance in Western thought. Ancient Egypt is an African society that has long been recognized as a great civilization by the West. What defined the African content of Afrocentrism was not African culture per se but European notions of civilization and "high culture." Afrocentrists were more interested in demonstrating an African equality or superiority to Western civilization than in examining exploitation and inequality in ancient Egypt and in African societies in general. So, for example, Afrocentrists were more interested in asserting their superiority to whites by saying that sexism never existed in Africa than in facing the realities of male-female relations in Africa.

Afrocentrism is fundamentally American. As Americans, blacks are influenced by American cultural ideas. We see this from the fact that black Afrocentrists were influenced by the work of Herskovits, a white Jewish scholar. Afrocentrism was influenced by other American intellectual currents in the 1980s and 1990s. Popular ideas about the "underclass," "self-esteem," "failing schools," "immigrant success," and even New Age thought all shaped Afrocentrism. The strongest set of American cultural ideas in Afrocentric thought is American racial ideology. The idea of race, the idea that blacks belong to Africa, and the one-drop rule for defining blackness all shape Afrocentric thought. Ancient Egyptians did not have a race concept or even our current conception of Africa. Although superficially "African," Afrocentrism was an Americanism in black American life.

7

Change in Black Nationalism
in the Twentieth Century

Black nationalism varies sociohistorically. Just as black social movements affect American society, other social movements and other forces in American society affect black social activism. This chapter examines broad historical changes in black nationalism. First, it details changes in the black public's support for black nationalism as measured by public opinion surveys. Second, it describes the broad historical patterns in black nationalist activism.

The analysis of public opinion data shows that the support for black nationalism among the black public in the Afrocentric era equaled or exceeded the level of support in the Black Power era. Also, contrary to the popular belief that black nationalism is a black lower-class ideology, in the Afrocentric era the black middle and upper classes were more likely to be nationalists than the lower classes.

Black nationalist activism, which is distinct from black public opinion, has undergone an interesting pattern of change over the twentieth century. Cultural nationalist activism has increased while political nationalist activism has decreased. It was Eurocentric black Americans in the nineteenth and early twentieth centuries who considered leaving the United States to develop a black nation modeled after Western nations, but it was Afrocentric black Americans in the late twentieth century who wished to stay in the United States and celebrate African culture. Black nationalism is a socially embedded ideology and, as such, it changes in accordance with broad societal trends.

Black Nationalism and Black Public Opinion

In addition to the renaissance of Africanisms in black America as discussed in chapter 6, the Afrocentric era was notable for having high degrees of support for black nationalism as measured by public opinion polls. In the late 1960s, black nationalism was far more popular among activists than it was among the general black population. Only a minority of blacks supported the goals of the activists. In the 1990s, a slight majority of the black public supported black nationalism. Among the general public, the black middle class showed stronger levels of support than the black lower classes. Certain conceptions of Afrocentrism also showed stronger middle-class support. When Afrocentrism was defined as being about culture and pride, the black middle class again showed stronger support. The level of public support for black nationalism generally, and the level of black middle-class support for black nationalism in particular, are additional factors that mark the Afrocentric era as a distinct and important era in the history of black nationalism in America.

Methodological Considerations

There are a number of important methodological points one should keep in mind when reviewing public opinion data. It is important to distinguish activists who give their time and skills to a social movement from a public that merely gives their opinion on a social issue. It is, of course, much easier to give one's opinion on issues than to be an activist. Social movements are typically the product of the activism of a small minority. For example, in 1963 only 12 percent of blacks reported that they had marched in a demonstration and even smaller numbers had participated in pickets and sit-ins.[1] Only a small minority of blacks were civil rights activists.

Activists also differ from the general public in that they tend to be ideologically clearer and more committed. As the sociologist Gary Marx observed, the general public tends to be "characterized by moderation, inconsistency, indifference, and a lack of all but the most rudimentary information."[2] One should never confuse an analysis of the general public with an analysis of activists, or vice versa.

The support, or lack thereof, for a social movement by the general public can be an important factor in a movement's ability to sustain itself and to grow. It is also sociologically and politically useful to know the extent to which a movement does or does not represent the desires of the public it claims to represent.[3] Scientifically administered public opinion surveys are the only way to gauge the opinions of a large population with precision. Substantial national surveys of black American public opinion have been available only since the 1960s. While there were a number of surveys in the 1960s, there is little useful data from the 1970s. There are good surveys covering the 1980s and 1990s. This means that it is not possible to use survey data to examine black public opinion on black nationalism before the 1960s. The analysis in this section will focus on the late 1960s and the early 1990s. For details about the data and survey questions used in the figures and tables below, see the Appendix.

The ideal situation for attempting to gauge changes in black public opinion from the Black Power era to the Afrocentric era would be to have a sequence of surveys where the only methodological variation would be the date on which the data were collected. This situation does not exist.[4] The data that will be compared vary in a number of ways. Nearly any variation from one survey to another can potentially introduce problems for making precise comparisons.[5] There are enough similarities, however, that rough comparisons are possible. These data are also a great methodological improvement over the research which attempted to gauge general black public opinion from studies of black activists.

The concept of black nationalism as measured by public opinion includes a broad range of ideas. It can refer to the desire for black people to have a separate black country or to a range of less politically extreme ideas. Attitudes expressing black pride, black solidarity, and black autonomy can all be understood as measuring support for black nationalism. For most of the twentieth century, black nationalist activism has been directed toward goals other than the establishment of a separate black state. These lesser ideas are therefore good ways of gauging the degree to which the general black public supports the goals of activists.

The Black Power Era versus the Afrocentric Era

The support for black nationalism among the general black public during the Afrocentric era equaled or exceeded that of the Black Power era. Louis Farrakhan, the leader of the Nation of Islam in the 1990s, was slightly more popular than his predecessor, Elijah Muhammad in the 1970s. The percentage of blacks favoring a number of black nationalist positions in the Afrocentric era is higher than in the Black Power era. Afrocentric-era black nationalism also appears to have been a more

TABLE 7.1
Civil Rights vs. Black Nationalism, 1966 (in %)

| | Civil Rights | | | |
	M. L. King	*SCLC*	*NAACP*	*C.R. Average*
Approve	88	55	81	75
Disapprove	3	6	7	5

| | Black Nationalism | | | |
	Elijah Muhammad	*Black Muslims*	*Stokely Carmichael*	*B.N. Average*
Approve	12	9	19	13
Disapprove	43	49	13	35

Notes: "Approve" refers to respondents who said that the person or group had done an "excellent" or "pretty good" job "in the fight for Negro rights." "Disapprove" refers to "only fair" or "poor." The "not sure" responses are not presented.
Source: William Brink and Louis Harris, *Black and White: A Study of U.S. Racial Attitudes Today* (New York: Simon and Schuster, 1967), 54, 244–54.

coherent and structurally oriented nationalism than Black Power black nationalism. In terms of black public opinion, the Afrocentric era was clearly a high point of black nationalism in the twentieth century.

Black approval of black nationalism increased over the 1960s and 1970s, though it never exceeded that of integrationism. In 1966, a large majority of the black public supported integrationist leaders, but black nationalist leaders received relatively little support. Instead of being neutral or undecided about black nationalist leaders, a significant number of blacks were opposed to them. (See Table 7.1.) By 1971, black nationalist leaders' relative standing had improved considerably, but they were still not as popular as integrationist leaders. While in 1966 black nationalist leaders were only about one-sixth as popular as integrationist leaders, in 1971 they were about one-half as popular. They were more popular but still not as popular as integrationists. (See Table 7.2.)

There are not enough data to be certain about the trends in black nationalist attitudes over the 1970s. The trends in support of black nationalist leaders as well as Howard Schuman and Shirley Hatchett's research suggest that support for black nationalism was increasing into the early 1970s.[6] Beyond the early seventies, it is not clear whether support for black nationalism peaked in the mid-1970s or late 1970s. Support for black nationalism did decline in the early 1980s. (See Appendix Table A1.)

In the mid-1990s, during the Afrocentric era, support for the black nationalist leader of the Nation of Islam, Louis Farrakhan, appears to

TABLE 7.2
Civil Rights vs. Black Nationalism, 1971 (in %)

| | Civil Rights | | | |
	Ralph Abernathy	*SCLC*	*NAACP*	*C.R. Average*
Approve	89	91	93	91
Disapprove	5	3	3	4

| | Black Nationalism | | | |
	Elijah Muhammad	*Black Panthers*	*Stokely Carmichael*	*B.N. Average*
Approve	46	49	48	48
Disapprove	26	36	33	32

Notes: "Approve" refers to respondents who said that they respected the person or group "a great deal" or "some." "Disapprove" refers to "hardly at all." The "not sure" responses are not presented.
Source: Louis Harris and Associates, Inc., *The Harris Survey Yearbook of Public Opinion, 1971: A Compendium of Current American Attitudes* (New York: Louis Harris and Associates, 1975), 340.

have been slightly higher than the support received by black nationalist leaders in 1971. In 1993–94,[7] Farrakhan received 70 percent of the level of approval Jesse Jackson received. In 1971, Elijah Muhammad, the then leader of the Nation of Islam, received about 60 percent of the civil rights leader, Ralph Abernathy's, level of approval. Relative to their civil rights contemporaries, black Americans were slightly more positive toward Farrakhan in the Afrocentric era than to Muhammad in the Black Power era. (See Table 7.3.)

These findings are informative but they do not show the degree to which civil rights and black nationalist leaders had moved closer toward each other in the Afrocentric era. For example, in the 1980s, Jesse Jackson, then a civil rights leader (with past involvement in black nationalist activism), and Louis Farrakhan were political allies. Other civil rights activists had also moved toward black nationalism.[8]

The black public lagged behind activists in their support for the Black Power movement. The 1968 Fifteen-Cities survey, which collected data from over three thousand blacks in fifteen major cities on black nationalism and other issues, is an excellent source for black public opinion during the early Black Power era.[9] In 1968, when the Black Power movement was rapidly gaining strength among activists, the Fifteen-Cities survey indicated only weak support among the black public. Black Americans were willing to endorse the shallower and more symbolic aspects of black nationalism, but only relatively small numbers expressed support for the structurally oriented idea that blacks should control black-community organizations and institutions.

Of the eight separate items in Table 7.4, only the question, "Negroes should shop in Negro-owned stores whenever possible," received support from the majority of blacks surveyed. This item was only weakly correlated with the idea that "stores in a Negro neighborhood . . . should be owned and run by Negroes." In 1968, blacks expressed a desire to support existing black stores, but they did not insist that stores in black neighborhoods be controlled by blacks.

The second most favored item, the idea that "Negro children should study an African language," was approved by 43 percent of respondents. The two items receiving the most support were weakly correlated with the other items. (For the correlation table, see Table A2 in the Appendix.) Those who favored "shopping black" and "African language" did not favor the more structural nationalist goals. Less than 20 percent of the surveyed blacks expressed support for the more structural

TABLE 7.3
Civil Rights vs. Black Nationalism, 1990s (in %)

1993–94	Civil Rights		Black Nationalism
	Jesse Jackson		*Louis Farrakhan*
Approve	80		57

1996	Civil Rights		Black Nationalism
	Jesse Jackson	*NAACP*	*Louis Farrakhan*
Approve	71	82	43

Notes: "Approve" equals a rating of greater than 50 degrees on a "thermometer" of 0 to 100 degrees.
Sources: *National Black Politics Study, 1993* [computer data file] and *National Black Election Study, 1996* [computer data file]. See Appendix for additional information.

TABLE 7.4
Black Power Black Nationalism (in %)

	Approving
There should be a separate black nation here.	6
Negroes should shop in Negro-owned stores whenever possible.	70
Negro children should study an African language.	43
Stores in a Negro neighborhood should be owned and run by Negroes.	18
A public school that is attended by mostly Negro children should have a Negro principal.	15
Negroes should not have anything to do with whites if they can help it.	9
Would rather that my children have only Negro friends.	5

Source: *Racial Attitudes in Fifteen American Cities, 1968* [computer data file]. See Appendix for additional information.

concern that stores in black neighborhoods have black owners and that black schools have black principals.

While there was little support for the more structurally oriented black nationalism in 1968, in 1993–94 there was a great deal. Table 7.5 shows that in 1993–94 structural nationalist questions were approved by a majority of blacks. A majority of blacks supported the idea that "blacks should have control over the economy in mostly black communities," that "blacks should have control over the government in mostly black communities," and that "blacks should participate in black-only organizations whenever possible." Also, the idea that "black people should shop in black stores whenever possible" is not a shallow measure of black solidarity, as it was in 1968. This item is fairly strongly correlated with the idea that "blacks should have control over the economy in mostly black communities" and that "blacks should have control over the government in mostly black communities." "Shopping black" captures structural nationalist sentiments. In 1993–94, the black public supported the structural nationalist goals of the Black Power movement more strongly than they did in 1968. (For the full 1993–94 correlation table, see Table A3 in the Appendix.)

The analysis so far has been less than ideal because of differences in the wording of questions. If we examine surveys that can be more closely compared, we again see evidence that black nationalist attitudes were strong in the Afrocentric era. They may even have peaked historically in this period, which followed the Los Angeles riots.[10]

Three questions about black nationalism are fairly similar in both the 1968 Fifteen-Cities survey and the 1993–94 survey. The least similar of these questions are the 1968 question, "There should be a separate black nation here," and the 1993–94 question, "black people should have their own separate nation." The other two questions differ between the two years only in that in 1993–94 "black" is substituted for 1968's "Negro." They are "Negroes/Black people should shop in Negro-owned/black stores whenever possible," and "Negro school children/Black children should study an African language."

The Fifteen-Cities survey is a survey of fifteen major cities and not a national sample of black Americans like the 1993–94 survey. Comparisons of urban black samples to national black samples have shown that urban samples can be good approximations of national results;[11] however, we still cannot be completely certain that differences between 1968 and 1993–94 are not due to differences in the samples. On the three re-

TABLE 7.5
Afrocentric Era Black Nationalism (in %)

	Approving
Black people should have their own separate nation.	15
Black people should shop in black-owned stores whenever possible.	83
Black children should study an African language.	70
Blacks should have control over the economy in mostly black communities.	66
Blacks should participate in black-only organizations whenever possible.	57
Africa is a special homeland and America is not the real home for black people here.	31

Notes: "Approve" refers to "strongly agree" and "agree."
Source: National Black Politics Study, 1993 [computer data file]. See Appendix for additional information.

TABLE 7.6
The Black Power Era vs. the Afrocentric Era

% *Approving of*	Black Power Era		Afrocentric Era
	1968	1979–80	1993–94
Black Nation	6		15
Black Political Party		45	49
Vote Black		39	26
Shop Black	70	64	83
African Language	43	56	70

Sources: Racial Attitudes in Fifteen American Cities, 1968 [computer data file], *National Survey of Black Americans, Wave 1, 1979–80* [computer data file], and *National Black Politics Study, 1993* [computer data file]. See Appendix for additional information.

peated questions, the level of support for black nationalism in 1993–94 exceeded the level in 1968. (See Table 7.6. All the differences with 1993–94 are statistically significant at the p < .05 level.)

There are data for comparisons with the 1993–94 data that largely remove the question of the comparability of the samples but are less than ideal in terms of date. From the end of the 1970s through the 1990s, national surveys were conducted that repeated four questions relevant to measuring black nationalism. Two questions from the 1968 Fifteen-Cities study were repeated in these later studies. The four questions are: (1) "Do you think blacks should form their own political party?" (2) "Blacks should always vote for black candidates when they run," (3) "Black people should shop in black stores whenever possible," and (4) "Black children should study an African language." In 1979–80 and in 1993–94, these items are only weakly correlated, which suggests that they are tapping into different aspects of black nationalism. (See Tables A4 and A5 in the Appendix.)

The general pattern revealed by these questions from the end of the 1970s through the mid-1990s is that black nationalist sentiments declined in the early 1980s and then rose dramatically in the early 1990s after the Rodney King beating and the Los Angeles riots. Support for black nationalist ideas began to decline again by the mid-1990s. (See Table A1 in Appendix.)

The repeated survey questions can be used to gauge the relative support for black nationalism among the general public in the Black Power and Afrocentric eras. So far, the analysis has shown that black public opinion lagged behind Black Power activism. Although 1975 is a common date used for the end of Black Power activism, it is possible that the effect of the Black Power movement on the attitudes of the black public was still strong after 1975. It is even possible that among the black public black nationalist sentiments peaked at the end of the 1970s.

The 1979–80 data will be used as a minimum for the levels of black nationalist attitudes in the 1970s. If black nationalism in the Afrocentric era exceeds the level observed in 1979–80, it will be considered comparable to that of the Black Power era. In 1993–94, on three of the four items gauging different aspects of black nationalism, the support for black nationalism was greater than in 1979–80. (See Table 7.6. All the differences between the 1979–80 and 1993–94 survey results are statistically significant at the the p < .05 level.)

Black nationalist attitudes in the Afrocentric era were at comparable, and possibly higher, levels than in the Black Power era. Support for a black nation in the Afrocentric era was higher than in the late 1960s. On three additional survey questions, the level of support for black nationalism in the early 1990s was higher than in the late 1960s and late 1970s. Louis Farrakhan's relative approval rating in the 1990s appears to be slightly higher than that of Elijah Muhammad in 1971. Support for black nationalism in the Afrocentric era was also more coherent and structurally oriented than during the Black Power era. In addition to a great deal of cultural activism, the Afrocentric era was also marked by a great deal of strong support for black nationalism by the black public.

Black Nationalism and Class

A number of scholars argue that black nationalism is the true political consciousness of the black lower classes. In 1970, John Bracey accused scholars of ignoring "the actions of the black masses and the many manifestations of black nationalism." In the 1990s, Rod Bush and William Sales argued, "[black] nationalism is the political orientation of the ordinary Black folk." Errol Henderson states, "for the black masses, many of them poor, the integrationist dream is not representative of their daily—and very separate—reality." For these and other scholars, black middle-class leaders have masked the true desires of the majority of black people.[12]

This argument is incorrect in several ways. As shown above, the strength of black nationalist sentiment varies historically. In the 1960s it was relatively weak among the black public, but in the early 1990s it was quite strong. The prevalence of black nationalist sentiment among any class segment of black Americans also varies historically. Black nationalism has not been a constant among blacks generally or among any class segment of black Americans.

The idea that black nationalism is a lower-class phenomenon is attributable in part to the lower-class constituencies of the early-twentieth-century black nationalist movements. The membership of Marcus Garvey's black nationalist Universal Negro Improvement Association movement and of the Nation of Islam was disproportionately lower class.[13] However, it is problematic to make conclusions about the general public based on activists. The public opinion data from the 1960s shows that the majority of lower-class blacks were not black nationalists. A *Newsweek* survey in 1966 reveals this fact clearly. Although the raw data is not available, useful crosstabulations were published, though unfortunately without the sample sizes. (The study as a whole interviewed 1,059 blacks.)[14] The tables with income crosstabulations were limited to the non-South. Since support for black nationalism was about equal or greater in the non-South than in the South, we can get a good picture of blacks nationally with the non-South tables.[15]

Tables 7.7 and 7.8 show that when asked specifically about black nationalism and the Nation of Islam (the "Black Muslims"), the low-income group is more than twice as likely to express its approval than the two other income categories. This appears to support the idea that black nationalism is a lower-class phenomenon. But since the support of the low-income group on both questions is only 9 percent and the opposition of the low-income group is nearly 70 percent, we cannot say that support for black nationalism represents the true political consciousness of the black lower class. Class is positively correlated to

TABLE 7.7
1966: Do You Approve or Disapprove of Black Nationalism? (in %)

	Non-South		
	Low Income	*Moderate Income*	*High Income*
Approve	9	4	4
Disapprove	68	60	72
Not Sure	23	36	24

Source: William Brink and Louis Harris, *Black and White: A Study of U.S. Racial Attitudes Today* (New York: Simon and Schuster, 1967), 260.

TABLE 7.8
1966: Do You Approve or Disapprove of the Black Muslim Movement? (in %)

	Non-South		
	Low Income	*Moderate Income*	*High Income*
Approve	9	4	4
Disapprove	71	64	78
Not Sure	20	32	18

Source: William Brink and Louis Harris, *Black and White: A Study of U.S. Racial Attitudes Today* (New York: Simon and Schuster, 1967), 262.

support for black nationalism, but a majority of the lower class opposes it. The black public's support for black nationalism in the 1960s was low, although it was an important ideology among black activists.[16]

We can explore the relationship between black nationalism and class and compare the Black Power and Afrocentric eras by analyzing community-oriented black nationalism and separatist-oriented black nationalism. The political scientists Robert Brown and Todd Shaw found these two distinct forms of black nationalism in their analysis of the 1993–94 survey data. They were able to distinguish what they identified as community nationalists from separatist nationalists. Community nationalists want blacks to control black community organizations and institutions. They want to improve the position of blacks within American society as it is presently structured. Separatist nationalists want to be separate from whites and would accept fairly radical changes in society to achieve that end. They want to improve the condition of blacks by either reorganizing American society to achieve more black autonomy or by even withdrawing completely from American society and forming a separate black nation.[17]

Few of the 1993–94 questions analyzed by Brown and Shaw were asked in the 1968 Fifteen-Cities survey. Comparable 1968 questions that had relatively strong correlations were substituted. In 1968, for each construct, only two questions were appropriate where there were four in 1993–94. See Table 7.9 for the questions that made up the 1968 and 1993–94 constructs.

In the following analyses, "poor" is defined as having a family income less than or approximately (due to rounding) equal to the U.S. Census Bureau poverty threshold for a family of four for the year of the survey. "Working class" is defined as between one and two times "poor." "Middle class" is defined as between two and five times "poor," and "rich" is greater than five times "poor." In 1968, "poor" was less than $4,000. In 1993–94, "poor" was less than $15,000.[18]

In 1968, less than 10 percent of poor and working-class blacks gave the community nationalist response to both questions. Separatist nationalism did not exceed 5 percent of support among the lower classes. Interestingly, it appears that the richest blacks were the most likely to support community nationalism. (See Tables 7.10 and 7.11.) Again, in

TABLE 7.9
1968 and 1993 Community and Separatist Nationalist Questions

Community Nationalism

1968

A public school that is attended by mostly Negro children should have a Negro principal.
Stores in a Negro neighborhood should be owned and run by Negroes.
(N = 3,073; Cronbach's alpha = .51)

1993–94

Black people should shop in black-owned stores whenever possible.
Blacks should have control over the government in mostly black communities.
Blacks should have control over the economy in mostly black communities.
Blacks should rely on themselves and not others.
(N = 1,113; Cronbach's alpha = . 70)

Separatist Nationalism

1968

Negroes should not have anything to do with whites if they can help it.
There should be a separate black nation here.
(N = 3,187; Cronbach's alpha = .61)

1993–94

Black people should always vote for black candidates when they run.
Blacks should form their own political party.
Black people should have their own separate nation.
Black people form a nation within a nation.
(N = 1,060; Cronbach's alpha = .51)

TABLE 7.10
1968: Community Nationalism by Class (in %)

	Poor	Working Class	Middle Class	Rich
Nationalist	7	9	6	17
Not Nationalist	93	91	94	83
100% =	(689)	(1,189)	(951)	(71)

x^2 = 16.331, df = 3, p = .001
Source: Racial Attitudes in Fifteen American Cities, 1968 [computer data file].
See Appendix for additional information.

TABLE 7.11
1968: Separatist Nationalism by Class (in %)

	Poor	Working Class	Middle Class	Rich
Nationalist	5	3	2	2
Not Nationalist	95	97	98	98
100% =	(700)	(1,239)	(975)	(82)

x^2 = 7.273, df = 3, p = .064
Source: Racial Attitudes in Fifteen American Cities, 1968 [computer data file].
See Appendix for additional information.

1968 we do not find evidence that black nationalism was the true political consciousness of the black lower class.

To gain a better understanding of which segments of the black public supported black nationalism, logistic regression analyses were conducted with control variables. Since in bivariate analyses, younger blacks and males were found to be more community and separatist nationalist, it is useful to control for age and sex in multivariate analyses. Because in 1968 so few blacks gave black nationalist responses to community or separatist questions, in the logistic regression blacks who provided the black nationalist response to one of the two questions are treated as black nationalists.

In 1968, controlling for age and sex, neither education nor income were found to be predictive of support for community nationalism. The results were different for separatist nationalism. Controlling for age and sex, blacks with less education and with lower incomes were found to be more separatist. (See Table A6.) Although in 1968 the black lower class was more likely to support separatist nationalism, it was still the case that 81 percent of poor and working-class blacks with an eighth-grade education or less rejected separatist nationalism.

Support for community nationalism was not only much higher during the Afrocentric era than during the Black Power era, but a slight majority of blacks were community nationalists. In 1993–94, 52 percent of all blacks took the community nationalist position on all four items. Separatism remained a small minority position as it was during the Black Power era. Only 5 percent of all blacks took the separatist position on all four items. For multivariate analyses, only those who made the nationalist response to all four items will be defined as community nationalists, but those making the nationalist response to three or four separatist items will be defined as separatists to provide more cases for analysis.

In 1993–94, controlling for age, sex, and education, higher-income blacks were more likely to be community nationalists. Education did not have a statistically significant relationship with community nationalism. One's level of education did not affect whether one supported or did not support community nationalism. With the same controls, education and income were both statistically significant in predicting whether one was a separatist nationalist. Blacks who were less educated and who had lower incomes were more likely to be separatists. (See Table A7.)

In 1993–94, community nationalism was an important part of the political consciousness of the black middle and upper class. Fifty-seven percent (without controls) of middle-class blacks were community nationalists. An even higher percentage, 68 percent, of rich blacks were community nationalists. Although the black lower class was more likely to be separatist nationalists, only about 20 percent (without controls) of poor and working-class blacks were separatists. (See Tables 7.12 and 7.13.) Recall that one needed only three nationalist responses to be classified as a separatist nationalist but four to be a community nationalist; so community nationalism had the more stringent criteria. Of blacks with less than a high school diploma, 19 percent of the poor and 25 percent of the working class were separatists. Even controlling for education, separatism remains a minority position.

In the Afrocentric era, black nationalist attitudes were stronger among the general black public than in the early years of Black Power. In the Black Power era, black nationalism was a minority position. In the Afrocentric era, it became a majority position. The strongest support for black nationalism in the Afrocentric era was among the middle and upper classes. In 1968, only rich blacks were more likely to be community nationalists and only 17 percent of rich blacks were strong community nationalists. During the Afrocentric era, 68 percent of rich blacks were strong community nationalists. In both periods, separatist

TABLE 7.12
1993–94: Community Nationalism by Class (in %)

	Poor	Working Class	Middle Class	Rich
Nationalist	45	50	57	68
Not Nationalist	55	50	43	32
100% =	(240)	(373)	(358)	(65)

$x^2 = 15.355$, df = 3, p = .002
Source: National Black Politics Study, 1993 [computer data file]. See Appendix for additional information.

TABLE 7.13
1993–94: Separatist Nationalism by Class

	Poor	Working Class	Middle Class	Rich
Nationalist	19	21	15	10
Not Nationalist	81	79	85	90
100% =	(207)	(344)	(335)	(62)

$x^2 = 7.758$, df = 3, p = .051
Source: National Black Politics Study, 1993 [computer data file]. See Appendix for additional information.

nationalism was a more lower-class phenomenon, but support for separatism among the lower class was about four times greater during the Afrocentric era than during Black Power.

The relationship of class to black nationalism therefore varies sociohistorically. We cannot say that black nationalism is more authentic to the black lower classes than the black middle classes. It depends on the time period and specific type of black nationalism one is examining. In the Afrocentric era, black nationalism was most notable among the black middle and upper class.

Who Supported Afrocentrism?

In chapter 6, we saw that blacks who engaged in the cultural nationalist activism and the cultural nationalist activities of Afrocentrism were largely middle and upper class. Since activists are not a random sample of the public, assumptions about the general pattern of black public support for Afrocentrism cannot be made from what is known about activists. Was the support for Afrocentrism among the general black public predominantly middle class or lower class, or was it equal across class segments? The answer appears to be "all of the above." When Afrocentrism is a type of cultural capital struggle with white elites, the black middle class is disproportionately in favor of it. When Afrocentrism is presented as separatist nationalism, the support for it is disproportionately from the lower class. When it is seen as a noncontroversial educational policy, class is not a predictor of support.

In the conclusion to chapter 6, I argued that Afrocentrism was a way for black middle-class activists to challenge and compete with the cultural capital of white elites. This perspective helps us interpret the results of analyses where the black middle class disproportionately supports a particular interpretation of Afrocentrism. In *Black Pride and Black Prejudice*, Paul M. Sniderman and Thomas Piazza found that the educational black middle class was more likely to support the idea that the achievements of African scientists and philosophers have not been acknowledged in American society. The educational black middle class also disproportionately supported the idea that building black pride was more important than building good relations with whites.[19]

An analysis of a 1994 General Social Survey question suggests that the black middle class disproportionately believes that minority history receives too little attention in high school and college curricula. (See Table A8 in Appendix.) The educational black middle class was also most likely to prefer the term "African American" over "black." (See Table A9 in Appendix.) The argument for the term "African American" was made by making reference to terms for white ethnic groups. If there were "Armenian Americans," "Jewish Americans," and "Italian Americans," Jesse Jackson argued, then there should be "African Americans." In other words, blacks should be treated like whites in terms of the name for the group.

Black middle-class support for acknowledging African thinkers, for black pride, for more black history, and for "African American" are all about valuing blacks and blackness more within a majority white context. When Afrocentrism is understood as being about improving the cultural prestige of blacks in American society, it disproportionately receives black middle-class support.

When Afrocentrism is presented as a more neutral educational policy, class does not predict who supports it. Support for Afrocentric education and for African language instruction for children did not receive more support from the middle class than from other classes. (See Appendix Tables A10 and A11.) Unlike the survey questions above, these questions did not give any clear indication of competition with or a relationship to whites.

An additional Afrocentric question did not have a class relationship. (See Appendix Table A12.) In 1993–94, respondents were asked whether "Africa is a special homeland for black people including blacks in the U.S." or whether "America is the real home for black people here." This question is somewhat confusing because "special homeland" is not the same as a "real home." It is possible for someone to view Africa as a "special homeland," meaning a place of ancestral origin, and see the United States as one's "real home," as in where one lives. About one-third of the respondents stated that "Africa is a special homeland," but there was no statistically significant class relationship. This question also does not indicate cultural competition with whites.

When Afrocentrism has a more separatist tenor, it receives disproportionately high lower-class support. The black lower class was most likely to support all-male schools for blacks. All-male schools were a more radical approach to attempting to improve the academic performance of black boys. This approach was attempted but formally stopped after it was legally challenged.[20] Black women were as likely as black men to support all-male schools for black boys. (See Appendix Table A13.) The black lower class disproportionately supported separatist nationalism and they also supported separate schools for boys.

In the Afrocentric era, black nationalism cannot be defined as a black lower-class phenomenon. Support for black nationalism was high among the black middle class. Different varieties of black nationalism had greater appeal among different classes. The black lower class favored a black nationalism that more radically pulled away from white society. It appeared that the black lower class, having achieved little in a predominantly white America, was more open to the idea of trying to build a separate black society. The black middle and upper class had achieved some success but were frustrated by continuing racial prejudice and discrimination by whites and by the perception that the prospects for improving the status of blacks generally was bad.[21] On the other hand, they had middle- and upper-class jobs. While the black middle and upper classes were disaffected, they were not willing to make a more radical break from white America. They hoped that through black-unity activities, like blacks supporting black businesses, the conditions of blacks could be improved. They expressed their frustration with white America through a type of cultural capital struggle with whites, and not through ideas that would require disrupting their political and economic opportunities in American society.

Black-Nationalist Activism in the Twentieth Century

The Nation of Islam, the Black Power movement, and the Afrocentric movement espoused different ideologies about who black people are and what black people should do to achieve liberation. The "first" Nation of Islam differed from the other movements in that its leaders saw black Americans as people of Middle Eastern descent. Because they were a millenarian religious movement, they did not see a need for blacks to engage in political activism. They believed that Allah would destroy America and produce the ultimate liberation of black Americans.

Although the Black Power movement had roots in the Nation of Islam, it was a different movement. While the Nation of Islam saw blacks as Asiatics, Black Power activists saw racially authentic blacks as either "Black" or "Afrikan," not Asiatic. Black Power activists generally felt that a nationalist *and* socialist movement was necessary to liberate black people. The Nation of Islam was not only against formal political activism; it was staunchly capitalist. Encouraging blacks to form their own private businesses was one of its central ideas.[22]

Afrocentrists may have had the best opportunity to realize the dreams of the Black Power movement. During the Afrocentric era, the black public's support for black control of black-community organizations and institutions was higher than during the Black Power era. However, the leaders during the Afrocentric era did not put these black nationalist attitudes to the political test. They stressed cultural pride and moral values, not structural issues. Afrocentrists were African-identified, like the Pan-Africanists or "cultural" nationalists of Black Power, but they were not concerned with leftist political and economic change as Black Power activists were.

These different movements are products of different historical periods. The Nation of Islam should be understood within the context of the "classical" black nationalism of nineteenth-century and early-twentieth-century America. Classical black nationalism was decidedly Eurocentric. The classical black nationalists rarely questioned the idea that Western society and its ideals were the only standards against which human development should be measured. They wanted to build a black nation, but the model would be based on European and American society.[23]

Therefore, Marcus Garvey, the leader of the early-twentieth-century black nationalist organization, the Universal Negro Improvement Association, could call on blacks to build their own civilization that would produce "a duplicate in Africa of what exist[s] in Europe."[24] This meant that black people had to reproduce not only the political structures of Europe, but also much of European culture. One of the goals of the Universal Negro Improvement Association was "[t]o assist in civilizing the backward tribes of Africa."[25] Garvey also declared that blacks liked spirituals and jazz only because they "did not know better music."[26] Another major figure in classical black nationalism, Alexander Crummell, called for the adoption of the English language and Christianity by Africans.[27]

After World War I, people in the West began to question ideas of Western superiority.[28] The Nation of Islam also challenged the superiority of the West. The rejection of Christianity in favor of Islam and the assertion of the racial superiority of Asiatics over whites were all manifestations of its rejection of notions of Western superiority. However, the Nation retained a pejorative view of African blackness. Like Marcus Garvey and other classical black nationalists, Elijah Muhammad viewed Africans as uncivilized and struggled against black Americans' increasing identification with Africa in the Black Power era.

The civil rights movement (its successes *and* its failures), African independence movements, and the other social movements of the 1960s and 1970s were the social forces that shaped the development of the Black Power movement. In a variety of ways, these movements challenged Western ideals and Western notions of civilization and superiority over non-Western societies. A product of this social context, the Black Power movement was therefore even more strongly anti-Western than the Nation of Islam. The black nationalists of the Black Power movement now saw blackness as being in opposition to, and often superior to, whiteness. Black Power activists could now embrace African culture to a degree that the Nation of Islam could not. The opposition to "traditional" American values found in Black Power could also be found in other social movements of the 1950s, 1960s, and 1970s such as the Beat, Hippie, and Women's movements.

By the late 1980s and 1990s, it was clear that Africa and much of the Third World had not developed into flourishing, modern, independent socialist countries. Pan-Africanists in the 1960s and 1970s could be optimistic about the future of African nations, but Afrocentrists in the 1980s and 1990s needed to look to ancient Africa for Africans who could be easily glorified.

Pan-Africanists who were once African socialists had to revise not only the Africa they looked to but also their economic philosophy. The socialist countries in Africa had not succeeded and, in 1991, even the Soviet Union had come to an end. Reaganism moved the United States powerfully to the political right. Afrocentric black nationalists also moved to the political right.

A number of Pan-Africanists of the 1960s and 1970s became Afrocentrists in the 1980s and 1990s. Maulana Karenga, Haki Madhubuti (Don L. Lee), and Molefi Kete Asante serve as interesting examples of this transformation. In the 1960s, the Pan-Africanist Karenga made immediate political change his priority. He argued that he "would sacrifice the discussion of philosophy for the satisfaction of any concrete need" of black communities. But in 1993, the Afrocentric Karenga received his second Ph.D. for a dissertation on the social ethics of ancient Egypt.[29] In the 1970s, the Pan-Africanist Haki Madhubuti presented blacks and whites as natural, historical, and logical enemies because he viewed white people as being warlike by nature. Madhubuti wrote:

> After thousands of years of white master-Black slave relationship it is clear that the great majority of white people under their ideology of *White World Supremacy*, can never live peacefully with Black people or other non-white people. The fact that white people don't live in harmony with white people is empirical evidence of their abnormality and killer instinct. . . .
>
> War, to white people, is a national, natural part of their psychic and physical momentum. The *kill* is in their blood and it doesn't matter who or what.[30]

However, in the 1990s the Afrocentric Madhubuti worked with Robert Bly, who is white, in Men's Movement activism.[31] Madhubuti even wrote a poem, "White People Are People Too."[32] The Pan-Africanist Molefi Kete Asante argued, "Pan-Africanism without socialism [is] self-defeating because otherwise the exploitation of the people would continue at the hands of the black exploiters."[33] The Afrocentric Asante, however, is happy to have black Americans work in mainstream capitalist companies.[34]

These examples should be seen as indicators of *social* change, not *individual* change (although that is a factor here too).[35] The transformations evident in these examples suggest that black nationalists, like other "Sixties Radicals," have tempered their views, focused on cultural identity over political economy, and have moved to the right from the Black Power era to the Afrocentric era.

Afrocentrism is also similar to classical black nationalism. Afrocentrism returns to the "civilizationism" of the classical black nationalists. While black nationalists during the Black Power era could celebrate, albeit ambivalently, the black lower classes,[36] Afrocentrists exhibit the recurring black middle-class need to reform and "uplift" the black lower classes. Afrocentrists are similar to classical black nationalists in that both groups looked to ancient Africa to redeem black people. The classical black nationalists used the achievements of the ancient African world as evidence that black people could be "civilized."[37] Afrocentrists hoped that African culture would provide lower-class blacks with the moral values for them to become middle class. Both groups are Eurocentric in that the standard of achievement—"civilization"—is a European one.

However, there are differences between classical black nationalists and Afrocentrists. Classical black nationalists overtly accepted the European standard of "civilization." Afrocentrists *say* that they reject measuring blacks by European standards. Classical nationalists could speak about making English the language of Africa and Christianity the religion of Africa. Afrocentrists stress the importance of black Americans adopting African religions, names, and bits of African culture. Afrocentrists are clearly more Afrocentric than the classical black nationalists, but they are similar in terms of their Eurocentric approach to the ancient African world.

Classical black nationalists exhibited the strongest and clearest desire for a political separation of blacks from American society and the strongest and clearest Eurocentrism. Wilson Jeremiah Moses largely defines "classical black nationalism" as "the effort of African Americans to create a sovereign nation-state."[38] Relative to classical black nationalists, Black Power activists were weaker political nationalists but stronger cultural nationalists. Black Power activists were more interested in organizations than in nations, but they did regard African culture positively. We can add that during the Black Power era, "cultural" nationalists were more interested in Africa than "revolutionary" nationalists. Afrocentrists are the strongest cultural nationalists, but the weakest political nationalists. They whole-heartedly support visiting Africa, but they do not propose permanently living in Africa or in any other black nation. Their desire to have blacks "center" themselves in Africa is about identity, not geography.

Conclusion

"[I]ntegration has been a material success but an ideological and spiritual failure; black nationalism, on the other hand, has been an ideological success but a material failure," writes Norman Kelley.[39] For at least the latter half of the twentieth century, Kelley is more correct than he realizes. He is correct that the support for black nationalism among black Americans has increased over time. But he does not fully appreciate his point about the material success of integration. Because of the material success of integration, black nationalism has been tempered. More blacks accept community and cultural nationalism than they do nationalism's more separatist and political forms. As Molefi Kete Asante suggested, many blacks worked for major American corporations, lived in middle-class suburbs, *and* were Afrocentric. Black nationalism in the Afrocentric era did not entail blacks separating themselves politically or economically from American society.

The black nationalism of the late twentieth century was what the sociologist Herbert Gans would call a "symbolic ethnicity." Gans writes:

> Symbolic ethnicity can be expressed in a myriad of ways, but above all, I suspect, it is characterized by a nostalgic allegiance to the culture of the immigrant generation, or that of the old country; a love for and a pride in a tradition that can be felt without having to be incorporated in everyday behavior. . . . People may even sincerely desire to "return" to these imagined pasts, which are conveniently cleansed of the complexities that accompanied them in the real past, but while they may soon realize that they cannot go back, they may not surrender the wish. Or else they displace that wish on churches, schools, and the mass media, asking them to recreate a tradition, or rather, to create a symbolic tradition, even while their familial, occupational, religious and political lives are pragmatic responses to the imperatives of their roles and positions in local and national hierarchical social structures.[40]

In the Afrocentric era, the love for and pride in a simplified African past was restricted largely to schools and symbolism in black popular

194 I Change in Black Nationalism in the Twentieth Century

culture. It did not affect blacks' pragmatic pursuit of political and economic life in America.

Gans also observed that "middle class ethnics . . . have in some cases
used ethnicity and ethnic organization as a psychological and political
defense against the injustices which they suffer in an unequal society."[41]
Although blacks advanced socially and economically due to integration,
they still faced injustices in American society. The resentment and frustration caused by racial discrimination were channeled into an Afrocentric symbolic ethnicity. But the material benefits of life in America
and of integration were also quite clear. The black nationalism of the
late twentieth century was therefore not a nationalism to separate from
American society but was compatible with a high degree of political and
economic integration—it was an *integrationist* black nationalism.

8

Making Races, Making Ethnicities

Scholars distinguish the concepts of race and ethnicity in a variety of ways. The most common distinction is that race refers to socially acknowledged differences in physical appearance while ethnicity refers to socially acknowledged differences in cultural background.[1] I have rejected the physical appearance-based definition of race in favor of one that builds race out of the belief that groups have heritable essential differences. Ideas of essential difference, racial stereotypes, and other racial ideas make up a racial ideology. Racial ideologies are developed in the interests of political and economic exploitation and competition. When race is fully developed, racial ideologies are created and social structural relationships are directly or indirectly racialized. These ideologies and structures produce people with racial identities. Although race is first developed to address a specific political or economic situation, once the idea of race exists in a society it becomes a tool that can be used in new or redefined situations of conflict. In my view, it is social ideologies, social practices, and social identities that make race, not the presence or absence of biological differences. Differences in appearance can be used to mark racial boundaries, but they are not necessary. In fact, I do not know of a single case where racial categories are defined solely and completely by differences in appearance. In the United States, for example, one could look "white" and be black or American Indian.

My understanding of race, therefore, removes one of the two distinctions—physical appearance—between race and ethnicity. When we reexamine my case studies, we see that they also remove the second distinction—cultural difference. Race and ethnicity are the same phenomenon but poor analyses of physical appearance and cultural difference have obscured this fact. The study of racial relations will benefit by reconceptualizing the race-ethnicity distinction. Scholars studying race are repeatedly led away from seeing and analyzing the social by a definition of race which rests on the biological. Biological and pseudobiological reasoning will continue to plague the study of racial relations—a *socially* constructed phenomenon—as long as race continues to be defined by biology.

The Cultures of Race

Cultural difference and, more often, the idea of cultural difference is important in all my case studies. Essentialized notions of culture are often used to construct racial categories. Aryan and Jew in Nazi Germany were cultural categories that were made into racial ones. Afrocentric scholars also construct racial categories based on essential notions of culture. They argue that African culture was formed in the ancient past and it has subsequently become a fixed aspect of black people. Ancient Egyptians and contemporary black Americans are essentially the same culturally, and contemporary blacks are essentially different culturally from whites. For Afrocentrists, blackness and whiteness are rooted in these notions of essentialist cultural difference.

Racial groups are also frequently stereotyped culturally. Racial discrimination is not about color aesthetics. It is not skin color that drives antiblack discrimination in the labor market but stereotypes about blacks lacking a strong work ethic, having a "bad attitude," and being oversensitive about race.[2] During the Black Power era Pan-Africanists also had cultural stereotypes about blacks and whites. According to Pan-Africanists, authentic black people valued black nationalism and opposed integration. Authentic black people were also collectivists who lived in harmony with nature. Whites were individualists who exploited other people and the natural world. Different races are often believed to have important differences in cultural values.

Cultural stereotypes can easily become self-fulfilling prophecies. People often try to conform to the stereotypes of their group. Black people consciously try to "act black" as opposed to "acting white," so that they can be seen as racially authentic or normal. The black economist Glenn Loury, for example, illustrates a common type of racial thinking. Loury once recounted how upset he was that his son was interested in ice hockey. Because many black males play basketball and very few play ice hockey, this descriptive fact has developed into a normative compulsion. Loury stated that he wanted his son to play something "respectable" for a black male, like basketball. For Loury, to have a son who played ice hockey was to have a racially deviant son.[3] Rock 'n' roll provides another interesting example. Although rock music emerged out of the black-dominated rhythm and blues, it came to be dominated by white artists and to have predominantly white consumers. By the 1980s, blacks interested in rock were marked as racial deviants. Black artists formed the Black Rock Coalition and had to assert their right to play a "white" music.[4] Unlike the members of the Black Rock Coalition and Loury's son, who was probably too young to appreciate the racial reading of his interest in ice hockey, many people choose to conform to stereotypes rather than to challenge them.

Just as black people feel some pressure to do things that the majority of black people do or are believed to do, a similar dynamic occurred in the "first" Nation of Islam. The members of the Nation of Islam believed that they were Asiatic people, not black people. Since the members of the Nation believed that Asiatic peoples have a Middle Eastern culture, they worked to incorporate this culture into their lives. They tried to learn Arabic, they bought Arabic records and pictures of the Middle East, and they learned to cook Middle Eastern food. In their desire to be Asiatic, they rejected a variety of cultural practices that they grew up with that were common among blacks in favor of cultural practices that they believed were common among Asiatics. In all my case studies, race is linked to a real or imagined culture.

Racial structures also have cultural consequences. If a racial group is prevented structurally from living as another racial group, then the social structure produces behavioral differences. For example, if one group is prevented from obtaining formal education, while another group is required to have it, then the cultural lives of the two groups will differ in a profound way. By producing racial inequality racial structures can produce a similar result in slightly more indirect ways. If one group is disproportionately poor, then because of poverty many members of that group will not be able to live like the group that is disproportionately well off. What are basically class differences can come to be seen as cultural differences resulting from race. A lower-class lifestyle is often seen as being more authentically black than a middle-class lifestyle.

The fact that different racial groups have different origins can also have cultural consequences. There can be real cultural survivals stemming from different cultural origins. John Shelton Reed and Dale Volberg Reed illustrate this point when they state:

> Soul food was simply the chic 1960s label for the funkier dishes of down-home Southern cooking. When black became beautiful, so did fried chicken, greens, and crackling cornbread. Leonard Bernstein served this food to the Black Panthers. Of course he could also have served it to the Knights of the Ku Klux Klan, if he'd wanted to make them feel at home. It's just the food of poor rural Southerners making the most of what's at hand, and there's been a lot of interracial recipe trading, too.[5]

The food of relatively poor, Southerners—black *and* white—became defined as "soul food"—an aspect of black culture which differed from white culture, because blacks (but not whites) moved out of the South in large numbers in the early twentieth century. To whites who were not familiar with Southern cuisine and to later generations of blacks outside the South who were not familiar with what white Southerners ate, it appeared that blacks had a racially distinctive cuisine. Again, what is important is what people believe to be true, not what is actually true. It is also the case that there are a few West African cultural survivals in black American life.[6] There may be some real cultural differences that result from the legacies of different histories.

When one recognizes the importance of culture, real and imagined, to race, it becomes clear that using cultural difference to define ethnicity and to distinguish between race and ethnicity does not work. Racial groups are commonly perceived as being culturally different. If one also acknowledges that racial categories do not require differences in physical appearance, then the major distinctions between the conventional notions of race and ethnicity have been removed.

What Is Ethnicity?

As Everett C. Hughes argues, the common understanding of ethnicity is backward. He states:

> An ethnic group is not one because of the degree of measurable or observable difference from other groups; it is an ethnic group, on the contrary, because the people in it and the people out of it know that it is

one; because both the ins and outs talk, feel and act as if it were a separate group.[7]

In other words, an ethnic group is a group that is defined as being ethnically different. It is a group that people *believe* is culturally different, regardless of whether or not it is objectively so. "If men define situations as real then they will be real in their consequences [for men's behavior]."[8] What we call ethnic relations rest on people's belief in difference. This belief affects their behavior and produces a social reality.

This is exactly the same ground on which race is built. We can note the similarity of Hughes's definition of ethnicity with Oliver C. Cox's definition of race. Cox stated, "For the sociologist a race may be thought of as simply any group of people that is generally believed to be, and generally accepted as, a race" regardless of the appearance of the groups.[9] Both race and ethnicity are made by social meanings and definitions, not by objective criteria. Once groups are categorized as racially or ethnically different, social practices lead to the highlighting and development of real and imagined cultural differences.

A careful examination of ethnicity reveals that like race, it is about heritable, essential differences. There are no cultural requirements for membership in an ethnic group. If someone's parents are Hispanic, the fact that he is born and raised in the United States and does not speak Spanish does not disqualify him from being Hispanic. If a non-Hispanic learns Spanish, she is no closer to being seen as Hispanic than before she learned Spanish. Ultraorthodox Jews are seen as sharing an ethnicity with secular Jews, although there are very important differences in their values and the way they live their lives. A secular Jew's cultural similarity to non-Jews does not disqualify him from Jewishness. Ethnicity is not based on objective cultural differences.

Groups may be ethnocentric, and may come into conflict with one another over cultural differences. Sometimes these real cultural conflicts map onto ethnic boundaries, but generally cultural conflict does not require ethnic difference, and ethnic conflict does not require cultural difference. Although there are important cultural conflicts in American society today, most of them are not regarded as ethnic conflict. For example, the division in cultural values for and against abortion has been a fairly strong one, but no one has defined the two sides as opposing ethnic groups. Members of most ethnic groups can be found on both sides of this issue.

Groups change culturally over time. The members of all modern societies live differently today than their coethnic ancestors did a century ago. When groups come into contact, cultural assimilation usually occurs quite rapidly. Groups who were very different when they first came into contact usually have more similarities than differences by the third or fourth generation.[10] However, ethnic conflict can persist and even intensify over the passing generations as different groups become more similar, because the conflict is not about objective cultural differences but about essentialist categories animated by political and economic conflict.[11]

In addition to cultural difference, differences in national origin are sometimes also included as criteria for ethnicity. National origin is used simply as an explanation for what the cultural difference is and where it comes from. While this way of thinking is a convenient shorthand, there are often important cultural differences between groups within a state. Italians and Italian Americans can provide us with an example of these differences. Scholars studying Italian immigrants to the United States in the early twentieth century note that Italian immigrants did not necessarily regard each other as having the same culture or cultural identity. Immigrants from different regions spoke different dialects. In American cities, Italians from Abruzzi, for example, associated with others from Abruzzi. Those from Sicily associated with other Sicilians, and so on. "[T]he Abruzzesi regarded Sicilians as dishonest and revengeful. Conversely, these latter considered the Calabresi as stubborn." Over time, these immigrants and their children developed an Italian identity in part because they were categorized and discriminated against by other Americans as *Italians* and not as Sicilians, Abruzzesi, Calabresi, and the like.[12] Common national origin does not necessarily mean that there is a common culture or cultural identity. Ethnicities have to be socially created. They do not emerge automatically from cultural differences or cultural similarities.

Common origin is also used to define racial categories, though with race the geographic boundaries are often larger than a state. For example, the U.S. Census Bureau states that whites are "people having origins in any of the original peoples of Europe, the Middle East, or North Africa."[13] The geographic region is much larger than a single state, but it is still a geographic region. Richard Jenkins provides a nice illustration of how arbitrary geography is in constructing cultural boundaries. Jenkins points out, "Although two groups may be differentiated from each other as A and B, in a different context they may combine as C in contrast to D (with which they may combine in yet other circumstances)."[14] He elaborates:

> Consider the following, very incomplete sequence. The opposition East Swansea is subsumed under Swansea: Cardiff, which is subsumed under South Wales: North Wales, which is subsumed under Wales: England, which is subsumed under Britain: Europe. Precisely where in this sequence could one say that identity based on community or locality becomes identity based on ethnicity? And why?[15]

There are no clear answers to these questions. What precisely is the cultural difference in each of these oppositions, and what happens to these supposed cultural differences when a more general identity is adopted? If East Swansea is different from the rest of Swansea, how are these differences dealt with when Swansea is opposed to Cardiff? It is completely arbitrary to see the state as a marker of ethnicity and not a larger or smaller unit. In fact, for those who regard Jews and Hispanics as ethnic groups, the state is not important. These are trans–state based ethnicities. It is the desired political and economic opposition that defines the ethnic group, not the culture.

A different way of distinguishing race from ethnicity is to argue that race is imposed by a dominant group and ethnicity is asserted by a subordinate group. Groups can therefore be racial and ethnic at the same time.[16] This is a neat theoretical distinction but it fails to account for people's actual experiences. The first problem with this conceptualization is that, within its assumptions and logic, a dominant group cannot be a racial group because no one imposes race on it. A second problem is that there is a great deal of interplay between the imposed and the asserted identities.[17] The West Africans who were captured to become slaves in the Americas, did not have black identities. Black identities arose out of racial domination.[18] Therefore, the assertion of a black identity is the assertion of an identity that is, at least in part, imposed by the dominant group. In other words, Europeans took a diverse population of Africans and transformed them into people with black racial identities. When black people assert some form of blackness, this blackness cannot be treated as if it is independent of the history of white domination. This "ethnic" assertion of blackness is therefore to some degree a "racial" assertion and the effect of racial domination.

A third problem is that the distinction between the imposed and the asserted assumes a common experience, common interests, and egalitarian relations within dominant and subordinate groups. For example, if one examines the "ethnic" assertion of "African American" as a name for blacks (discussed in chapter 6), one sees that Jesse Jackson *imposed* this "ethnic" marker on black Americans. A majority of blacks did not believe that they should be "African Americans" when he declared it the proper term for blacks. "African American" was not arrived at by consensus or by majority vote.[19] The idea of an "asserted" identity assumes that there is a real egalitarian, communal group which makes these assertions. We should never forget that even minority groups are hierarchical. "Asserted" identities may very well be imposed by one faction of a minority group upon the rest.

Not only are there power relationships among blacks, but blacks and whites also have a great deal of culture in common, including racial ideology. For example, as discussed in chapters 5 and 6, Afrocentric ideas are influenced by mainstream American ideas. When Molefi Asante defends the one-drop rule or Asa Hilliard argues that blacks should be more like the stereotypical Asian or Jew, should these ideas be seen as a perspective emerging from a distinctive black experience or as conservative ideas from American thought? Even the ideas of blackness asserted by black nationalists are often linked to mainstream stereotypes and dichotomies.[20] Because blacks are part of American culture and contribute to American culture, it is often difficult to determine a "black thing" from a "white thing." Just as other Americans do, blacks also reproduce American cultural ideas. The idea that race is imposed and ethnicity is asserted fails to deal with the real inequalities within racial groups and the real shared cultural ideas among racial groups.

As discussed in chapter 1, racial categories are defined on the basis of a variety of criteria. To varying degrees physical appearance, ancestry, geography, and *beliefs* about culture are used to define racial groups. All these criteria are also used to define ethnic groups. Although it frustrates some social scientists, people often do believe that ethnic groups differ in appearance. Stephen Cornell and Douglas Hartmann inform us that groups they define as ethnic groups, the Hutus and Tutsis, are commonly believed to differ in appearance by Hutus and Tutsis. Richard Schaefer informs us that "many people believe they can tell a Jew from a non-Jew," although he defines Jews as an ethnic group. Although Italians are supposed to be only culturally (but not physically) different from other whites, even scholars report that early-twentieth-century Italian immigrants differed in appearance from the people of Northern European descent who already resided in America. As I will discuss below, it is not easy to determine whether these statements about the physical differences of such "ethnic groups" are true or false. Ultimately, what is important is that people believe there are physical differences. That people believe there to be differences, as Cox states, "is detail enough" if we are interested in social interaction as opposed to biology. It is not uncommon for people to believe there are physical differences between groups that scholars define as ethnic groups.[21]

Ancestry, geography, and *beliefs* about culture are also used to construct ethnic categories. As Alain Corcos points out, in the United States "if a descendant of the original people who lived in North America before its 'discovery' by Columbus lives north of the Rio Grande, he or she is considered an American Indian, but if that individual lives south of the River, he or she is considered Hispanic."[22] Geography and ancestry, not an objective measure of culture, ultimately define which people are referred to as being of Latino ethnicity. This category is based on the *belief* that there is a basic cultural commonality among people from this region. If one's ancestors came from Latin America although one was born and raised in the United States, one is still Latino. This is based on the *belief* that one inherits the culture of one's ancestors. All the criteria that are used to define racial categories are used to define ethnic ones as well.

It is common for people to see culture as an inherited essence rather than a social product. Francisco J. Gil-White illustrates this point by reporting an exchange with his Russian teacher:

> Recently, my Russian teacher, herself a Russian Jew, told me that to her I was a Jew, because I am descended from Jews. She will not budge, and maintains this view despite being aware that (1) I have to go back about four generations (perhaps more) to find an ancestor who practised Judaism (after that they are all Roman Catholic); (2) I did not grow up with a Jewish identity; and (3) my parents and I did not even know that any of our ancestors were Jewish until I was about ten years old, when a genealogy buff in the family uncovered this information.[23]

For the Russian teacher, Jewishness is not only a religious belief system or a set of cultural practices or even a claimed identity; it is an essence passed on by one's ancestors. This is the general logic of ethnicity. Gil-White finds the same type of thinking among people from a variety of ethnic groups. People often assume that one's culture emerges automatically from one's ancestry. This way of thinking does not acknowledge that people's culture is determined by a social context that is larger than their family. Nor does it acknowledge cultural change. All cultures change over time. No one lives the same way as their ancestors did a century ago.[24]

This inability to acknowledge diversity and change is a feature of essentialist thinking. To understand social relations, the fact that people's ideas about culture are inaccurate is irrelevant. Gil-White's Russian teacher probably feels a different bond with him than with her non-Jewish students. She would probably feel more comfortable inviting him to Jewish events than her non-Jewish students. Her behavior toward him may be shaped by her definition of him as Jewish, although he feels that there is nothing objectively Jewish about himself. Ethnic groups do not have to be culturally different, but they are *believed* to be so.

Ethnicity therefore rests on *essentialist beliefs* of cultural similarity within a group and cultural difference between groups, not on objective measures of cultural similarity and difference. As with race, this is a heritable essence, an essence that one receives from one's parents and passes on to one's children. Cultural essentialism is intrinsic to race and ethnicity. Racial groups are assumed to share a common geographic origin, have common ancestry, and share important cultural traits. The same assumptions apply to ethnic groups. Both racial groups and ethnic groups are often seen as differing in physical appearance by the general public. Upon careful examination, the supposed differences between race and ethnicity disappear.

The only potential difference between the two concepts is that of physical appearance. For scholars adhering to the race-ethnicity distinction, racial categories can be *objectively* distinguished by physical appearance while ethnic categories cannot. The fact that it is possible to look "white" and be black, and the common perception that many ethnic groups differ in appearance, shows that this scholarly distinction has not dealt with the complications of social life. For the distinction between race and ethnicity to be a sociologically valid one, differences in physical appearance would have to make a difference in social relations. Before one can address that issue one has to determine which groups differ in physical appearance.

The Complexity of Seeing "Races"

Although scholars think that the question of whether or not there are physical differences is obvious,[25] it is, in fact, quite complicated. How much physical difference does one need to make a racial difference? Should imagined or perceived physical differences be considered equivalent to real physical differences? If one takes the black and white racial distinction in the United States as a standard, one sees that the fact that some blacks look "white" does not lead scholars to say that the distinction is ethnic and not racial. If one does not need 100 percent of all blacks to differ in appearance from 100 percent of all whites, what percentage is enough for physical differences to serve as a racial marker? There are a number of questions about whether or not a physical difference exists which have not been answered.

People's perception and beliefs about physical differences can differ significantly from objective measures of physical differences. If we had two groups—say, the Green race and the Blue race—people might perceive that a majority of Greens were physically different from Blues although objectively this might not be the case. If 30 percent of Greens were physically distinguishable from Blues, this could be enough of a difference for the perception that a majority of Greens differed in appearance from Blues. If 30 percent of Greens differed in appearance from Blues and someone observing a random pairing of 100 Blues with 100 Greens was asked to pick the Green, she would be able to do so easily 30 percent of the time. If she were correct for half of the remaining times just by chance, she would have correctly identified 65 Greens out of 100 for an *apparent* accuracy rate of 65 percent. In this scenario, only 30 percent of Greens differed in appearance, and the remaining 70 percent of Greens and 100 percent of Blues did not differ in appearance.

A more realistic scenario for two groups with some history of geographic separation is for 30 percent of Greens to have a distinctive appearance and for 30 percent of Blues to be physically distinctive in some other way. In this new scenario, the *apparent* accuracy rate would be even higher than 65 percent. A *perceived* physical difference more than 65 percent of the time could be enough for people to believe that Greens and Blues generally look different, even if the majority, 70 percent of each group, look the same.

In real life, because the accuracy or inaccuracy of our ability to classify people racially is never tested, assessments are highly subjective. We can easily persuade ourselves that our ability to classify others on the basis of physical appearance is better than it actually is. One would expect this type of bias if there were a racial ideology claiming that there are clear physical differences between groups. In real life we also have any number of clues beyond physical appearance to help us make identifications. It is clear that people use these social clues. Based on analyses of telephone survey data, we know that black Americans can distinguish black Americans from nonblacks when both groups are reading the same interview text, based only on vocal clues, with an accuracy rate of about 70 percent.[26] In the South during the Jim Crow era, with its rigid segregation, people could quite easily identify blacks who looked "white" as blacks, based on where they lived and whether they interacted with blacks as equals. If a "white" person lived in the black part of town, everyone knew that the person was black. If a "white" person dealt with blacks as equals, most likely the person was black.[27] Because race shapes social relations, there are many social clues to help us with identifications. We may not be conscious of them and therefore may think that we are making our classifications on the basis of physical differences alone, when social differences may play an important part.

With 30 percent of Greens possessing some distinctive trait and 30 percent of Blues possessing some other distinctive trait, plus social clues, plus some luck due to chance, it is possible for Greens and Blues to accurately classify each other nearly 100 percent of the time. If there is an ideology that Greens and Blues differ in appearance, Greens and Blues may believe that they are merely seeing "obvious" physical differences when they classify people. This type of scenario may explain why people say that there are physical differences between groups, while social scientists say that there are not. If social scientists looking for objective biological criteria encounter my society of Blue and Green races, they would say that since 70 percent of Blues are not distinguishable from 70 percent of Greens, there are no physical differences between the groups. In day-to-day life, however, Greens and Blues know that they can easily identify Greens and Blues the vast majority of the time. Greens and Blues are convinced that the groups are physically distinct; social scientists are convinced that they are not.

We do see these disagreements between average people and social scientists. For example, discussing the Hutus and the Tutsis, Cornell and Hartmann state that the groups believe each other to be physically dif-

Fig. 8.1. If Colin Powell (*right*) looks "obviously" black, it is not because of his physical appearance. Powell's skin color is closer to the average white American's than it is to the average black American's. His hair texture and some of his facial features are intermediate between "black" and "white." For Americans, Powell may be "obviously" black because American eyes have been trained to see race through the American cultural category that defines people with "one drop of black blood" as black. In a society without the one-drop rule, it would be quite "obvious" that Powell and Kofi Annan (*left*) are racially different. The "races" that we see are not independent of our cultural categories. (UN/DPI photo)

ferent. However, Cornell and Hartmann state that the conflict between the Hutus and the Tutsis "is ethnic rather than racial" because "outside observers have found these [physical] stereotypes difficult to confirm."[28] Richard Schaefer argues that although "many people believe they can tell a Jew from a non-Jew, . . . actual distinguishing physical traits are absent."[29] Why do people believe they see physical differences, when social scientists insist that there are none? Although people's "incorrect" beliefs should be a topic for sociological study, scholars have chosen to dismiss them instead. When scholars do so, they are letting biological reality displace social reality; but as social scientists, social reality is supposed to be the object of our study.[30]

"Incorrect" was placed in quotation marks above because in fact it is not clear whether scholars or average people are correct. It is not clear whether Cornell and Hartmann's "outside observers" or Hutu and Tutsi "insiders" are correct on the presence or absence of physical differences between Hutus and Tutsis. There is no clear standard for how much physical difference makes a racial difference. There is no clear standard for what percentage of a racial group needs to have this racial difference for the group to be defined as a racial group. There is no validated procedure for measuring these things. In addition to these problems, both "insiders" and "outsiders" are potentially biased in their perception of physical differences. Studies of people's ability to identify individuals in racial groups show that they are better at identifying people of their own race than they are at identifying those of another. It appears that one's experience with a racial group affects one's ability to make distinctions among them. The more we interact with a racial group and need to distinguish within that group, the better we become at doing so.[31] Therefore, our ability to make physical distinctions may depend on social learning.

Seeing physical differences is analogous to hearing linguistic differences. A French speaker from France can distinguish a French accent from France from a French accent from Quebec, although both accents sound the same to me since I do not speak French. In this case there is a real difference, but the "outsider" is not sensitive to it. Do "outside observers" not see physical differences because they are not sensitized to them or because they do not exist? Do "insiders" see physical differences because of racial ideology and social clues or because they really do exist? We do not know.

Social scientists have not developed a methodology to carefully assess when differences in appearance exist and when they do not. They have not distinguished between objective differences in appearance and the perception of differences in appearance. Consequently, they have not appreciated the complexities involved in racial perception. This discussion illustrates the larger and more important point that even the perception of differences in physical appearance is a social phenomenon and is socially constructed. In a society where Malays are defined as a different race from the Chinese, people will become skilled at distinguishing Malay from Chinese.[32] In a society where both Malay and Chinese are Asian, more people will perceive no physical difference between the two groups. Even when we think we are addressing the biology of race, we are dealing with social facts.

Are Racial Relations More Severe than Ethnic Relations?

This discussion of "seeing 'races'" was initiated as a first step in trying to determine the significance of objective physical differences in social relations. Determining the significance of biology is difficult because there is no clear methodology to determine when populations differ or, more importantly, when they do not differ in appearance. The best way to address the significance of physical differences, therefore, is to examine cases where there is agreement that groups generally do differ in appearance. Then we need to see if physical differences yield any pattern in social relations in these cases.

When we do this analysis we see that differences in appearance do not have any sociological significance. When populations that clearly differ in physical appearance encounter each other, they do not automatically produce racial relations. If racial relations do develop, the form and degree of racial inequality varies independently of physical features. In other words, we can hold differences in physical appearance constant and have racial relations or not have racial relations. Holding differences in physical appearance constant, we can have racial conflict based on bringing a group into a society so that it can be exploited or based on expelling a group from a society; we can have severe forms of inequality, or mild forms of inequality, or no inequality. The observed social relations are not determined by the differences in physical appearance. Biology does not make racial relations; people do.

Peoples of relatively extreme differences in physical appearance have come in contact with each other without one or both groups regarding the other as an essentially different category of humanity. Africans and Europeans encountered each other in the ancient Mediterranean without developing a race concept. Asians and Europeans interacted as equals in ancient Eurasia. American Indians encountered Europeans and Africans without seeing them as racially different. Africans and Europeans interacted in colonial America as equals before the development of racial slavery. Physical differences in appearance do not produce races.[33]

Even when races are created, biology does not dictate the racial categories. Malaysians have three races—Malay, Chinese, and Indian[34]—where Americans today have only one—Asian. Americans see just black people, where Brazilians see a range of racial categories.[35] The physical differences acknowledged in one social context are dismissed in another.

The fact that different societies have divided the same range of differences in physical appearance in different ways shows that physical differences do not in and of themselves create racial categories.

Nor do differences in appearance dictate any particular form of racial relations. In the United States, Africans were enslaved and American Indians were removed and exterminated. Both forms of racial persecution eventually ended. Examining physical appearances will not help us understand why Africans were initially treated so differently from Indians or why the discrimination faced by both groups has changed and has been reduced over time.

If we examine the racial stereotypes that shape the discriminatory practices of employers, we see that they have nothing to do with skin color or any other aspect of physical appearance. Today, many employers prefer Asians and Latinos over blacks and whites for low-wage manufacturing jobs. This preference cannot be explained as a preference for lighter skin over darker skin since light and dark skin are in both the preferred and not-preferred categories. Employers prefer Asians and Latinos because they perceive them to be more docile and dedicated workers.[36] It is their beliefs about the culture and psychology of racial groups that explain employers' behavior, not the racial groups' skin color. In all these examples social factors drive the relations, while the biology per se is meaningless.

One probably finds the greatest commitment to distinguishing race from ethnicity in the United States. Here scholars wish to distinguish the experiences of white groups from those of nonwhite groups. What they are really distinguishing are relative differences in the degree of discrimination and inequality, not differences in the type of social boundaries. Outside the United States, people are often more aware that what might be called ethnic conflict and inequality can be as brutal as any of the racial conflicts and inequality in the United States. For example, many of the most notorious genocides involved people who were supposedly not distinguishable by physical appearance (e.g., the Holocaust, the Rwandan genocide, the Cambodian genocide). The fact that people are similar in physical appearance places no limits on the brutality to which they may subject each other. The assumption of some American scholars that conflict and inequality is less durable or less severe when people are similar in appearance is false.[37]

The race-as-physical-difference position also suffers from an inability to acknowledge change in social relations. Because it is based on physical appearance, a racial group is always a racial group and an ethnic group is always an ethnic group. In this perspective, races are not created at a point in history, they just are. And they cannot be unmade, because they just are. The same applies to ethnic groups. Again, although everyone claims to be a social constructionist, rather anticonstructionist ideas are common.[38]

Since races are social creations, races are created at a particular time in history and can be unmade. The degree and form of discrimination to which a group is subjected also changes over time. For scholars who do not rely on biology to define races, the anti-Irish sentiment and discrimination in the nineteenth-century United States justifies seeing the Irish as a racial group at that time.[39] The Irish were described by whites as savage, groveling, bestial, lazy, wild, simian, ignorant, and dangerous.[40] As Andrew Greeley observed:

> Practically every accusation that has been made against the American blacks was also made against the Irish: Their family life was inferior, they had no ambition, they did not keep up their homes, they drank too much, they were not responsible, they had no morals, it was not safe to walk through their neighborhoods at night, they voted the way crooked politicians told them to vote, they were not willing to pull themselves up by their bootstraps, they were not capable of education, they could not think for themselves, and they would always remain social problems for the rest of the country.[41]

In the nineteenth century, there was also clear anti-Irish discrimination. The Irish and their communities were occasionally attacked by whites. Their homes and churches were occasionally burned. It was not uncommon for them to be paid less than white workers.[42] In the South, they were seen as preferable to slaves for dangerous work because of their perceived inferiority. White Southern employers put the Irish to work "ditching and draining plantations, building levees and sometimes clearing land because of the danger of death to valuable slave property (and, as one account put it, to mules) in such pursuits." As one Southerner put it, "niggers are worth too much to be risked here; if the Paddies are knocked overboard . . . nobody loses anything."[43] Today, there are no attacks on Irish neighborhoods. The Irish are so well integrated into white America that there are no Irish neighborhoods. While there are still some negative stereotypes about people of Irish descent, no one sees them as half-apes as they did in the past. The stereotyping and discrimination of the Irish has been reduced drastically since the nineteenth century. The Irish have almost completely been unmade as a group racially different from whites.[44]

Detractors will say that this type of transformation is not possible for people who do not look white. But this view reifies race as biology. Differences in physical appearance do not automatically have a racial meaning. People of African descent and those of European descent have interacted without a race concept at earlier points in human history. If we understand whiteness socially—as being about having full access to the rights and opportunities accorded to white Americans—then we will see that blacks have become considerably whiter over the course of American history. Not only are blacks no longer slaves, but they have access to a host of social spaces and activities that were once explicitly forbidden to them. While antiblack discrimination and racial inequality still exist today, in nearly every area blacks have advanced considerably. It is possible—but by no means guaranteed—that black Americans will be completely white, in a social sense, in the future. It took the Irish over a century to become almost completely white. Given that black Americans suffered greater institutional inequality than the Irish for a longer period of time, we should expect their whitening to take even longer. An examination of American history shows that the differences in physical appearance between blacks and whites have not led to any one specific and permanent type of social relations. Social change has occurred independent of biology.

What scholars regard as ethnicity is actually the same as what they regard as race. Because people of European descent in the United States have faced less severe forms of discrimination than others, scholars have assumed that differences in physical appearance are significant for shaping social relations. This analysis has failed to appreciate that the sense of difference between peoples of European descent in the United States was quite strong in the nineteenth and early twentieth centuries. If the Irish were not similar in appearance to whites, no one would have hesitated to call their relations with whites in the nineteenth century racial relations. If we are interested in social relations as opposed to biology, the relations between the Irish and whites have to be placed in the same category as other, similar social relations.

When we take a comparative and historical look at racial relations, we see that no pattern of social relations follows from physical appearance. When people who differ in physical appearance come in contact with each other, they do not automatically create a race concept. When they do form racial relations, these relations vary over time according to social factors, not biology. A biological conception of race hides and distorts the social process of racialization and therefore invites flawed and antisociological analyses. This biologically based conception of race leads scholars to privilege biology over social relations in the analysis of race. Henry Louis Gates looks at the people of Kizimkazi, and rather than investigating the social processes by which they became Arab and Persian and the social consequences that follow from that definition, he simply sees them as a people suffering from delusions. For him, biology preempted social analysis and real understanding. As for the Nation of Islam, scholars reflexively defined them as Pan-African and problack despite the fact that their founder and their Allah was not of African descent. If the members looked "black," scholars assumed that their racial identity must be oriented toward Africa. Again, biology preempted careful analysis. Recently, Michael Banton has wondered "why differences of physical appearance seem more important in North America and Britain than in Spain and France where hostility towards North Africans is greater than towards West Africans."[45] If we understand that physical appearance does not make race or determine the nature of racial relations, we need not ask this question. Social factors—not physical appearance—determine the degree of hostility toward groups in North America and Britain as well as in Spain and France.

The greatest error that the biologically based definition of race produces is the attempt by social scientists to explain racial relations in terms of biological and pseudobiological theories. Richard J. Herrnstein and Charles Murray's *The Bell Curve* was only the latest of these. The more scholars understand that race is not based on biological differences, the more likely they are to understand that biological differences cannot explain racial hierarchies in society. By acknowledging that race and ethnicity are the same phenomenon, and by removing biological ideas from our definition of race, we will take a step in the right direction.

Appendix

This Appendix lists the full citation for the computer data file sources and includes some additional figures and tables.

Data Sources

Many of the figures and tables presented in chapter 7 are based on analyses conducted by the author. The datasets analyzed by the author were often referred to only by the year their data collection began. The full citation is listed here.

1968 Fifteen Cities

Angus Campbell and Howard Schuman, *Racial Attitudes in Fifteen American Cities, 1968* [computer data file], 2d ICPSR version, conducted by University of Michigan, Institute for Social Research, Survey Research Center [producer], 197? (Ann Arbor, MI: Inter-University Consortium for Political and Social Research [distributor], 1997).

1979–80

James S. Jackson and Gerald Gurin, *National Survey of Black Americans, Wave 1, 1979–80* [computer data file], ICPSR version, conducted by University of Michigan, Survey Research Center (Ann Arbor, MI: Inter-University Consortium for Political and Social Research [producer and distributor], 1997).

Note: Data collection for this study began in 1979 but it was completed in 1980.

1984

James S. Jackson, *National Black Election Panel Study, 1984* [computer data file], ICPSR version, conducted by University of Michigan,

Research Center for Group Dynamics (Ann Arbor, MI: Inter-University Consortium for Political and Social Research [producer and distributor], 1997).

1991 "African American"

"Some people say the term 'African-American' should be used instead of the word 'black.' Which term do you prefer—'African-American' or 'black' or doesn't it matter to you?"

Gallup News Service Survey: June Omnibus, Wave 2 [computer data file], conducted by the Gallup Organization, 1991 (Storrs, CT: Roper Center for Public Opinion Research, USAIPOGNS1991-222002 [distributor]).

1993–94

Michael Dawson, Ronal Brown, and James S. Jackson, *National Black Politics Study, 1993* [computer data file], ICPSR version, conducted by University of Chicago, Wayne State University, and University of Michigan, 1994 [producers] (Ann Arbor, MI: Inter-University Consortium for Political and Social Research [distributor], 1998).

Note: Data collection for this study began in 1993 but it was completed in 1994.

1994 "Minority History"

"In history classes in high school and college, do the experiences of racial and ethnic minority groups in America receive too much attention now, too little attention, or about the right amount?"

James A. Davis, Tom W. Smith, Peter V. Marsden, *General Social Survey 1994* [computer data file] (Chicago, IL: National Opinion Research Center at the University of Chicago, 1994 [producer and distributor]).

1996

Katherine Tate, *National Black Election Study, 1996* [computer data file], ICPSR version, conducted by Ohio State University, 1997 [producers] (Ann Arbor, MI: Inter-University Consortium for Political and Social Research [distributor], 1998).

TABLE A1
Trends in Black Nationalism

% Approving of	1979–80	1984	1993–94	1996
Black Pol. Party	46	31	52	34
African Language	62	37	71	na
Shop Black	65	57	84	62
Vote Black	40	19	27	12

Note: "Don't Know" responses were not available in the 1984 National Black Election Panel Study, consequently all "Don't Knows" have been removed from all years.

TABLE A2
1968: Fifteen-Cities Correlations (Correlation Coefficients)

	Black Nation	Shop Black	African Language	Black-Owned Stores	Black School, Black Principal	Avoid Whites	Black Friends for Child
Black Nation	1.00						
Shop Black	.10	1.00					
African Language	.15	.13	1.00				
Black-Owned Stores	.13	.18	.13	1.00			
Black School, Black Principal	.13	.07	.09	.36	1.00		
Avoid Whites	.45	.14	.15	.21	.15	1.00	
Black Friends for Child	.24	.07	−.01 (n.s.)	.21	.24	.28	1.00

Note: Minimum N = 2,959; all $p < .01$ except n.s. (not significant).

TABLE A3
1993–94: National Black Politics Study Correlations (Correlation Coefficients)

	Black Nation	Shop Black	African Language	Community Control: Econ.	Community Control: Govt.	Black-Only Organizations	Africa Homeland
Black Nation	1.00						
Shop Black	.10	1.00					
African Language	.23	.30	1.00				
Community Control: Econ.	.22	.43	.28	1.00			
Community Control: Govt.	.27	.40	.25	.60	1.00		
Black-Only Organizations	.30	.30	.33	.35	.30	1.00	
Africa Homeland	.21	.10	.24	.17	.16	.16	1.00

Note: Minimum N = 1,115; all $p < .01$.

TABLE A4
Repeated Black Nationalism Questions, 1979–80 Correlations
(Correlation Coefficients)

	Black Party	Vote Black	Shop Black	African Language
Black Party	1.00			
Vote Black	.26	1.00		
Shop Black	.10	.28	1.00	
African Language	.17	.23	.26	1.00

Note: Minimum N = 1,795; all *p* < .01.

TABLE A5
Repeated Black Nationalism Questions, 1993–94 Correlations
(Correlation Coefficients)

	Black Party	Vote Black	Shop Black	African Language
Black Party	1.00			
Vote Black	.24	1.00		
Shop Black	.13	.11	1.00	
African Language	.20	.23	.30	1.00

Note: Minimum N = 1,106; all *p* < .01.

TABLE A6
*1968: Logistic Regression Coefficients Predicting Support for
Black Nationalism*

	Community Nationalism		Separatist Nationalism	
	b	s.e.	b	s.e.
Education	−.008	(.017)	−.163 ***	(.023)
Income	.003	(.014)	−.107 ***	(.020)
Age	−.014 ***	(.003)	−.028 ***	(.005)
Male	.367 ***	(.088)	.496 ***	(.122)
Constant	−.679 **	(.247)	.966 **	(.342)
−2 log-likelihood	3265.855		2039.919	
Nagelkerke R-sq	.019		.086	
N =	2,896		2,994	

*p < .05 **p < .01 ***p < .001

TABLE A7
1993–94: Logistic Regression Coefficients Predicting Support for Black Nationalism

| | Community Nationalism | | Separatist Nationalism | |
	b	s.e.	b	s.e.
Education	.014	(.023)	−.098 ***	(.028)
Income	.103 ***	(.029)	−.100 *	(.039)
Age	−.009 ᵃ	(.004)	−.008	(.006)
Male	.197	(.137)	.497 **	(.182)
"White" Interviewer	−.564 ***	(.171)	−.933 **	(.277)
Constant	−.143	(.359)	.454	(.453)
−2 log-likelihood	1239.157		782.573	
Nagelkerke R-sq	.051		.077	
N=	923		854	

*p < .05 **p < .01 ***p < .001
ᵃ p = .051

TABLE A8
Logistic Regression Coefficients Predicting Support for More Minority History

	b	s.e.
Education	.031	(.080)
Income	.109 **	(.038)
Age	−.015	(.013)
Male	−.055	(.383)
Constant	−.433	(1.193)
−2 log-likelihood	175.078	
Nagelkerke R-sq	.125	
N =	146	

*p < .05 **p < .01 ***p < .001
Note: This analysis is between those saying that there is "too little" minority history, and that they would like there to be more, and those saying that there is the "right amount." The 11 responses of "too much" were removed to simplify the analysis.

TABLE A9
Multinomial Logistic Regression Coefficients Predicting Support for "African American" and "Black" (omitted) or "Doesn't Matter" (reference)

	b	s.e.
Education	.302 ***	(.083)
Poor	.842 *	(.344)
Working Class	.329	(.307)
Middle Class reference		
18–29 years old	.589 ^	(.350)
30–49 years old	.544 ^	(.324)
50–99 years old reference		
Constant	−3.813 ***	(.647)
−2 log-likelihood	347.55	
Nagelkerke R-sq	.062	
McFadden R-sq	.029	
N =	489	

*p < .05 **p < .01 ***p < .001
^p < .10

TABLE A10

1996: Logistic Regression Coefficients Predicting Support for Afrocentric Education

	b	s.e.
Education	.087	(.063)
Income	−.037	(.042)
Age	−.023 **	(.007)
Male	−.069	(.205)
"White" Interviewer	−.671 ***	(.191)
Constant	−.055	(.416)
−2 log-likelihood	676.952	
Nagelkerke R-sq	.064	
N =	644	

*p < .05 **p < .01 ***p < .001
[a] p = .051

TABLE A11

1993–94: Logistic Regression Coefficients Predicting Support for African Language Study

	b	s.e.
Education	−.029	(.025)
Income	−.050	(.032)
Age	−.017 ***	(.005)
Male	.041	(.149)
"White" Interviewer	−.541 **	(.178)
Constant	2.355	(.405)
−2 log-likelihood	1103.87	
Nagelkerke R-sq	.038	
N =	962	

*p < .05 **p < .01 ***p < .001

TABLE A12

1993–94: Logistic Regression Coefficients Predicting Support for Africa as a Special Homeland

	b	s.e.
Education	−.015	(.024)
Income	−.024	(.032)
Age	−.044 ***	(.006)
Male	.390 **	(.148)
"White" Interviewer	−.311	(.190)
Constant	1.272 **	(.390)
−2 log-likelihood	1077.552	
Nagelkerke R-sq	.127	
N =	898	

*p < .05 **p < .01 ***p < .001

TABLE A13

1993–94: Logistic Regression Coefficients Predicting Support for All-Male Schools

	b	s.e.
Education	−.060 *	(.025)
Income	−.100 **	(.031)
Age	−.024 ***	(.005)
Male	−.165	(.142)
"White" Interviewer	−.358 *	(.174)
Constant	2.937 ***	(.404)
−2 log-likelihood	1174.075	
Nagelkerke R-sq	.077	
N =	937	

*p < .05 **p < .01 ***p < .001

Notes

NOTES TO THE PREFACE

1. Nicholas Wade, "Race-Based Medicine Continued . . . ," *New York Times*, 14 November 2004, Section 4, 12.

2. Ari Patrinos, "'Race' and the Human Genome," *Nature Genetics Supplement* 36, no. 11 (November 2004): 51–52.

3. Francis S. Collins, "What We Do and Don't Know about 'Race,' 'Ethnicity,' Genetics and Health at the Dawn of the Genome Era," *Nature Genetics Supplement* 36, no. 11 (November 2004): 513–15.

NOTES TO CHAPTER 1

1. *Wonders of the African World*: [tape 1] *Black Kingdoms of the Nile; The Swahili Coast*, Wall to Wall Television for the BBC and PBS in association with ITEL, written and presented by Henry Louis Gates, Jr. (Alexandria, VA: Distributed by PBS Home Video, 1999), videorecording.

2. David Levering Lewis, *W. E. B. Du Bois: Biography of a Race, 1868–1919* (New York: Henry Holt, 1993), 3–4, 5, 26, 30, 64, 76, 107, 113, 120, 136, 144.

3. Brazil is famous for its complex system of racial categorization. Brazilians have a variety of categories between black and white that are not used in the United States. Michael Hanchard, Introduction to *Racial Politics in Contemporary Brazil* (Durham, NC: Duke University Press, 1999), 1–29. The "mulatto" Yannick Noah also reports that "in Africa I am white, and in France I am black." Sharan Begley, "Three Is Not Enough," *Newsweek*, 13 February 1995, 68. In South Africa, Du Bois would be classified as colored (mixed race), not black. F. James Davis, *Who Is Black? One Nation's Definition* (University Park: Pennsylvania State University Press, 1991), 90–98. At one time, in Ghana the Ashanti term for whites was also applied to black Americans. Malcolm X was once described as "a *white man* with astonishing ideas." Today, in Ghana black Americans are generally not seen as white though Asians still are. David R. Roediger, *Towards the Abolition of Whiteness: Essays on Race, Politics, and Working Class History* (London: Verso, 1994), 4. Emphasis in original.

4. See, for example, among Gates's numerous works, *"Race," Writing and Difference* (Chicago: University of Chicago Press, 1986) and *Loose Canons: Notes on the Culture Wars* (New York: Oxford University Press, 1992). For discussions of Gates's position in and on African American Studies, see Greg Thomas, "The Black Studies War: Multiculturalism versus Afrocentricity," *New York Village Voice*, 17 January 1995, 23(6), and Henry Louis Gates, Jr., "A Debate on Activism in Black Studies: A Plea to Protect Academic Integrity from Politics," *New York Times*, 4 April 1998, Section B, 11.

5. Allan G. Johnson, *The Blackwell Dictionary of Sociology* (Cambridge, MA: Basil Blackwell, 1995), 223. See also Roediger, *Abolition of Whiteness*, 2.

6. For example, Diana Fuss understands social constructionism as emerging from poststructuralism. Fuss's understanding of social constructionism informs the work of Michael Omi and Howard Winant. David Roediger also understands social constructionism as a recent development based on insights from a range of disciplines including biology and poststructuralist theory. Ira Berlin and Tracy Heather Strain, the authors of the videorecording *Race, The Power of an Illusion*, see advances in human genetics as very important to understanding race as socially constructed. I follow the lead of sociologists such as Peter Berger, Thomas Luckmann, Jodi O'Brian, and Peter Kollock and understand social constructionism as emerging from basic sociological theory. See Diana Fuss, "'Race' under Erasure? Poststructuralist Afro-American Literary Theory," in *Essentially Speaking: Feminism, Nature & Difference* (New York: Routledge, 1989), 73–96; Michael Omi and Howard Winant, *Racial Formation in the United States: From the 1960s to the 1990s*, 2d ed. (New York: Routledge, 1994), 54, 181n6; Roediger, *Abolition of Whiteness*, 2; Ira Berlin, "Prologue: Making Slavery, Making Race," *Many Thousands Gone: The First Two Centuries of Slavery in North America* (Cambridge, MA: The Belknap Press of Harvard University Press, 1998), 1, 379n1; *Race, the Power of an Illusion*: [part 1] *The Difference between Us*, written, produced, and directed by Tracy Heather Strain, California Newsreel, 2003, videorecording; Peter L. Berger and Thomas Luckmann, *The Social Construction of Reality: A Treatise in the Sociology of Knowledge* (New York: Anchor Books, 1966); Jodi O'Brien and Peter Kollock, *The Production of Reality: Essays and Readings on Social Interaction*, 2d ed. (Thousand Oaks, CA: Pine Forge Press, 1997).

7. Quoted in Johnson, *Blackwell Dictionary*, 356.

8. Meredith F. Small, *Our Babies, Ourselves: How Biology and Culture Shape the Way We Parent* (New York: Anchor Books, 1998), 204–12.

9. Quoted in O'Brien and Kollock, *The Production of Reality*, 57–60.

10. See "Kasey Madden and Charlotte Allen discuss whether mothers should be able to breast-feed in public places," National Public Radio's *Weekend All Things Considered*, 22 August 2004.

11. Oliver C. Cox, *Caste, Class and Race: A Study in Social Dynamics* (New York: Monthly Review Press, 1948), 319.

12. Ibid.

13. *Wonders*, videorecording; Henry Louis Gates, Jr., *Wonders of the African World*, with photographs by Lynn Davis (New York: Alfred A. Knopf, 1999), 158, 162–63, 165, 169, 190, 265n9.

14. Although we commonly use the term "racial group," it is important to realize that we are really discussing "categories." Groups are the product of some degree of social interaction. Categories are merely created by the power of the categorizer. Racial categories are also too large and dispersed to be communities developed out of social interaction. The effect of racialization does produce a collective identity that groups also possess, but we should avoid the common mistake of homogenizing racial categories by assuming that they are a community in the sense that groups are a community. For further discussions on these issues, see Richard Jenkins, "Rethinking Ethnicity: Identity, Categorization and Power," *Ethnic and Racial Studies* 17, no. 2 (1994): 197–223; Richard Jenkins, "'Us' and 'Them': Ethnicity, Racism and Ideology," in *The Racism Problematic: Contemporary Sociological Debates on Race and Ethnicity*, edited by Rohit Barot (Lewiston, NY: Edwin Mellen Press, 1996), 69–88; Adolph Reed, Jr., "The Curse of 'Community,'" in *Class Notes: Posing as Politics and Other Thoughts on the American Scene* (New York: New Press, 2000), 10–13.

15. Richard Schaefer, *Racial and Ethnic Groups*, 8th ed. (Upper Saddle River, NJ: Prentice Hall, 2000), 8.

16. Omi and Winant, *Racial Formation*, 55. Emphasis in original.

17. Stephen Cornell and Douglas Hartmann, *Ethnicity and Race: Making Identities in a Changing World* (Thousand Oaks, CA: Pine Forge Press, 1998), 24.

18. Some scholars add, often just as an aside, that racial categorization can be based on imagined physical differences as well as real differences. See, for example, Joe R. Feagin and Clairece Booher Feagin, *Racial and Ethnic Relations*, 5th ed. (Upper Saddle River, NJ: Prentice Hall, 1996), 7; Jenkins, "'Us' and 'Them,'" 74; Cornell and Hartmann, *Ethnicity and Race*, 33. While this conception of racial categorization is an improvement over the "real-biology" definition, it is still inadequate. These scholars do not explain how real difference and imaginary differences can function in the same way. They also miss the point that physical differences—real or imaginary—are not the only basis for racialization. This point will be explained below.

19. Bill Dedman, "Midwest Gunman Had Engaged in Racist Acts at 2 Universities," *New York Times*, 6 July 1999, Section A, 1; Jo Thomas, "New Face of Terror Crimes," *New York Times*, 16 August 1999, Section A, 1; Dennis B. Roddy, "Interviews Show Troubled Mind; Baumhammers Told Psychologists What He Did in Chilling Detail," *Pittsburgh Post-Gazette*, 2 May 2001, Local,

A-1; "Boston Couple Plotted Blasts to Incite Race War, Prosecutor Says," *New York Times*, 16 July 2002, Section A, 11; Thanassis Cambanis, "27-Year Sentence Sought for Neo-Nazi," *Boston Globe*, 10 December 2002, Metro/Region, B3.

20. Ibid.

21. Cornell and Hartmann, *Ethnicity and Race*, xvii, 41; see also 39–41, 68–71.

22. Schaefer, *Racial and Ethnic Groups*, 384.

23. Ibid., 385.

24. Abby L. Ferber, "The Construction of Race, Gender and Class in White Supremacist Discourse," *Race, Gender and Class* 6, no. 3 (1999): 67–89.

25. "The 'Jews' of Africa," *Economist*, 21 August 2004, 37–39.

26. Ferber, "White Supremacist Discourse"; Michael Burleigh and Wolfgang Wippermann, *The Racial State: Germany 1933–1945* (Cambridge: Cambridge University Press, 1991), 40–41.

27. "The 'Jews' of Africa," *Economist*, 21 August 2004, 37–39.

28. U.S. Census Bureau, "Overview of Race and Hispanic Origin: Census 2000 Brief," by Elizabeth M. Grieco and Rachel C. Cassidy (Washington, DC: U.S. Department of Commerce, 2001), 2, http://www.census.gov/prod/2001pubs/c2kbr01-1.pdf, accessed 19 October 2004.

29. Richard Goldsby, who is primarily concerned with biology, divides whites into four types. Richard A. Goldsby, *Race and Races*, 2d ed. (New York: Macmillan, 1977), 37, 41.

30. Quoted in Feagin and Feagin, *Racial and Ethnic Relations*, 135.

31. Quoted in Matthew Frye Jacobson, *Whiteness of a Different Color: European Immigrants and the Alchemy of Race* (Cambridge, MA: Harvard University Press, 1998), 84.

32. Ibid., 83–84.

33. Richard A. Goldsby, who is primarily concerned with biology, divides the Mongoloid race into five groups. He also divides the Sub-Saharan Negroids into five groups. Goldsby, *Race and Races*, 45, 31–35.

34. For example, in Malaysia, the Malay, Chinese, and Indian populations are seen as different races although they are all Asian in the United States. In South Africa, blacks and coloureds (mixed race) were distinguished while the United States defined both categories as black. In Central Africa, Tutsis are said to be tall and thin and have a thin nose. In other words, they are what Goldsby would call the East African Negroid, while Hutus are the West African Negroid. Since factors beyond physical appearance are involved in making races, it is incorrect to view these categories as simply defined by physical characteristics. Additionally, it is more difficult to determine whether groups differ than is generally acknowledged. I discuss this issue in chapter 8. Goldsby, *Race and Races*, 45, 31–35; Charles Hirschmann, "The Making of Race in Colonial Malaya: Political Economy and Racial Ideology," *Sociological Forum* 1, no. 2 (Spring

1986): 330–61; Eugene K. B. Tan, "From Sojourners to Citizens: Managing the Ethnic Chinese Minority in Indonesia and Malaysia," *Ethnic and Racial Studies* 24, no. 6 (November 2001): 949–78; Davis, *Who Is Black?* 90–98; "The 'Jews' of Africa," *Economist*, 21 August 2004, 37–39.

35. There have been blacks who could pass as white probably from as early as the late eighteenth century. Thomas Jefferson's children with the slave Sally Hemings were "seven-eighths white," for example. The 1890 Census listed 70,000 octoroons—people who were assumed to have only one great grandparent who was black. A very conservative estimate of the number of blacks who passed as white is 2,000 per year. In the sixty prime years for passing, from 1880 to 1940, it is likely that many, many more than 120,000 blacks looked white, since the vast majority of blacks who could pass did not do so. (Other estimates of the number of blacks who pass go as high as 12,000 blacks per year during Jim Crow and as high as 50,000 today.) Joseph John Ellis, "'Tom and Sally': The Jefferson-Hemings Paternity Debate," *Encyclopedia Britannica Online*, http://search.eb.com/eb/article?tocId=9126494, accessed 19 October 2004; Davis, *Who Is Black?* 54–56; Frank W. Sweet, "The Rate of Black-to-White 'Passing,'" *Essays on the Color Line and the One-Drop Rule*, http://backintyme.com/Essay040915.htm, accessed 29 October 2004.

36. Gates, *Wonders*, 158, 162–63, 165, 169, 190, 265n9.

37. Dunstan M. Wai, *The African-Arab Conflict in the Sudan* (New York: African Publishing Company, 1981), 23.

38. Kirk Johnson, "Tribal Rights: Refining the Law of Recognition," *New York Times*, 17 October 1993, Section E, 6.

39. U.S. Census Bureau, "Overview of Race and Hispanic Origin."

40. Based on physical features, Goldsby sees South Asians as a separate race from Mongoloid peoples. Goldsby, *Race and Races*, 31–35, 45.

41. U.S. Census Bureau, "Overview of Race and Hispanic Origin."

42. Clara E. Rodríguez, *Changing Race: Latinos, the Census, and the History of Ethnicity in the United States* (New York: New York University Press, 2000), 130, 152; Vilna Bashi, "Racial Categories Matter Because Racial Hierarchies Matter: A Commentary," *Ethnic and Racial Studies* 21, no. 5 (1998): 962.

43. Rodríguez, *Changing Race*, 83.

44. Ibid. For political reasons, in recent censuses the major Asian subgroups are listed as separate races. Yen Le Espiritu, *Asian American Panethnicity: Bridging Institutions and Identities* (Philadelphia: Temple University Press, 1992), 112–33.

45. Ronald Takaki, quoted in Ian F. Haney Lopéz, *White by Law: The Legal Construction of Race* (New York: New York University Press, 1996), 87–88.

46. Just before the rise of the Nazi Party Jews in Germany were fairly well assimilated into the society. For example, the intermarriage rate for men was 25 percent and that for women 16 percent. Most of the children of these marriages

were raised as Christians. For many Jews, Nazism, not Jewishness, produced the social separation of Jews from non-Jews. Marion A. Kaplan, *Between Dignity and Despair: Jewish Life in Nazi Germany* (New York: Oxford University Press, 1998), 10–13, 229.

47. John F. Szwed, "Race and the Embodiment of Culture," *Ethnicity* 2 (1975): 19–33; Davis, *Who Is Black?* 24.

48. Winthrop Jordan, *White over Black: American Attitudes toward the Negro, 1550–1812* (New York: W. W. Norton), 17, 18.

49. Ibid., 56; George M. Fredrickson, *The Black Image in the White Mind: The Debate on Afro-American Character and Destiny, 1817–1914* (Hanover, NH: Wesleyan University Press, 1971), 60–61, 87.

50. Richard A. Apostle, Charles Y. Glock, Thomas Piazza, and Marijean Suelzle, *The Anatomy of Racial Attitudes* (Berkeley: University of California Press, 1983), 24.

51. Southern Poverty Law Center, "Hate Violence and White Supremacy: A Decade Review, 1980–1990," *Klanwatch Intelligence Report* #47, December 1989, 6. See also Jo Thomas, "New Face of Terror Crimes," *New York Times*, 16 August 1999, Section A, 1.

52. Mary C. Waters, *Ethnic Options: Choosing Identities in America* (Berkeley: University of California Press, 1990), 17.

53. One of Mary Waters's respondents with a Slovenian identity adopted a son who had Irish, Austrian, and English ancestors. The adoptive mother felt that the family had to participate in Saint Patrick's Day and bought the child lederhosen in acknowledgment of the child's "culture." She felt that because of his ancestry he could not be Slovenian. In her view, ancestry determined "culture." Waters, *Ethnic Options*, 91.

54. William J. Wilson, *Power, Racism, and Privilege: Race Relations in Theoretical and Sociohistorical Perspectives* (New York: Macmillan, 1973), 190.

55. Jordan, *White over Black*, 97.

56. Ibid., 94.

57. Wilson, *Power, Racism, and Privilege*, 78–80, 190.

58. Apostle et al., *Anatomy of Racial Attitudes*, 20–37. Because Apostle et al. do not understand that cultural ideas can be essentialist, they decide that some "culturalists" really believe that differences are biological.

59. Quoted in Eduardo Bonilla-Silva, *White Supremacy and Racism in the Post–Civil Rights Era* (Boulder, CO: Lynne Rienner, 2001), 94.

60. Edward J. Park, "Racial Ideology and Hiring Decisions in Silicon Valley," *Qualitative Sociology* 22, no. 3 (1999): 231.

61. Cornell and Hartmann, *Ethnicity and Race*, 40.

62. Apostle et al., *Anatomy of Racial Attitudes*, 23–32.

63. Quoted in Johnson, *Blackwell Dictionary*, 356.

64. Frank M. Snowden, Jr., *Before Color Prejudice: The Ancient View of Blacks* (Cambridge, MA: Harvard University Press, 1983).

65. James Axtell, "The White Indians of Colonial America," *William and Mary Quarterly* 32, no. 1 (1975): 55–88; Peter Stern, "The White Indians of the Borderlands," *Journal of the Southwest* 33, no. 3 (1991): 262–81; Kenneth W. Porter, "Chapter One: Their Best Soldiers Are Black," *The Black Seminoles: History of a Freedom-Seeking People* (Gainesville: University Press of Flor-ida, 1996), 3–12.

66. Gary L. Morrison, "Loulan Beauty: Encountering the Xinjiang Mum-mies," *World Order* 32, no. 2 (Winter 2000–01): 33–38.

67. T. H. Breen and Stephen Innes, *"Myne Owne Ground": Race and Free-dom on Virginia's Eastern Shore, 1640–1676* (New York: Oxford University Press, 1980), 5.

68. Peter Kolchin, *American Slavery, 1619–1877* (New York: Hill and Wang, 1993), 14; Eric Williams, *Capitalism and Slavery* (London: André Deutsch, 1964), 3–29.

69. My thinking about the dimensions of race is based on J. Milton Yinger's. Figures 1.1 and 1.2 were developed from his diagram "The Field Context of Ethnic Discrimination." J. Milton Yinger, *Ethnicity: Source of Strength? Source of Conflict?* (Albany: State University of New York Press, 1994), 167–98, 171.

70. Burleigh and Wippermann, *The Racial State.*

71. Yinger, *Ethnicity*, 167–98.

72. Davis, *Who Is Black?* Tomas Almaguer, *Racial Fault Lines: The Histori-cal Origins of White Supremacy in California* (Berkeley: University of California Press, 1994); Virginia Dominguez, *White by Definition: Social Classification in Creole Louisiana* (New Brunswick, NJ: Rutgers University Press, 1986).

73. Rodríguez, *Changing Race*; Clyde Tucker and Brian Kojetin, "Testing Racial and Ethnic Origin Questions in the CPS Supplement," *Monthly Labor Review*, September 1996, 5.

74. My discussion of twentieth-century black nationalist movements will show that they rely on and do not challenge racial ideology. To argue that blacks are racially superior to whites does not free people from the idea of race. In this sense, they are racially conservative. The political scientist Dean Robin-son addresses the political conservatism of the major black nationalist move-ments. I emphasize the conservatism of Afrocentric-era nationalism and show some of the conservatism of the Nation of Islam. Dean E. Robinson, *Black Nationalism in American Politics and Thought* (Cambridge: Cambridge Univer-sity Press, 2001), 133–35.

75. John H. Bracey, Jr., August Meier, and Elliott Rudwick, eds., Introduc-tion to *Black Nationalism in America* (Indianapolis: Bobbs-Merrill, 1970), xxv–lxvii, quotation, xxvi.

76. To see the range of black nationalist activity and scholarship, see Bracey, Meier, and Rudwick, *Black Nationalism in America*; Wilson Jeremiah Moses, ed., *Classical Black Nationalism: From the American Revolution to Marcus Garvey* (New York: New York University Press, 1996); William L. Van Deburg, ed., *Modern Black Nationalism: From Marcus Garvey to Louis Farrakhan* (New York: New York University Press, 1997); Madhu Dubey, *Black Women Novelists and the Nationalist Aesthetic* (Bloomington: Indiana University Press, 1994); Robinson, *Black Nationalism in American Politics*; Michael C. Dawson, *Black Visions: The Roots of Contemporary African-American Political Ideologies* (Chicago: University of Chicago Press, 2001).

77. Patrick Hossay, "French Canada: A Province Unlike the Others," in *Contentions of Nationhood: Nationalist Movements, Political Conflict, and Social Change in Flanders, Scotland, and French Canada* (Lanham, MD: Lexington Books, 2002), 161–204; Colin H. Williams, "Recognition and National Justice for Québec: A Canadian Conundrum," in *Ethnonational Identities*, eds. Steve Fenton and Stephen May (New York: Palgrave Macmillan, 2002), 21–47; Daniel Latouche, "Globalization in a Very Small Place: From Ethnic to Civic Nationalism in Quebec," in *Minority Nationalism and the Changing International Order*, eds. Michael Keating and John McGarry (Oxford: Oxford University Press, 2001), 179–202.

NOTES TO CHAPTER 2

1. Quoted in Karl Evanzz, *The Messenger: The Rise and Fall of Elijah Muhammad* (New York: Pantheon Books, 1999), 86.

2. See Winthrop Jordan, *White over Black: American Attitudes Toward the Negro, 1550–1812* (New York: W. W. Norton), 94.

3. Ibid., 97.

4. Clara E. Rodríguez, *Changing Race: Latinos, the Census, and the History of Ethnicity in the United States* (New York: New York University Press, 2000), 83. For political reasons, in recent censuses the major Asian subgroups are listed as separate races. Yen Le Espiritu, *Asian American Panethnicity: Bridging Institutions and Identities* (Philadelphia: Temple University Press, 1992), 112–33.

5. Louis E. Lomax argues that the Asiatic identity of the Nation of Islam was just a "tinge" to "plug up the emotional and ideological leaks" in the political arguments. Claude Andrew Clegg sees the Nation's appeals to orthodox Muslims as purely strategic and not an integral part of the organization's belief system. Clifton E. Marsh, Richard Brent Turner, and Karl Evanzz state that the Nation of Islam was a Pan-Africanist organization. C. Eric Lincoln sees it as a black protest organization. Essien-Udom and Marth E. Lee argue that the organization worked to build positive black identities. Louis E. Lomax, *When the Word Is Given . . . : A Report on Elijah Muhammad, Malcolm X, and the Black*

Muslim World (Cleveland, OH: World Publishing Company, 1963), 62; Claude
Andrew Clegg, III, *An Original Man: The Life and Times of Elijah Muhammad*
(New York: St. Martin's Press, 1997), 122–23, 254–56; Clifton E. Marsh, *From
Black Muslims to Muslims: The Resurrection, Transformation and Change of
the Lost-Found Nation of Islam in America, 1930–1995,* 2nd ed. (London:
Scarecrow Press, 1996), xiv, 79–99; Richard Brent Turner, *Islam in the African-
American Experience* (Bloomington: Indiana University Press, 1997), 159;
Evanzz, *The Messenger,* 65, 78–79, 91; C. Eric Lincoln, *The Black Muslims in
America,* 3d. ed. (Grand Rapids, MI: William B. Eerdmans Publishing Com-
pany, 1994), 228–53; Essien-Udom, *Black Nationalism*; Martha F. Lee, *The
Nation of Islam, an American Millenarian Movement* (Lewiston, NY: Edwin
Mellen Press, 1988), 1.

6. I discuss the two main "Nations of Islam" but there are several offshoots.
Evanzz, *The Messenger,* 434–41; Mattias Gardell, *In the Name of Elijah Muhammad: Louis Farrakhan and the Nation of Islam* (Durham, NC: Duke University Press, 1996), 224–25.

7. Clegg, *An Original Man,* 20, 276–79.

8. Lee, *An American Millenarian Movement,* 78–79, 88, 90; Salim Muwakkil, "Into the Breach," *In These Times,* 27 June 1994, 24; Ernest Allen, Jr.,
"Religious Heterodoxy and Nationalist Tradition: The Continuing Evolution of
the Nation of Islam," *Black Scholar* 26, no. 3–4 (1996): 2–34; Manning Marable, "Louis Farrakhan and the White Conservatives," *Committees of Corre-
spondence Newletter* 6, no. 2 (April/June 1997), 8–9; Salim Muwakkil, "Louis
Farrakhan's New Song: The Nation of Islam's Leader Tones Down His Rhetoric," *In These Times,* 5 April 1998, 11–13.

9. William Clairborne, "Rival U.S. Black Muslim Groups Reconcile; Nation
of Islam Embraces Orthodoxy as Farrakhan, Founder's Son Pledge Loyalty,"
Washington Post, 26 February 2000, Section A, 2.

10. Michele Dillon, *Catholic Identity: Balancing Reason, Faith, and Power*
(Cambridge: Cambridge University Press, 1999).

11. George Gallup, Jr. and Jim Castelli, *The American Catholic People: Their
Beliefs, Practices, and Values* (Garden City, NY: Doubleday, 1987), 162–77.

12. Evanzz, *The Messenger,* 398–417; John Woodford, "Testing America's
Promise of Free Speech: Muhammad Speaks in the 1960s, a Memoir," *Voices of
the African Diaspora* (Fall 1991): 12–13.

13. Clegg, *An Original Man,* 14–40.

14. Ibid., 103.

15. Essein-Udom, *Black Nationalism,* 207–9; Clegg, *An Original Man,*
103–4, 228–29, 261–63; Aubrey Barnette, "The Black Muslims Are a Fraud,"
Saturday Evening Post, 27 February 1965, 23–29; Woodford, "Testing America's Promise," 14.

16. Lomax, *When the Word Is Given,* 115.

17. Vivian Hudson Ross, "Black Muslim Schools: Institutionalization of Black Nationalism" (Ph.D. diss., University of Michigan, 1976), 76; Sonsyrea Tate, *Little X: Growing Up in the Nation of Islam* (New York: HarperCollins Publishers, 1997), 31.

18. Ross, "Black Muslim Schools," 76–77; Clegg, *An Original Man*, 27.

19. Elijah Muhammad, *The Supreme Wisdom: Solution to the So-Called Negroes' Problem*, vol. 1 (Atlanta, GA: Messenger Elijah Muhammad Propagation Society, 1957), 33.

20. Muhammad, *The Supreme Wisdom*, vol. 1, 30–33, 50; Clegg, *An Original Man*, 41–73.

21. Essien-Udom, *Black Nationalism*, 43, 315.

22. Elijah Muhammad, *The Supreme Wisdom*, vol. 2 (Hampton, VA: U.B. & U.S. Communications Systems, n.d.). Emphasis added, 27.

23. Elijah Muhammad, *Message to the Blackman in America* (Chicago: Muhammad's Temple No. 2, 1965), 183–84.

24. The 2000 Census, for example, defines whites as "people having origins in any of the original peoples of Europe, the Middle East, or North Africa." U.S. Census Bureau, "Overview of Race and Hispanic Origin: Census 2000 Brief," by Elizabeth M. Grieco and Rachel C. Cassidy (Washington, DC: U.S. Department of Commerce, 2001), 2, http://www.census.gov/prod/2001pubs/c2kbr01-1.pdf, accessed 19 October 2004.

25. Evanzz, *The Messenger*, 398; Woodford, "Testing America's Promise," 3–16; Clegg, *An Original Man*, 137. Clegg, believing that being Asiatic is a physical description, assumes that the physical "whiteness" of the Turkish people should cause Elijah Muhammad to reject them. He reports, "Muhammad found the Turkish people to be good Muslims" and he "drew inspiration from selected features of Turkish worship and history." Muhammad would not have felt this way if he believed the people of Turkey to be white. Just as Fard Muhammad looked "white" but was not racially white, the Turks were not racially white. They were Asiatic.

26. Turner, *Islam in the African-American Experience*, 200; Kenneth B. Clark, *King, Malcolm, Baldwin: Three Interviews* (Middletown, CT: Wesleyan University Press, 1985), 39.

27. Clegg, *An Original Man*, 137.

28. Turner, *Islam in the African-American Experience*, 200.

29. Elijah Muhammad, *The Fall of America* (Atlanta: Messenger Elijah Muhammad Propagation Society, 1973), 12. The entire book addresses the coming destruction of America.

30. Muhammad, *Message to the Blackman*, 308; see also Muhammad, *The Fall of America*, 2, 12.

31. Clegg, *An Original Man*, 48.

32. For example, when Malcolm X taught the "Black Man's History" he

only mentioned that the Original People lived in Mecca. Malcolm X, *The End of White World Supremacy: Four Speeches*, edited and with an Introduction by Imam Benjamin Karim (New York: Arcade Publishing, 1971), 47–48.

33. Muhammad, *The Supreme Wisdom*, vol. 1. Emphasis in original, 45.

34. Clegg, *An Original Man*, 46–47.

35. Malcolm X, *White World Supremacy*, 48.

36. Allen, "Religious Heterodoxy," 27n10.

37. Muhammad, *Message to the Blackman*, 290–94; Clegg, *An Original Man*, 41–73.

38. Muhammad, *The Supreme Wisdom*, vol. 1, 12–18, 43–44; Ross, "Black Muslim Schools," 64–65; Malcolm X, *White World Supremacy*, 25; Clegg, *An Original Man*, 47.

39. Muhammad, *The Supreme Wisdom*, vol. 1, 30, 31, 34.

40. John F. Szwed, "Race and the Embodiment of Culture," *Ethnicity* 2 (1975): 19–33.

41. Stephen Cornell and Douglas Hartmann, *Ethnicity and Race: Making Identities in a Changing World* (Thousand Oaks, CA: Pine Forge Press, 1998), 30, 135–41, 179. This process works for all identities. Males consciously learn to act masculine, for example.

42. Lomax, *When the Word Is Given*, 71.

43. Lincoln, *The Black Muslims*, 210–27; Clegg, *An Original Man*, 68; Turner, *Islam in the African-American Experience*, 170–71. Ernest Allen sees the organization as "Islamic only in name" in the 1930s. It is not clear whether Allen feels that the move toward orthodox Islam in the 1950s would qualify seeing the organization as Islamic. The more important point is that the members saw themselves as practicing Islam. On this point, Allen agrees. Allen, "Religious Heterodoxy," 8, 11.

44. Muhammad, *The Supreme Wisdom*, vol. 1, 46–47, 50; Muhammad, *The Supreme Wisdom*, vol. 2, 63, 66.

45. Clegg, *An Original Man*, 143, 255.

46. Clegg, *An Original Man*, 123.

47. Lincoln, *The Black Muslims*, 105–6, 112; Essien-Udom, *Black Nationalism*, 203–5, 218, 240–41.

48. Essien-Udom, *Black Nationalism*, 205–6.

49. *Muhammad Speaks*, 1 January 1971, 12.

50. *Muhammad Speaks*, 4 February 1972.

51. Tate, *Little X*, 66.

52. Ibid., 78–80.

53. Ibrahim M. Shalaby, "The Role of the School in Cultural Renewal and Identity Development in the Nation of Islam in America" (Ph.D. diss., University of Arizona, 1967), 130, 250.

54. *Muhammad Speaks*, 19 February 1965.

55. Ibid.

56. *Muhammad Speaks*, 23 October 1964.

57. *Muhammad Speaks*, December 1961, 3 June 1966, 4 February 1972.

58. *Muhammad Speaks*, 27 May 1966, 24 June 1966, 8 July 1966.

59. See Woodford, "Testing America's Promise," 3–16; Leon Forrest, *Relocations of the Spirit* (Wakefield, RI: Asphodel Press, 1994); Allen, "Religious Heterodoxy" 13–14.

60. *Muhammad Speaks*, 28 February 1964, 27 May 1966.

61. Erdmann Doane Beynon, "The Voodoo Cult among Negro Migrants in Detroit," *American Journal of Sociology* 43, no. 6 (1938), 908.

62. Ibid., 901.

63. Hatim A. Sahib, "The Nation of Islam" (M.A. diss., University of Chicago, 1951), 215–18.

64. Allen, "Religious Heterodoxy," 5.

65. Peter Abrahams, "The Meaning of Harlem," *Holiday* (June 1960), 142.

66. Essien-Udom, *Black Nationalism*, 264; see also 291.

67. Goldman, *Death and Life*, 38.

68. *Muhammad Speaks*, 22 November 1963, 6 December 1963. Emphasis added.

69. Another example is Herbert Muhammad, a *Muhammad Speaks* correspondent, who reported on his travels to India and Japan in 1963. *Muhammad Speaks*, 18 February 1963, 4 March 1963. See also Lincoln, *The Black Muslims*, 169; Essien-Udom, *Black Nationalism*, 291.

70. Muhammad, *The Supreme Wisdom*, vol. 1, 37; Muhammad, *The Supreme Wisdom*, vol. 2, 54.

71. Allen, "Religious Heterodoxy," 11; Clegg, *An Original Man*.

72. Ernest Allen, Jr., "When Japan Was 'Champion of the Darker Races': Satokata Takahashi and the Flowering of Black Nationalism," *The Black Scholar* 24, no. 1 (1994): 23–46.

73. Clegg, *An Original Man*, 296–97.

74. Turner, *Islam in the African-American Experience*, 168.

75. Clegg, *An Original Man*, 296.

76. Clegg, *An Original Man*, 82, 91–92; Lomax, *When the Word Is Given*, 54–55.

77. Frank McCoy, "Black Business Courts the Japanese Market," *Black Enterprise*, June 1994, 216.

78. Charles Mount, "Muhammad's Heirs to Share in Fortune," *Chicago Tribune*, 11 July 1986, 1(2).

79. Robert Lucas, "How Negroes Look at Whites," *Tomorrow*, May 1950, 6; Essien-Udom, *Black Nationalism*, 184. Middle Easterners and Asians were allowed to attend public speeches by Elijah Muhammad, though, even after whites were banned. After a conflict over getting white police officers to disarm

for a public speech, Elijah Muhammad vowed "never again to permit white people to sit in our meeting—armed or unarmed." Muhammad made a point of adding, "This does not include the Turkish people, Chinese, Japanese, Filipinos, those of Pakistan; Arabs, Latin Americans, Egyptians and those of other Asiatic Muslim and non-Muslim nations." Elijah Muhammad, "Open Letter to Non-Whites," *Muhammad Speaks*, 22 November 1963, 1.

80. Essien-Udom, *Black Nationalism*, 185.

81. Quoted in Lomax, *When the Word Is Given*, 67. East Asians were refused with the excuse that the time was not right. Lucas, "How Negroes Look at Whites," 6.

82. Ibid., 6. Lucas, an undercover reporter posing as a member of the Nation of Islam, initially was able to use the idea of Asiatic kinship to bring a Chinese woman to a mosque.

83. Lincoln, *The Black Muslims*, 111.

84. Clegg, *An Original Man*, 122–23, 131–32.

85. Sahib, "The Nation of Islam," 55–56.

86. This is how Muhammad and others perceived the relationship. Naeem was an FBI informant. Evanzz, *The Messenger*, 238, 557n39. The important point here is that Muhammad would value his public and private association with a nonblack. Because of the importance of the Middle East and South Asia to Muhammad, a person from this region was probably the best choice for a spy. Middle Easterners and South Asians were probably more likely to be trusted than a black American. A white American, of course, was out of the question.

87. Abdul Basit Naeem, "The South Chicago Moslems," *Moslem World & the U.S.A.*, April–May 1956, 22–23; Abdul Basit Naeem, "The Rise of Elijah Muhammad," *Moslem World & the U.S.A.*, June–July 1956, 19–27; Abdul Basit Naeem, "Pakistani Muslim Asserts: 'Will Forever Serve Messenger of Allah,'" *Muhammad Speaks*, 31 July 1964, 9.

88. Naeem, "'Will Forever Serve Messenger of Allah,'" 9.

89. Turner, *Islam in the African-American Experience*, 194–95.

90. Clegg, *An Original Man*, 136–44, 189, 224.

91. *Muhammad Speaks*, 18 February 1963, 4 March 1963, 22 November 1963, 6 December 1963.

92. See Abdul Basit Naeem, "The South Chicago Moslems," *Moslem World & the U.S.A.*, April–May 1956, 22–23; Abdul Basit Naeem, "The Rise of Elijah Muhammad," *Moslem World & the U.S.A.*, June–July 1956, 19–27; *Muhammad Speaks*, 15 October 1962, 14 February 1964.

93. Lincoln, *The Black Muslims*, 224–27; Lomax, *When the Word Is Given*, 72.

94. *Muhammad Speaks*, June 1962.

95. *Muhammad Speaks*, 1 April 1963.

96. *Muhammad Speaks*, 27 April 1964.

97. *Muhammad Speaks*, 1 October 1965.

98. *Muhammad Speaks*, 13 June 1967.

99. See also Lincoln, *The Black Muslims*, 168–69.

100. *Muhammad Speaks*, April 1962.

101. Clegg, *An Original Man*, 224–25.

102. Lincoln, *The Black Muslims*, 166–67; Essien-Udom, *Black Nationalism*, 310–19; Clegg, *An Original Man*, 262–63.

103. Lincoln, *The Black Muslims*, 169. Emphasis added.

104. The following is a generic description of the Universities of Islam. Details vary depending on the particular school and over time for each school.

105. Ibrahim M. Shalaby and John H. Chilcott, *The Education of a Black Muslim* (Tuscon, AZ: Impresora Sahuaro, 1972), 7–11; William Alfred Marshall, "Education in the Nation of Islam during the Leadership of Elijah Muhammad, 1935–1975" (Ed.D. diss., Loyola University, 1976), 92. There are contradictory reports about the number of Universities of Islam in existence in the 1970s. Marshall reports that "the Muslims operated twenty-four schools" in fourteen cities "during the leadership of Elijah Muhammad" (76, 92). *Newsweek* (25 September 1972) also states that there were twenty-four schools. However, Vivian Hudson Ross's "Black Muslim Schools" reports that "by 1975, forty-six Muslim schools were known as the University of Islam" (59). Barbara Jeanne Taylor Whiteside, in "A Study of the Structure, Norms, and Folkways of the Educational Institutions of the Nation of Islam in the United States from 1932 to 1975" (Ed.D. diss., Wayne State University, 1987), identifies forty-three schools (107–9). Ross's and Whiteside's numbers seem extrordinarily high. It is possible that they counted all the existing mosques. However, not every mosque had the resources to establish a school. Or they may have included Saturday schools or Nation of Islam general education classes.

106. Essien-Udom, *Black Nationalism*, 241–42; Tate, *Little X*, 27–32; Clegg, *An Original Man*, 37, 40; Shalaby and Chilcott, *The Education of a Black Muslim*, 10.

107. Shalaby and Chilcott, *The Education of a Black Muslim*, 10–11; Essien-Udom, *Black Nationalism*, 237.

108. Allen, "Religious Heterodoxy," 6; Essien-Udom, *Black Nationalism*, 234.

109. Essien-Udom, *Black Nationalism*, 239–43; Shalaby and Chilcott, *The Education of a Black Muslim*, 10–11. The "Actual Facts" included the speed of light, the height of Mount Everest, the circumference of the Earth, and other physical science facts. Ross, "Black Muslim Schools."

110. Essien-Udom, *Black Nationalism*, 239–43; Shalaby and Chilcott, *The Education of a Black Muslim*, 10–11; Whiteside, "Structure, Norms, and Folkways," 51.

111. Essien-Udom, *Black Nationalism*, 240. See also Hatim A. Sahib, "The Nation of Islam," 187–89.

112. Essien-Udom, *Black Nationalism*, 238n12; Marshall, "Education in the Nation of Islam," 83.

113. See Alvin Adams, "Inside a Black Muslim School," *Jet*, 12 July 1962, 16–22; Christine Johnson, *ABC's of African History* (New York: Vantage Press, 1971).

114. Given the choice between moral values and academic efficiency, Elijah Muhammad chose morality. See Essien-Udom, *Black Nationalism*, 235–36. Ibrahim M. Shalaby, "Role of the School," 181–211, demonstrates how this education counters black stereotypes, and he discusses discipline on 274. Shalaby observed the following motto on a classroom wall: "There is no substitute for intelligence; the nearest thing to it is silence"(199). "Islam Economics" is discussed in L. Daniel Hammit, "Senator Gottschalk Meets the Muslims," *Muhammad Speaks*, July 1962, 9.

115. Shalaby, "Role of the School," 151–54. Clemmont E. Vontress, "Threat, Blessing, or Both? The Black Muslim Schools," *Phi Delta Kappan* 48 (2 October 1965): 86–90, quotation, 88.

116. "The Muslim Way," *Newsweek*, 25 September 1972, 110; Whiteside, "Structure, Norms and Folkways," 15, 51. Shalaby, "Role of the School," 100–2, 154–59; Cynthia S'Thembile West, "Nation Builders: Female Activism in the Nation of Islam, 1960–1970" (Ph.D. diss., Temple University, 1994), 173–87; Tate, *Little X*, 80–96.

117. Tynnetta Deanar, "Muslim Woman Is Model Personality," *Muhammad Speaks*, June 1962; West, *Nation Builders*, 177–78.

118. Shalaby, "Role of the School," 248.

119. Essien-Udom, *Black Nationalism*, 238n13.

120. Naeem, "'Will Forever Serve Messenger of Allah,'" 9.

121. All notable visitors to the Nation of Islam were reported in *Muhammad Speaks*, which students read for Social Studies. But a number of the visitors to the Nation, discussed above, specifically visited the University of Islam.

122. Lincoln, *The Black Muslims*, 210.

123. Lincoln, *The Black Muslims*, 113–14; Essien-Udom, *Black Nationalism*, 188–89; Lomax, *When the Word Is Given*, 67; Malcolm X, *White World Supremacy*, 13.

124. Elijah Muhammad, *The Theology of Time*, transcribed by Abass Rassoull (Hampton, VA: UBUS Communications Systems, 1992), 54; see also Essien-Udom, *Black Nationalism*, 321–22.

125. Muhammad, *The Fall of America*, 150, see also 16–17.

126. *Muhammad Speaks*, 28 June 1968, 4.

127. Muhammad, *Message to the Blackman*.

128. Lincoln, *The Black Muslims*, 88–90; Clegg, *An Original Man*, 252–53.

Barnette argues that the Nation destroyed successful black businessmen. Barnette, "The Black Muslims Are a Fraud," 27.

129. Bracey, Meier, and Rudwick identified the Nation of Islam as a religious black nationalist organization. John H. Bracey, Jr., August Meier, and Elliot Rudwick, eds., Introduction to *Black Nationalism in America* (Indianapolis: Bobbs-Merrill, 1970), xxvii.

130. Lincoln, *The Black Muslims*, 57–58; William L. Van Deburg, *New Day in Babylon: The Black Power Movement and American Culture, 1965–1975* (Chicago: Chicago University Press, 1992).

131. See Turner, *Islam in the African-American Experience*, 159; Marsh, *From Black Muslims to Muslims*, xiv, 79–99; Evanzz, *The Messenger*, 65, 78–79, 91.

132. See chapters 3 and 4 for discussions of the Pan-Africanism of the Black Power movement; *Muhammad Speaks*, 28 June 1968, 4.

133. Clegg, *An Original Man*, 255.

134. Essien-Udom, *Black Nationalism*, 321.

135. See Van Deburg, *New Day in Babylon*.

136. Essien-Udom, *Black Nationalism*, 35, 43; Amina Beverly McCloud, *African American Islam* (New York: Routledge, 1995), 10–18; Lincoln, *The Black Muslims*, 48–52; Evanzz, *The Messenger*, 62–71.

137. Essien-Udom, *Black Nationalism*, 35, 43.

138. These issues will be discussed in detail in chapters 3 and 4.

139. Lomax, *When the Word Is Given*, 115.

NOTES TO CHAPTER 3

1. W. E. B. Du Bois, *Dusk of Dawn: An Essay toward An Autobiography of a Race Concept* (New Brunswick, NJ: Transaction Books, 1940), 153.

2. Ibid., 101.

3. Charles A. Lofgren, *The Plessy Case: A Legal-Historical Interpretation* (New York: Oxford University Press, 1987), 41, 55, 87–88.

4. Howard N. Rabinowitz, "Segregation," in *The Reader's Companion to American History*, ed. Eric Foner and John A. Garraty (Boston: Houghton Mifflin, 1991), 976–78.

5. John L. Jackson, Jr., *Harlemworld: Doing Race and Class in Contemporary Black America* (Chicago: University of Chicago Press, 2001), 12; Sarah Susannah Willie, *Acting Black: College, Identity, and the Performance of Race* (New York: Routledge, 2003), 126–27.

6. Willie, *Acting Black*, 126–27.

7. Charles Payne, *I've Got the Light of Freedom: The Organizing Tradition and the Mississippi Freedom Struggle* (Berkeley: University of California Press,

1995), 7–15; Paula Giddings, *When and Where I Enter: The Impact of Black Women on Race and Sex in America* (New York: Bantam Books, 1984), 17–31.

8. While in "street talk" blacks have called whites "ofay," "honky," "cracker," and "white boy" (said disparagingly), there are many more terms, both "street" and scholarly, which indicate an incorrect, deviant, or pathological blackness, as for example: "Negro" (said disparagingly), "nigger" (said disparagingly), "Uncle Tom," "Aunt Jemima," "self-hating," "oreo," "incognegro," "assimilated" (said disparagingly), "deracinated," "color struck," and the related "has a color complex" which is related to "inferiority complex," "miseducated," "sellout," "bougy" (from "black bourgeoisie"), "sididdy," and "crossover." This list is probably incomplete.

9. Peter Goldman, *The Death and Life of Malcolm X* (Urbana: Univesity of Illinois Press, 1973), 22–23, 397; Phillip Brian Harper, *Are We Not Men? Masculine Anxiety and the Problem of African-American Identity* (New York: Oxford University Press, 1996), 39–53, especially 48–49.

10. Willie, *Acting Black*, 54.

11. Bob Blauner, *Black Lives, White Lives: Three Decades of Race Relations in America* (Berkeley: University of California Press, 1989), 112.

12. Ibid., 111, 113.

13. Virginia Dominguez, *White by Definition: Social Classification in Creole Louisiana* (New Brunswick, NJ: Rutgers University Press, 1986), 173.

14. Blauner, *Black Lives*, 12.

15. Cynthia S'Thembile West, "Nation Builders: Female Activism in the Nation of Islam, 1960–1970" (Ph.D. diss., Temple University, 1994), 98–187; Elijah Muhammad, *Message to the Blackman in America* (Atlanta: Messenger Elijah Muhammad Propagation Society, 1965), 58–61.

16. Malcolm X, *The Autobiography of Malcolm X* (New York: Grove Press, 1964; reprint, New York: Ballantine Books, 1990), 225–26 (page numbers from the reprint edition). For some presumably pre-Nation views, see 91, 92.

17. Malcolm X, *Autobiography*, 226. Malcolm's views on women can be found throughout his *Autobiography*. In recounting his life before joining the Nation, he told about his affair with a white woman, Sophia: "It seems that some women love to be exploited. When they are not exploited, they exploit the man. . . . Always, every now and then, I had given her [Sophia] a hard time, just to keep her in line. Every once in a while a woman seems to need, in fact *wants* this, too. But now, I would feel evil and slap her around worse than ever, some of the nights when Shorty was away." Emphasis in original, 135.

18. Malcolm X, *Autobiography*, 389.

19. Adolph L. Reed, *Stirrings in the Jug: Black Politics in the Post-Segregation Era* (Minneapolis: University of Minnesota Press, 1999), 198–99.

20. Quoted in Goldman, *Death and Life*, 385.

21. Ibid.

22. "The Time Has Come (1964–1965)," *Eyes on the Prize II*, prod. Blackside, Inc. and Corporation for Public Broadcasting, PBS Video, 1989–1990, videocassette.

23. For a black feminist response to the castration and matriarchy argument, see Toni Cade, *The Black Woman: An Anthology* (New York: New American Library, 1970), 113–18. Daryl Michael Scott places the arguments in a broader political and intellectual history. Scott, *Contempt and Pity: Social Policy and the Image of the Damaged Black Psyche, 1880–1996* (Chapel Hill: University of North Carolina Press, 1997), 150–56.

24. Giddings, *When and Where*, 317.

25. For overviews of "the Masculine Decade," see Giddings, *When and Where*, 314–24; Cade, *The Black Woman*, especially 113–18; Toni Morrison, "What the Black Woman Thinks about Women's Lib," *New York Times Magazine*, 22 August 1971, 15(5). Since the sexism of "cultural" nationalists is often highlighted, it is useful to note that the Black Panthers were also antibirth control. The Panthers argued that the birth control pill was an attempt at black genocide. "Educate your woman to stop taking those pills. You and your woman—replenish the earth with healthy black warriors," demanded a female Panther. It is interesting to note that the Panther directs her message to males so that they can then direct females to make reproductive decisions. Philip S. Foner, ed., *The Black Panthers Speak* (New York: HarperCollins, 1970; reprint New York: Da Capo Press, 1995), 26 (page citations are from reprint edition). A Panther newspaper cover story in response to a new abortion law in New York informed readers, "Black people know that part of our revolutionary strength lies in the fact that we out number the pigs—and the pigs realize this too. This is why they are trying to eliminate as many people as possible before they reach their inevitable doom!" *The Black Panther*, 4 July 1970. The Nation of Islam also argued that birth control was an attempt at black genocide. Muhammad, *Message*, 65–66.

26. Ibid.

27. Young-Hee Yoon, "African-American Women and Work," in *Women and Work: A Handbook*, eds. Paula J. Dubeck and Kathryn Borman (New York: Garland Publishing, 1996), 35–38.

28. Steven Estes, "'I Am a Man!'": Race, Masculinity, and the 1968 Memphis Sanitation Strike," *Labor History* 41(2), 2000: 143–70.

29. Aldon D. Morris, *The Origins of the Civil Rights Movement: Black Communities Organizing for Change* (New York: Free Press, 1984), 83.

30. Ibid., 103.

31. Morris, *Origins*, 114; see also Giddings, *When and Where*, 311–13.

32. Quoted in Giddings, *When and Where*, 313.

33. Randall Kennedy, "From Protest to Patronage," *The Nation*, 29 September 2003.

34. *The Quotable Karenga*, ed. Clyde Halisi and James Mtume (Los Angeles: US Organization, 1967), 20–21.

35. Angela Davis, *Angela Davis: An Autobiography* (New York: International Publishers, 1988), 161.

36. Tracye Matthews, "'No One Ever Asks, What a Man's Place in the Revolution Is': Gender and the Politics of the Black Panther Party, 1966–1971," in *The Black Panther Party [Reconsidered]*, ed. Charles E. Jones (Baltimore: Black Classic Press, 1988), 267–304.

37. Ibid., 290.

38. Regina Jennings, "Why I Joined the Party: An Africana Womanist Reflection," in *The Black Panther Party [Reconsidered]*, ed. Charles E. Jones (Baltimore: Black Classic Press, 1988), 257.

39. Ibid.

40. Quoted by Eugene Victor Wolfenstein, who discusses Elaine Brown in "New Souls for Old? Race, Gender and the Transformational Effects of Social Movements," *Studies in Gender and Sexuality* 1, no. 4, Fall 2000: 403. Emphasis in original. See also 412–13, 416–17.

41. Ibid., 416.

42. Amiri Baraka, *Home: Social Essays* (New York: William Morrow & Co., 1966), 216.

43. Amiri Baraka, *Black Art* (Newark, NJ: Jihad Productions, 1966), 3.

44. *Black News*, October 1969, 2; 15 November 1969, 8.

45. *Black News*, 12 May 1970, 7.

46. *Black News*, 19 December 1969, 3.

47. Goldman, *Death and Life*, 397; Harper, *Are We Not Men?* 39–53, especially 48–49.

48. Dean Robinson, *Black Nationalism in American Politics and Thought* (Cambridge: Cambridge University Press, 2001), 49; Goldman, *Death and Life*, 190.

49. Malcolm X, *Autobiography*, 238; C. Eric Lincoln, *The Black Muslims in America*, 3d ed. (Boston: Beacon Press, 1961; reprint, Grand Rapids, MI: Wm. B. Eerdmans Publishing Co. and Trenton, NJ: Africa World Press, 1994), 102–3 (page citations are to the reprint edition); Goldman, *Death and Life*, 63.

50. Goldman, *Death and Life*, 75, 183, 229–30, 383–84.

51. For discussions of some of these organizations, see Roberta Gold, "The Black Jews of Harlem: Representation, Identity and Race, 1920–1939," *American Quarterly* 55, no. 2 (2003): 179–225; E. U. Essien-Udom, "The Nationalist Movements of Harlem," *Freedomways* 3, no. 3 (Summer 1963), 335–42.

52. Payne, *I've Got the Light*, 436.

53. Martin Luther King, Jr., argued, "At the center of nonviolence stands the principle of love," in *Stride toward Freedom: The Montgomery Story* (New York: Harper and Brothers, 1958), 103–4.

54. Goldman, *Death and Life*, 101. Emphasis in original.

55. Ibid., 386. Emphasis in original.

56. Clayborne Carson, *In Struggle: SNCC and the Black Awakening of the 1960s* (Cambridge, MA: Harvard University Press, 1981), 236–42; Meier and Rudwick, *CORE*, 420.

57. Imamu Halisi, ed., *Kitabu: Beginning Concepts in Kawaida* (Los Angeles: US Organization, 1972?), 5.

58. Huber C. Palmer, "Three Black Nationalist Organizations and Their Impact upon Their Times" (Ph.D. diss., Claremont Graduate School, 1973), 28, 32.

59. Ed Decker, "Maulana Karenga," in *Contemporary Black Biography* (Detroit: Gale Research, 1996), 119.

60. Halisi, *Kitabu*, 3n4, 4n8.

61. Claude Andrew Clegg III, *An Original Man: The Life and Times of Elijah Muhammad* (New York: St. Martin's Press, 1997), 143.

62. Halisi, *Kitabu*, 5n9; *The Quotable Karenga*, iii.

63. Halisi, *Kitabu*, 7; Muhammad, *Message*, 68–85.

64. Muhammad, *Message*, 54.

65. The idea that black men were gods was also present in the Nation offshoot called the Five Percent Nation of Islam or the Nation of Gods and Earths (black men are "Gods" and black women "Earths"), which began in 1963. Mattias Gardell, *In the Name of Elijah Muhammad: Louis Farrakhan and the Nation of Islam* (Durham: Duke University Press, 1996), 170–74, 224–25.

66. Emphasis added. Vivian Hudson Ross, "Black Muslim Schools: Institutionalization of Black Nationalism" (Ph.D. diss., University of Michigan, 1976), 76; Sonsyrea Tate, *Little X: Growing Up in the Nation of Islam* (New York: HarperCollins, 1997), 31.

67. *Quotable Karenga*, 9–15; Goldman, *Death and Life*, 6, 12, 73–74, 134; Muhammad, *Message*, 217–19, 319.

68. Carson, *In Struggle*, 279.

69. The Nation and Panther's Programs, taken from their respective newspapers, are reprinted in John H. Bracey, Jr., August Meier, and Elliott Rudwick, eds., *Black Nationalism in America* (Indianapolis, IN: Bobbs-Merrill, 1970), 404–7, 531–34. Emphasis in original.

70. Bobby Seale, *Seize the Time: The Story of the Black Panther Party and Huey P. Newton* (New York: Random House, 1970; reprint, Baltimore: Black Classic Press, 1991, ix, x, 4 (page citations are from the reprint edition); Goldman, *Death and Life*, 6, 12, 73–74, 134.

71. Carson, *In Struggle*, 3, 135–36, 192; Meier and Rudwick, *CORE*, 206–7, 302–3, 331–32, 374, 429.

72. Robinson, *Black Nationalism in American Politics*, 47–49.

73. Goldman, *Death and Life*, 70, 397.

74. Kasisi Jitu Weusi, "Around Our Way," *Fundisha: Congress of African People* 1, no. 3, in *Black News* 2, no. 8, 8 September 1973, 13. Emphasis in original.

75. Malcolm X, *Autobiography*, 186, 187, 207, 258–59; Goldman, *Death and Life*, 80–81.

76. Malcolm X, *Autobiography*, 221.

77. Ibid. Emphasis in original.

78. Elijah Muhammad, *How to Eat to Live* (Newport News, VA: National Newport News and Commentator, 1972), 63–64.

79. Aminah Beverly McCloud, *African American Islam* (New York: Routledge, 1995), 51–52.

80. Imamu Amiri Baraka, ed., *African Congress: A Documentary of the First Modern Pan-African Congress* (New York: William Morrow, 1972), 32, 44, 92; *Black Power Conference Reports* (Harlem, NY: Afram Associates, 1970), 23, 50; Madeleine Coleman, ed., *Black Children Just Keep on Growing: Alternative Curriculum Models for Young Black Children* (Washingtion, DC: Black Child Development Institute, 1977), 4. Joy Davis, a former student at a "cultural" nationalist school, recalls saying a school pledge that ended with "All praise is due to Allah," although the school was not a Muslim one. Interview by author, 11 March 2003.

81. The leftist politics of Black Power will be addressed in more detail in chapter 4. Martin Luther King, Jr., *Where Do We Go from Here: Chaos or Community?* (Boston: Beacon Press, 1967), 186.

82. Muhammad, *Message*, 192–205; Clegg, *Original Man*, 157–63, 251–54.

83. Robert L. Allen, *Black Awakening in Capitalist America: An Analytic History* (Garden City, NY: Doubleday, 1969; reprint, Trenton, NJ: Africa World Press, 1990), 183n37, 214–21 (page citations are to the reprint edition). See also Meier and Rudwick, *CORE*, 423–24.

84. Goldman, *Death and Life*, 3–5, 13, 239–56, 380.

85. Ibid.

86. Malcolm X, *Autobiography*, 246, 292. Emphasis in original. See also Goldman, *Death and Life*, 48.

87. Muhammad, *Message*, 308.

88. Elijah Muhammad, *The Fall of America* (Atlanta: Messenger Elijah Muhammad Propagation Society, 1973), 12. The whole book addresses the coming destruction of America.

89. Goldman, *Death and Life*, 96. Emphasis in original.

90. Ibid., 92–106.

91. Clegg, *An Original Man*, 172; see also Goldman, *Death and Life*, 93–94. Emphasis in original.

92. Malcolm X, *Autobiography*, 289.

93. Walter D. Abilla, *The Black Muslims in America: An Introduction to the Theory of Commitment* (Kampala, Uganda: East African Literature Bureau, 1977).

94. William W. Sales, Jr., *From Civil Rights to Black Liberation: Malcolm X and the Organization of Afro-American Unity* (Boston: South End Press, 1994), 109; Malcolm X, *Autobiography*, 452.

95. Sales, *Afro-American Unity*, 109–11; Malcolm X, *Autobiography*, 416–17, 419–20; Goldman, *Death and Life*, 221–38.

96. Kwame Ture and Charles V. Hamilton, *Black Power: The Politics of Liberation in America* (New York: Vintage Books, 1976; reprint New York: Vintage Books, 1976), 19 (page citations are to the reprint edition); Payne, *Light*, 361; Adolph Reed, Jr., Introduction to *Race, Politics, and Culture: Critical Essays on the Radicalism of the 1960s* (New York: Greenwood Press, 1986), 3–10.

97. Ture and Hamilton, *Black Power*; Carson, *In Struggle*, 101, 134–35, 198, 276–77.

98. Keith Danner, review of *Black Power: A Record of Reactions in a Land of Pathos* by Richard Wright, *MELUS*, Fall–Winter, 2000; available from http://www.findarticles.com/cf_dls/m2278/2000_Fall–Winter/74483374/print.jhtml; accessed 11 December 2003. "Wright's Life: 1951–1955"; available from http://home.gwu.edu/~cuff/wright/chronology/1951_1955.html; accessed 20 January 2004.

99. Paul Bohannan and Philip Curtin, *Africa and Africans*, 3d ed. (Prospect Heights, IL: Waveland Press), 365.

100. Martin Luther King, Jr., *Why We Can't Wait* (New York: Signet Books, 1963; reprint New York: Signet Books, 1964), 87–88 (page citations are from the reprint edition). See also *Freedomways* journal and Carson's *In Struggle* to gain an appreciation of Africa for the civil rights movement in general.

101. King, *Can't Wait*, 22.

102. John Henrik Clarke, "The New Afro-American Nationalism," *Freedomways* 1, no. 3 (Fall 1961): 385–95, quotation from 385; E. U. Essien-Udom, "The Nationalist Movements of Harlem," *Freedomways* 3, no. 3 (Summer 1963): 335–42.

103. Clarke, "The New Afro-American Nationalism," 290.

104. Ibid., 294.

105. Ibid., 295.

106. Ibid.

107. Scot Brown, *Fighting for Us: Maulana Karenga, the US Organization, and Black Cultural Nationalism* (New York: New York University Press, 2003).

108. "Jomo Kenyatta," *Encyclopedia Britannica* from Encyclopedia Britan-

nica Online, accessed 3 December 2004, http://search.eb.com/eb/article?tocId=3882.

109. Jomo Kenyatta, *Facing Mount Kenya: The Tribal Life of the Gikuyu* (New York: Vintage Books, 1965), 297.

110. Brown, *Fighting*, 10–17, quotation from 14.

111. Brown, *Fighting*, 10–17, 31–32; Philip S. Foner, ed., *The Black Panthers Speak* (New York: HarperCollins, 1970; reprint New York: Da Capo Press, 1995), ix (page citations are from reprint edition); Max Elbaum, *Revolution in the Air: Sixties Radicals Turn to Lenin, Mao, and Che* (London: Verso, 2002).

112. Clegg, *An Original Man*, 114–15.

113. Chuck Stone, "The National Conference on Black Power," in *The Black Power Revolt: A Collection of Essays*, ed. Floyd B. Barbour (Boston: Extending Horizons Books, 1968), 189.

NOTES TO CHAPTER 4

1. Allen, *Black Awakening*, 193–94, 197–98; Bob Blauner, *Black Lives, White Lives: Three Decades of Race Relations in America* (Berkeley: University of California Press, 1989), 4, 17–20; Max Elbaum, *Revolution in the Air: Sixties Radicals Turn to Lenin, Mao, and Che* (London: Verso, 2002).

2. Norman Kelley, "Memoirs of a Revolutionist," *The Nation*, 8 December 2003, 13–14, 18.

3. See Harvard Sitkoff, *The Struggle for Black Equality, 1954–1980* (New York: Hill and Wang, 1981), 167, 215; Robert Cook, *Sweet Land of Liberty? The African-American Struggle for Civil Rights in the Twentieth Century* (London: Longman, 1998), 201–16; Doug McAdam, *Political Process and the Development of Black Insurgency, 1930–1970* (Chicago: University of Chicago Press,1982), 181–229; Robert Weisbrot, *Freedom Bound: A History of America's Civil Rights Movement* (New York: W. W. Norton, 1990), 259–61.

4. Nikhil Pal Singh, "The Black Panthers and the 'Undeveloped Country' of the Left," in *The Black Panther Party [Reconsidered]*, ed. Charles E. Jones (Baltimore: Black Classic Press, 1988), 61.

5. Scot Ngozi-Brown, "The Us Organization, Maulana Karenga, and Conflict with the Black Panther Party: A Critique of Sectarian Influences on Historical Discourse," *Journal of Black Studies* 28, no. 2 (November 1997), 163. It is credible that "US" originally stood for "United Seven." Huber C. Palmer, "Three Black Nationalist Organizations and Their Impact upon Their Times" (Ph.D. diss., Claremont Graduate School, 1973), 31.

6. From the mid-1960s Maulana Karenga revealed the influence of Marxist ideas in his ideology of "cultural" black nationalism. For example, he argued,

"You cannot have political freedom without an economic base," and "Capitalism is an individual concept. Blacks can only reach a stage of economic force through a co-operative economic system." *The Quotable Karenga*, ed. Clyde Halisi and James Mtume (Los Angeles: US Organization, 1967), 18. The idea for a book of quotations was no doubt modeled on Mao Zedong's *Little Red Book* of quotations. In 1969, Karenga explained how his ideas conformed to Maoist ideas. Maulana Ron Karenga, "Karenga: Revolution Must Wait for the People," *Los Angeles Free Press*, 16 May 1969, 14. Amiri Baraka also makes it clear that "cultural" nationalism embraces socialism. Amiri Baraka, *Kawaida, National Liberation, and Socialism*, Deering Special Collections, Northwestern University Library, Evanston, Illinois. I discuss the socialist ideas and practices of "cultural" nationalists in more detail later in the chapter. For the Panther idea that "cultural" nationalists were black capitalists, see Robert L. Allen, *Black Awakening in Capitalist America: An Analytic History* (Garden City, NY: Doubleday, 1969; reprint, Trenton, NJ: Africa World Press, 1990), 167–68, 191 (page citations are to the reprint edition); Singh, "'Undeveloped Country,'" 66; Tracye Matthews, "'No One Ever Asks, What a Man's Place in the Revolution Is': Gender and the Politics of the Black Panther Party, 1966–1971," in *The Black Panther Party [Reconsidered]*, ed. Charles E. Jones (Baltimore: Black Classic Press, 1988), 271; Brian Ward, "Jazz and Soul, Race and Class, Cultural Nationalists and Black Panthers: A Black Power Debate Revisited," in *Media, Culture, and the Modern African American Freedom Struggle*, ed. Brian Ward (Gainesville: University Press of Florida, 2001), 181.

7. A few scholars are beginning to reappraise the "cultural" nationalism of Black Power. See Komozi Woodard, *A Nation within a Nation: Amiri Baraka (LeRoi Jones) and Black Power Politics* (Chapel Hill: University of North Carolina Press, 1999) and Scot Brown, *Fighting for Us: Maulana Karenga, the US Organization, and Black Cultural Nationalism* (New York: New York University Press, 2003).

8. *Quotable Karenga*, 1.

9. Alexander J. Motyl, ed., "Cultural Nationalism," in *The Encyclopedia of Nationalism* (San Diego, CA: Academic Press, 2001), 107–8; John H. Bracey, Jr., August Meier, and Elliott Rudwick, eds., *Black Nationalism in America* (Indianapolis, IN: Bobbs-Merrill, 1970), xxvi–xxvii.

10. Philip S. Foner, ed., *The Black Panthers Speak* (New York: HarperCollins, 1970; reprint New York: Da Capo Press, 1995), 3–4, xxvii (page citations are from reprint edition); Manning Marable, *Race, Reform, and Rebellion: The Second Reconstruction in Black America, 1945–1990*, rev. 2d ed. (Jackson: University Press of Mississippi, 1991), 109.

11. Karenga, "Revolution Must Wait for the People."

12. For a good discussion of the biased literature on US Organization, see Ngozi-Brown, "The Us Organization."

13. Alphonso Pinkney, *Red, Black and Green: Black Nationalism in the United States* (Cambridge: Cambridge University Press, 1976), 121, 147; Marable, *Race, Reform, and Rebellion*, 107, 134–37; Brown, *Fighting for Us*, 109–13.

14. See, for example, Don L. Lee, *From Plan to Planet: Life Studies: The Need for Afrikan Minds and Institutions* (Detroit and Chicago: Broadside Press and Institute of Positive Education, 1973), 45–46.

15. For the "revolutionary" perspective on African culture, see Huey Newton, "Huey Newton Talks to the Movement about the Black Panther Party, Cultural Nationalism, SNCC, Liberals and White Revolutionies," in Philip S. Foner, *The Black Panthers Speak* (New York: Da Capo Press, 1995), 50; Linda Harrison, "On Cultural Nationalism," in Philip S. Foner, *The Black Panthers Speak* (New York: Da Capo Press, 1995), 151.

16. John H. Bracey, Jr., August Meier, and Elliott Rudwick, *Black Nationalism in America* (Indianapolis, IN: Bobbs-Merrill, 1970), 553, 554, 555.

17. Matthews, "No One Ever Asks," 298n19, and Brown, *Fighting for Us*, 117–18, briefly discuss the interest in African-based religions among Party members.

18. Freedom Library Day School was part of the cultural nationalist confederation called the Council of Independent Black Institutions (CIBI). This confederation will be discussed below. CIBI subscribed to Maulana Karenga's Nguzo Saba. Council of Independent Black Institutions, "Summary from 1st Work Meeting," June 30th–July 3rd, 1972, Labadie Pamphlets, Special Collections Library, University of Michigan, Ann Arbor, 19, 28.

19. William L. Van Deburg, *New Day in Babylon: The Black Power Movement and American Culture, 1965–1975* (Chicago: University of Chicago Press, 1992), 129.

20. Jim Williams, "Death to the Pusher," *Black News*, October 1972, vol. 1, no. 43, 3.

21. Eugene Perkins, "The Need for a Pan-Africanist Alternative to the Street Institution," *Black Books Bulletin* 2, no. 3/4 (Winter 1974): 9–11. See also "Afrikan Youth Day: South Bend, Indiana," *Fundisha: Congress of African People* 1, no. 3, in *Black News* 2, no. 8 (8 September 1973): 9, and Kasisi Jitu Weusi, interview by Carlos E. Russell, 15 January 1977, in "Project Demonstrating Excellence: Perspectives on Power: A Black Community Looks at Itself (Profiles in Political Acumen)," by Carlos E. Russell, submitted to the Union Graduate School, 595. Robert Beecher Papers, Manuscripts, Archives and Rare Books Division, Schomburg Center for Research in Black Culture, New York, NY.

22. Ward, "Jazz and Soul," 187.

23. Angela Y. Davis, "Afro Images: Politics, Fashion, and Nostalgia," in *Soul: Black Power, Politics, and Pleasure*, ed. Monique Guillory and Richard C. Green (New York: New York University Press, 1998), 23.

24. Halisi and Mtume, *Quotable Karenga*, 7.

25. Karenga, *Kawaida Theory: An Introductory Outline* (Inglewood, CA: Kawaida Publications, 1980), 16–20, quotations from 18 and 19.

26. Ward, "Jazz and Soul," 187; Foner, *Black Panthers Speak*, 4–6.

27. See for example, Van Deburg, *New Day in Babylon*; Monique Guillory and Richard C. Green, ed., *Soul: Black Power, Politics, and Pleasure* (New York: New York University Press, 1998).

28. Van Deburg, *New Day in Babylon*, ix.

29. Ibid., 9.

30. Sitkoff, *The Struggle for Black Equality*, 215; McAdam, *The Development of Black Insurgency*, 181–229; Weisbrot, *Freedom Bound*, 259, 261.

31. Adolph Reed, Jr., has an excellent critique of the reification of the civil rights and Black Power movements in historical analyses in his Introduction to *Race, Politics, and Culture: Critical Essays on the Radicalism of the 1960s* (Westport, CT: Greenwood Press, 1986), 3–10, quotation 5. Doug McAdam's *Black Insurgency* presents a good dialectical theory of social movements but he does not really apply this perspective to his understanding of Black Power.

32. Martin Luther King, Jr., *Stride toward Freedom: The Montgomery Story* (New York: Harper and Brothers, 1958), 63.

33. Payne, *I've Got the Light of Freedom*, 361. We can also take Martin Luther King, Jr.'s title "Stride toward *Freedom*" as additional evidence. King, *Stride*. See also Reed, Introduction to *Race, Politics, and Culture*, 3–10.

34. See Ture and Hamilton, *Black Power*, 16–23; Allen, *Black Awakening*, 23–28.

35. Hugh Davis Graham, "The Role of Ideas in the African-American Civil Rights Movement: The Problem of the Color-Blind Constitution," in *Ideas, Ideologies and Social Movements: The United States Experience since 1800*, ed. Peter A. Coclanis and Stuart Bruchey (Columbia: University of South Carolina Press, 1999), 131. See also Cook, *Sweet Land*, 217; Payne, *Light*, 437.

36. Aside from SNCC and CORE, the only other organization that receives any substantial attention is the Black Panther Party. See Sitkoff, *The Struggle for Black Equality*; McAdam, *The Development of Black Insurgency*; Cook, *Sweet Land*; Mary Frances Berry and John W. Blassingame, *Long Memory: The Black Experience in America* (New York: Oxford University Press, 1982).

37. Carson, *In Struggle*; Meier and Rudwick, *CORE*.

38. Baraka, *African Congress*, vii.

39. Chuck Stone, "The National Conference on Black Power," in *The Black Power Revolt: A Collection of Essays*, ed. Floyd B. Barbour (Boston: Extending Horizons Books, 1968), 189.

40. Adam Clayton Powell, "Seek Audacious Power," *Negro Digest*, August 1966, 6.

41. Ibid.

42. Powell, "Seek Audacious Power," 6; the Black Power Conference resolution is quoted in Allen, *Black Awakening*, 65.

43. Leslie Campbell, "The Black Teacher and Black Power," in *What Black Educators Are Saying*, ed. Nathan Wright, Jr. (New York: Hawthorn Books, 1970), 23.

44. *Black Power Conference Reports*, 15.

45. Baraka, *African Congress*, 107.

46. Halisi and Mtume, *Quotable Karenga*, 18.

47. Baraka, *African Congress*, 107–11.

48. See also McCartney, *Black Power Ideologies*, 122–23; Charles E. Jones, ed., *The Black Panther Party [Reconsidered]* (Baltimore: Black Classic Press, 1998), 26, 31, 162.

49. Manning Marable, *Race, Reform, and Rebellion: The Second Reconstruction in Black America, 1945–1990*, rev. 2d ed. (Jackson: University Press of Mississippi, 1991), 133–34.

50. Baraka, *African Congress*, 108.

51. Ibid., 107–8. Emphasis in original.

52. Ibid., 108.

53. Stone, "National Conference," 189; *Black Power Conference Reports*; Baraka, *African Congress*, 94; Charlayne Hunter, "New Party Urged for World Blacks," *New York Times*, 5 September 1970; Woodard, *Nation within a Nation*, 159–218; Rudy Johnson, "Neighbors Look at Black Parley," *New York Times*, 1 September 1968.

54. See Allen, *Black Awakening*, 1–20; Ture and Hamilton, *Black Power*, 2–32.

55. *Eyes on the Prize II: America at the Racial Crossroads, 1965–1985*, prod. and dir. by Blackside Inc. and Corporation for Public Broadcasting (Alexandria, VA: distributed by PBS Video, 1989–1990).

56. Payne, *Light*, 361, 437; Reed, *Race, Politics*, 3–10.

57. For a good overview of Black Power and the diversity of black organizations, see Robert C. Smith, "Black Power and the Transformation from Protest to Politics," *Political Science Quarterly* 96(3), Autumn 1981: 436–37. For more detailed discussions of some Black Power political parties, see Ture and Hamilton, *Black Power*; Hardy Thomas Frye, "The Rise of a Black Political Party [of Alabama]: Institutional Consequences of Emerging Political Consciousness" (Ph.D. diss., University of California, Berkeley, 1975); "Historically Black Political Party [of South Carolina] Still Alive," *The Crisis*, November/December 2002, 9; Woodard, *A Nation within a Nation*; Warren N. Holmes, "The National Black Independent Political Party: Political Insurgency or Ideological Convergence?" (Ph.D. diss., University of Cincinnati, 1995).

To appreciate the Congressional Black Caucus as a product of Black Power, see Robert Singh, *The Congressional Black Caucus: Racial Politics in the U.S.*

Congress (Thousand Oaks, CA: Sage Publications, 1998), 54–57, 74–75; and Manning Marable's discussions of the Black Caucus's involvement with black nationalist politics in *Race, Reform, and Rebellion*. Jerry Gafio Watts discusses the formation of black caucuses of various sorts during Black Power, in *Heroism and the Black Intellectual: Ralph Ellison, Politics, and Afro-American Intellectual Life* (Chapel Hill: University of North Carolina Press, 1994), 6. For references to support for African independence movements, see Doughty, "The Contemporary Independent Black School Movement," 213; Lee, *From Plan to Planet*, 7.

For general overviews of Black Power activism, see Bracey, Meier, and Rudwick, *Black Nationalism*; William L. Van Deburg, ed., *Modern Black Nationalism: From Marcus Garvey to Louis Farrakhan* (New York: New York University Press, 1997); Marable, *Race, Reform, and Rebellion*.

58. This analysis is derived from Robert C. Smith. Dates were available for only 166 of the 350 organizations. If we assume that all the organizations without dates were founded before the Black Power era, then 21 percent (73 out of 350) would have been from the Black Power era. If we assume that the organizations missing dates are randomly dispersed, then the dated sample should be roughly equivalent to the whole sample. Smith makes this assumption and concludes that 44 percent (73 out of 166) were from the Black Power era. Smith, "The Transformation," 436.

59. Smith, "The Transformation," 436–37; Charles L. Sanders and Linda McLean, *Directory: National Black Organizations*, 2d printing (Harlem, NY: Afram Associates, 1972), 11, 45–48,

60. McAdam, *Political Process*, 182–86; Sitkoff, *Black Equality*, 215; Meier and Rudwick, *CORE*, 425.

61. For example, the anthropologist Melville J. Herskovits, in *The Myth of the Negro Past*, observes that in comparing the then existing research on African and Afroamerican culture, "we find far more attention paid to the religious aspect of Afroamerican cultures than to their social or economic forms, while in African research emphasis is laid almost exclusively on social, political and economic institutions" (Boston: Beacon Press, 1958), xxxiv. For Herskovits, religious, social, political, and economic institutions were all separate aspects of "culture." See also Brown, *Fighting for Us*, 11.

62. See Berry and Blassingame, *Long Memory*, 412–14, 420–21; Weisbrot, *Freedom Bound*, 222–34; Marable, *Race, Reform, and Rebellion*, 106–7, 146.

63. "Nikki Giovanni: Biographic Sketch," *BookSlave: Poetry by Women*, accessed 3 December 2004, http://pages.ivillage.com/crowyne/nikkibio.html.

64. Nikki Giovanni's poems are quoted in Marable, *Race, Reform, and Rebellion* (106 and 107), as part of a discussion of the "cultural" nationalist leaders Amiri Baraka, Maulana Karenga, and Black Power poetry. It is clear that for Marable, Giovanni is a "cultural" nationalist (see also 146), yet there is

no reason why Giovanni's ideas should not be seen as "revolutionary" as those of Malcolm X, who Marable considers a revolutionary nationalist (see 87–90).

65. See Berry and Blassingame, *Long Memory*, 412–14, 420–21; Weisbrot, *Freedom Bound*, 222–34.

66. Maulana Karenga, *In Love and Struggle: Poems for Bold Hearts* (San Diego, CA: Kawaida Publications, 1978).

67. Scot Ngozi-Brown, "The Us Organization, Maulana Karenga, and Conflict with the Black Panther Party: A Critique of Sectarian Influences on Historical Discourse," *Journal of Black Studies* 28, no. 2 (November 1997): 157–70.

68. Huey Newton, "Huey Newton Talks to the Movement about the Black Panther Party, Cultural Nationalism, SNCC, Liberals and White Revolutionaries," in Philip S. Foner, *The Black Panthers Speak* (New York: Da Capo Press, 1995), 50. See also Ngozi-Brown, "The Us Organization," 157–70.

69. Linda Harrison, "On Cultural Nationalism," in Philip S. Foner, *The Black Panthers Speak* (New York: Da Capo Press, 1995), 151.

70. Ibid.

71. Ngozi-Brown, "The Us Organization," 157–70.

72. "Kenyatta, Jomo," *Encyclopedia Britannica* from Encyclopedia Britannica Online, http://search.eb.com/eb/article?tocId=3882, accessed 12 December 2004.

73. They are also known as Kikuyu, Giguyu, Gekoyo, and Agekoyo.

74. Jomo Kenyatta, *Facing Mount Kenya: The Tribal Life of the Gikuyu* (New York: Knopf, 1962; reprint, New York: Vintage Books, 1965), 126, 263, 309 (page citations are from the reprint edition); Brown, *Fighting for Us*, 11–12.

75. Brown, *Fighting for Us*, 11–12.

76. Brown, *Fighting for Us*, 163. According to the Kamusi Project dictionary, "maulana" means "lord" or "master," http://www.yale.edu/swahili/, searched 13 December 2004.

77. Kenyatta, *Facing Mount Kenya*, 297.

78. Ibid., 305.

79. Brown, *Fighting for Us*, 10–17, quotation from 14.

80. Maulana Ron Karenga, "Karenga: Revolution Must Wait for the People," *Los Angeles Free Press*, 16 May 1969, 14.

81. Halisi and Mtume, *Quotable Karenga*, 7.

82. Karenga, "Revolution Must Wait for the People."

83. Halisi, *Kitabu*, 8.

84. Ibid., 8n14.

85. Ngozi-Brown, "The Us Organization." We should note that US Organization and other "cultural" nationalists saw themselves as revolutionary and believed the tactics of the Black Panther Party incapable of bringing about social change. See Karenga, "Revolution Must Wait for the People." For loosely veiled

criticisms of the Panthers' tactics by "cultural" nationalists, see Imamu Amiri Baraka, ed., *African Congress: A Documentary of the First Modern Pan-African Congress* (New York: William Morrow, 1972), 95, 98–99; Don L. Lee, *From Plan to Planet: Life Studies: The Need for Afrikan Minds and Institutions* (Detroit and Chicago: Broadside Press and Institute of Positive Education, 1973), 24.

86. Foner, *Black Panthers Speak*, ix; Palmer, "Three Black Nationalist Organizations," 7.

87. Foner, *Black Panthers Speak*, ix–x; Brown, *Fighting for Us*, 22–25.

88. Kenneth O'Reilly, *"Racial Matters": The FBI's Secret File on Black America, 1960–1972* (New York: Free Press, 1989), 305.

89. "Partial List of Black Congress," *Harambee*, 28 December 1967, 8.

90. Ngozi-Brown, "The Us Organization," 165–66.

91. Angela Davis, *Angela Davis: An Autobiography* (New York: International Publishers, 1988), 167.

92. Matthews, "'No One Ever Asks,'" 272.

93. Brown, *Fighting for Us*, 53–55, 88–91.

94. Brian Ward points out the similarities between the two organizations in relation to the arts in "Jazz and Soul," 161–96. For samples of the poetry from *The Black Panther* newspaper, see Foner, *Black Panthers Speak*, 20, 25, 26, 29, 31, xl for the national anthem and 16–18 for their views on revolutionary art. Regina Jennings talks about late-night poetry reading and community dances sponsored by the Party in "Why I Joined the Party: An Africana Womanist Reflection," in *The Black Panther Party [Reconsidered]*, ed. Charles E. Jones (Baltimore: Black Classic Press, 1988), 261. Eugene Victor Wolfenstein discusses Elaine Brown in "New Souls for Old? Race, Gender and the Transformational Effects of Social Movements," *Studies in Gender and Sexuality* 1, no. 4 (Fall 2000): 414. The "cultural" nationalist schools will be discussed in detail below. For information about Panther schools, see Foner, *Black Panthers Speak*, 170–73, and Charles E. Jones, ed., *The Black Panther Party [Reconsidered]* (Baltimore: Black Classic Press, 1988), 185–86. Matthews, "No One Ever Asks," 298n19, and Brown, *Fighting for Us*, 117–18, briefly discuss the interest among Party members in African-based religions.

95. Brown, *Fighting for Us*, 119. Moreover, the "revolutionary" Young Lords Organization who were allies of the Black Panther Party were also allies of Amiri Baraka's "cultural" nationalist organization. See Foner, *Black Panthers Speak*, 229–39; Baraka, *African Congress*, 359.

96. In response to the murder of the Chicago Panthers Mark Clark and Fred Hampton, the editor of *Black News*, the Brooklyn, New York, "cultural" nationalist newspaper, argued that "When the law zeroes in on a political party movement with the intention of murdering the leaders, the agents of the law must be frightened." Therefore the Black Panthers *"must be doing something*

right." The editor concluded by making clear his support for the aims of the Black Panthers as opposed to the aims of the NAACP.

> The object of politics is to govern. To control. To make the decisions. The Black Panthers among others have begun to challenge the pig power structure. The murders are the reaction to this challenge. Self defense and community control are the tools for acquiring that political control. The NAACP and some of the nation's fat cat business lawyers want another "investigation" of the Chicago Black Panther killings. At its best, this can only mean a whitewash of this racist system. They serve up a pig fall guy. But the system survives to kill other blacks.

Black News, 19 December 1969, 2.

For a "cultural" nationalist critiquing "reactionary nationalism," see Baraka, *African Congress*, 323; John Churchville, "On Correct Black Education," in *What Black Educators Are Saying*, ed. Nathan Wright, Jr. (New York: Hawthorn Books, 1970), 177–82; Jitu Weusi, "From Relevance to Excellence: The Challenge of Independent Black Educational Institutions," *Black Books Bulletin*, vol. 2, no. 3/4 (Winter 1974): 21.

97. Brown's *Fighting for Us* provides the best history of US Organization as a political organization and its dealings with the Black Panther Party. Angela Davis also provides an account of black nationalist politics in Southern California in the late 1960s. She mentions US Organization having a violent conflict with the United Front and discusses the attempts of both US and the Panthers to dominate her and her organization. Davis, *Autobiography*, 158–76.

98. Berry and Blassingame, *Long Memory*, 421; Weisbrot, *Freedom Bound*, 227–28, 230.

99. Marable, *Race, Reform, and Rebellion*, 132. Komozi Woodard provides the best history of Amiri Baraka and the political activities of his organization. For a discussion of the organizing that led to the Gary Convention, see Komozi Woodard, *A Nation within a Nation: Amiri Baraka (LeRoi Jones) and Black Power Politics* (Chapel Hill: University of North Carolina Press, 1999), chapter 5.

100. Afrikan Free School Inc., *Afrikan Free School: Education Text*; Woodard, *A Nation*, 134–35.

101. Carol D. Lee, "Profile of an Independent Black Institution," 162; Lee, *From Plan to Planet*, 7; http://www.thirdworldpressinc.com/message.htm, accessed 13 February 2004.

102. Brown, *Fighting for Us*, 154–55; Kalamu ya Salaam, "Art for Life: My Story, My Song," *Chicken Bones: A Journal for Literary and Artistic African-American Themes*, http://www.nathanielturner.com/artforlife10.htm, accessed 13 February 2004.

103. Uhuru Sasa Shule, *The Parent Handbook*, 4.

104. Weusi, Interview by Carlos E. Russell, 591.

105. *Black News*, 29 April 1970, 9.

106. Halisi and Mtume, *Quotable Karenga*, 18; see also Halisi, *Kitabu*, 10–11.

107. Halisi and Mtume, *Quotable Karenga*, 1, 5, 17, 29; Churchville, "On Correct Education," 177–82; Doughty, "Independent Black School Movement," 235–36; Foner, *Black Panthers Speak*, 51–52.

108. Halisi, *Kitabu*, 10–11.

109. Brown, *Fighting for Us*, 151–53.

110. Lee, *From Plan to Planet*, 45–46.

111. The only difference is in the "survival programs" like the free-breakfast program. But certainly these programs are not the basis for distinguishing the "cultural" from the "revolutionary."

112. On the educational activities of the Panthers, see Jones, *[Reconsidered]*, 185–86.

113. Gerald David Jaynes and Robin M. Williams, Jr., *A Common Destiny: Blacks and American Society* (Washington, DC: National Academy Press, 1989), 76, 332.

114. The Africa Free School was part of Amiri Baraka's CFUN. New Concept Development Center was part of Haki Madhubuti's Institute for Positive Education. Uhuru Sasa Shule was part of Kasisi Jitu Weusi's East confederation. US Organization's School of Afroamerican Culture was not part of CIBI.

115. Doughty, "The Contemporary Independent Black School Movement"; Baraka, *African Congress*, 314–33; Frank J. Satterwhite, ed., *Planning an Independent Black Institution* (New York: Afram Associates, 1971), 29.

116. Doughty, "The Contemporary Independent Black School Movement"; Baraka, *African Congress*, 314–33.

117. Baraka, *African Congress*, 315.

118. Ibid., 315–16.

119. Ibid., 317. Emphasis in original.

120. Ibid. Emphasis in original.

121. Ibid. Emphasis in original.

122. See also *Black Power Conference Reports* (Harlem, NY: Afram Associates, 1970), 61–67, 72–74.

123. Council of Independent Black Institutions, "Summary from 1st Work Meeting," June 30th–July 3rd, 1972, Labadie Pamphlets, Special Collections Library, University of Michigan, Ann Arbor, 22.

124. Ibid., 19.

125. Ibid., 5, 28.

126. Doughty, "The Contemporary Independent Black School Movement."

127. Craig C. Brookins, "A Descriptive Analysis of Ten Independent Black Educational Models" (M.A. Thesis, Michigan State University, 1984), 22.

128. Baraka, *African Congress*, 285.

129. For example, six months before CIBI was established, activists in Alabama formed the Federation of Child-Care Centers of Alabama which advocated black community control of educational resources in Alabama. This organization and the existence of CIBI schools and non-CIBI black nationalist schools in the South shows that Black Power was a national movement, not one restricted to the North. Wekesa Madzimoyo, "African-Americans Educate Their Own," *Southern Exposure* 3, 1980, 44.

130. Nairobi Day School, Nairobi College, the Center for New Horizons, Uhuru Sasa Shule ("Freedom Now School") and Umoja Sasa Shule ("Unity Now School") are some of the schools that had this philosophy. Daniels, *A Profile of Several Black Community Schools*; Coleman, *Black Children Just Keep on Growing*; Hoover, "The Nairobi Day School," *Journal of Negro Education* 61, no. 2 (1992): 203–4; Doughty, "The Contemporary Independent Black School Movement," 235–36.

131. Afrikan Free School Inc., *Afrikan Free School: Education Text* (Newark, NJ: Jihad Publishing Co., 1974), 6–7.

132. Carol D. Lee, "Profile of an Independent Black Institution: African-Centered Education at Work," *Journal of Negro Education* 61, no. 2 (1992): 172–73; Doughty, "The Contemporary Independent Black School Movement."

133. Doughty, "The Contemporary Independent Black School Movement," 153–58.

134. Kasisi Yusef Iman, *The Weusi Alfabeti* (Brooklyn, NY: Uhuru Sasa School, n.d.), Schomburg Center for Research on Black Culture, New York Public Library; Seitu Jim Dyson, ed., *Yesterday . . . Today and Tomorrow: A Black Reading Experience* (Brooklyn, NY: An East Publication: Uhuru Sasa School, 1972), Schomburg Center for Research on Black Culture, New York Public Library.

135. Dyson, *Yesterday . . . Today and Tomorrow*, 16, 56, 59.

136. Afrikan Free School Inc., *Afrikan Free School*; Coleman, *Black Children Just Keep on Growing*, 41–52.

137. Ovid Abrams, "Uhuru Sasa: A School Devoted to Freedom and Education," *Fundiasha* in *Black News*, 28 January 1974, vol. 2, no. 13, Schomburg Center for Research on Black Culture, New York Public Library, 7.

138. Doughty, "The Contemporary Independent Black School Movement," 252.

139. Ibid., 133.

140. Doughty, "The Contemporary Independent Black School Movement," 236. Other black nationalists at this time saw the black lower classes as the most authentic blacks. See Don L. Lee, *Think Black* (Detroit: Broadside Press, 1967), 7, 12–14; Ben Martin, "From Negro to Black to African American: The Power of Names and Naming," *Political Science Quarterly* 106, no. 1 (1991): 83–107.

141. Daniels, *A Profile of Several Black Community Schools*, 63.

142. Joy Davis, former Weusi Shule student, personal communication. The Martin Luther King, Jr. Community School in Atlanta taught boys carpentry. Coleman, *Black Children Just Keep on Growing*, 110. Centers for New Horizons, Inc., in Chicago instructed parents and staff in carpentry. Daniels, *A Profile of Several Black Community Schools*, 3–7.

143. Afrikan Free School Inc., *Afrikan Free School*.

144. Daniels, *A Profile of Several Black Community Schools*, 59–65.

145. Carol D. Lee, Kofi Lomotey, and Mwalimu Shujaa, "How Shall We Sing Our Sacred Song in a Strange Land? The Dilemma of Double Consciousness and the Complexities of an African-Centered Pedagogy," *Journal of Education* 172, no. 2 (1990): 53–54.

146. Iman, *The Weusi Alfabeti*.

147. Uhuru Sasa Shule, *The Parent Handbook* (Brooklyn, NY: Uhuru Sasa Shule, 1980), Schomburg Center for Research on Black Culture, New York Public Library, 8.

148. Dyson, *Yesterday . . . Today and Tomorrow*, 8, 13.

149. Ibid., 72–73.

150. Baraka, *African Congress*, 315–16.

151. Halisi and Mtume, *Quotable Karenga*, 20–21; Angela Davis, *Angela Davis*, 161, 374.

152. Coleman, *Black Children Just Keep on Growing*, 35–52.

153. Ibid., 110.

154. Doughty, "The Contemporary Independent Black School Movement," 130.

155. Shalewa Crowe, presentation for Mariame Kaba's course, "Black Education: Problems and Promise," Department of Sociology, Northwestern University, 5 May 2000; Dyson, *Yesterday . . . Today and Tomorrow*.

156. Doughty, "The Contemporary Independent Black School Movement," 256.

157. Afrikan Free School Inc., *Afrikan Free School*.

158. Lee, "Profile of an Independent Black Institution," 162.

159. Uhuru Sasa Shule, *The Parent Handbook*, 4.

160. Shalewa Crowe, presentation for "Black Education"; A. Dahleen Glanton, "An Afrocentric School Breaks from the Norm," *Chicago Tribune*, 19 October 1990, Section 2C, 1; Council of Independent Black Institutions, *Positive Afrikan Images for Children: Social Studies Curriculum* (Trenton, NJ: Red Sea Press, 1990), 51.

161. See Afrikan Free School Inc., *Afrikan Free School*; Dyson, *Yesterday . . . Today and Tomorrow*.

162. Doughty, "The Contemporary Independent Black School Movement," 213.

163. Baraka, *African Congress*, 310.

164. *Black News*, 21 March 1970, vol. 1, no. 11, 1.

165. Baraka, *African Congress*, 22.

166. Ibid., 32.

167. Sitkoff, *Struggle for Black Equality*, 216; Van DeBurg, *New Day in Babylon*, 9, 306.

168. Baraka, *African Congress*, 323. Emphasis in original.

169. Council of Independent Black Institutions, "Summary from 1st Work Meeting," 6.

170. John Churchville, "On Correct Black Education," in *What Black Educators Are Saying*, ed. Nathan Wright, Jr. (New York: Hawthorn Books, 1970), 177–82. See also Jitu Weusi, "From Relevance to Excellence: The Challenge of Independent Black Educational Institutions," *Black Books Bulletin*, vol. 2, no. 3/4 (Winter 1974): 21.

171. See Churchville, "On Correct Black Education"; Molefi Kete Asante, "Systematic Nationalism: A Legitimate Strategy for National Selfhood," *Journal of Black Studies* 9, no. 1 (September 1978): 115.

NOTES TO CHAPTER 5

1. *Newsweek*, 23 September 1991, has several articles on Afrocentrism and provides a brief overview of the Afrocentric era upto 1991. Peter C. Murrell, "Chartering the Village: The Making of an African-Centered School," *Urban Education* 33, no. 5 (1999): 566, provides the estimate of the growth in Afrocentric public schools but he does not provide a source for this estimate. It is credible based on my research. See the following for discussion of specific Afrocentric schools and curricula: Carol Ascher, "School Programs for African-American Males . . . and Females," *Phi Delta Kappan*, June 1992, 777; Clifford Watson and Geneva Smitherman, *Educating African American Males: Detroit's Malcolm X Academy Solution* (Chicago: Third World Press, 1996), 23–34; Zollie Stevenson, Jr., and Lillian Gonzalez, "Contemporary Practices in Multicultural Approaches to Education among the Largest American School Disticts," *Journal of Negro Education* 61, no. 3 (1992): 359–61; Jeffrey R. Henig et al., *The Color of School Reform: Race, Politics, and the Challenge of Urban Education* (Princeton: Princeton University Press, 1999), 77.

2. For a discussion of these competing definitions, see Imani Perry, "'I Am Still Thirsty': A Theorization on the Authority and Cultural Location of Afrocentism," in *Freedom's Plow: Teaching in the Multicultural Classroom*, ed. Theresa Perry and James W. Fraser (New York: Routledge, 1993), 261–70.

3. Molefi Kete Asante, *Afrocentricity*, new rev. ed. (Trenton, NJ: Africa World Press, 1988), 39.

4. William L. Van Deburg claimed that the Black Power movement *was*

"essentially cultural" in *New Day in Babylon: The Black Power Movement and American Culture, 1965–1975* (Chicago: University of Chicago Press, 1992), 9.

5. Melville J. Herskovits, *The Myth of the Negro Past* (Boston: Beacon Press, 1958), 32.

6. Wade W. Nobles, "African Philosophy: Foundations for Black Psychology," in *Black Psychology*, ed. Reginald L. Jones (New York: Harper & Row, 1972), 18.

7. Wade W. Nobles, "Ancient Egyptian Thought and the Development of African (Black) Psychology," in *Kemet and the African Worldview: Research, Rescue and Restoration*, ed. Maulana Karenga and Jacob H. Carruthers (Los Angeles: University of Sankore Press, 1986), 100–118.

8. Maulana Karenga and Jacob H. Carruthers, eds., *Kemet and the African Worldview: Research, Rescue and Restoration* (Los Angeles: University of Sankore Press, 1986), xiii, 164; Molefi Kete Asante, *The Afrocentric Idea* (Philadelphia: Temple University Press, 1987), 9.

9. Molefi Kete Asante, "African and African American Communication Continuities" (Buffalo: State University of New York at Buffalo: Council of International Studies, 1975), 1, 3; Asante, *Afrocentricity*, ix. For some other Afrocentrists bearing Herskovits's influence, see Janice E. Hale, *Black Children: Their Roots, Culture, and Learning Styles* (Baltimore: Johns Hopkins University Press, 1986), 12–17, and Reginald L. Jones, ed., *Black Psychology*, 3d ed. (Berkeley, CA: Cobb & Henry, 1991) which has a number of Afrocentric articles.

10. Asa G. Hilliard, III, Lucretia Payton-Stewart, and Larry Obadele Williams, eds., *Infusion of African and African American Content in the School Curriculum: Proceedings of the First National Conference* (Chicago: Third World Press, 1990), xx–xxi.

11. Asante, *Afrocentricity*, 2.

12. Asante, *Afrocentric Idea*, 10.

13. See Karenga and Carruthers, *Kemet and the African Worldview*, 4, 25, 128; Jawanza Kunjufu, *Lessons from History: A Celebration in Blackness, Jr.-Sr. High Edition* (Chicago: African American Images, 1987), 9–10.

14. Jacob H. Carruthers, "The Wisdom of Governance in Kemet," in *Kemet and the African Worldview: Research, Rescue and Restoration*, ed. Maulana Karenga and Jacob H. Carruthers (Los Angeles, University of Sankore Press, 1986), 4. Notes omitted from quoted text.

15. Asante, *Afrocentric Idea*, 18.

16. Curriculum and Instruction Department, Portland Public Schools, "Portland Model," rev., 26 May 1993 [unpublished document]. Very similar information is reproduced on the Portland Public Schools website. See www.pps.k12.or.us/district/depts/essays.shtml and www.pps.k12.or.us/district/depts/philosophy.shtml.

17. Carruthers, "The Wisdom of Governance in Kemet," 4. Notes omitted from quoted text.

18. Maulana Karenga, "Restoration of the Husia: Reviving a Sacred Legacy," in *Kemet and the African Worldview: Research, Rescue and Restoration*, ed. Maulana Karenga and Jacob H. Carruthers (Los Angeles, University of Sankore Press, 1986), 89, 94.

19. Kwame Kenyatta, *Guide to Implementing Afrikan-Centered Education* (Detroit: Afrikan Way Investments, 1998), 9–10.

20. Nobles lists "Individuality," "Uniqueness," and "Differences" as "Psychobehavioral Modalities" of the "European World View," and "Groupness," "Sameness," and "Commonality" as representing the modalities of the "African World View." Nobles's chart is cited in Nsenga Warfield-Coppock, *Afrocentric Theory and Applications*, vol. 1: *Adolescent Rites of Passage* (Washington, DC: Baobab Associates, 1990), 12.

21. Nobles's chart is cited in Warfield-Coppock, *Afrocentric Theory and Applications*, vol. 1, 24.

22. John Henrik Clarke, Introduction to *The Cultural Unity of Black Africa: The Domains of Patriarchy and Matriarchy in Classical Antiquity* by Cheikh Anta Diop (Chicago: Third World Press, 1978), iii; Ife Jogunosimi, "The Role of Royal Women in Ancient Kemet," in *Kemet and the African Worldview: Research, Rescue and Restoration*, ed. Maulana Karenga and Jacob H. Carruthers (Los Angeles: University of Sankore Press, 1986), 31–42; Marian Ma' At-Ka Re Monges, "Reflections on the Role of Female Dieties and Queens of Ancient Kemet," *Journal of Black Studies* 23(4), June 1993: 561–70.

23. Valethia Watkins, "Womanism and Black Feminism: Issues in the Manipulation of African Historiography," in *African World History Project: The Preliminary Challenge*, ed. Jacob H. Carruthers and Leon C. Harris (Los Angeles: Association for the Study of Classical African Civilizations, 1997), 249, 284.

24. Algernon Austin, "Theorizing Difference within Black Feminist Thought: The Dilemma of Sexism in Black Communities," *Race, Gender and Class* 6, no. 3 (1999): 60–61.

25. T. Owens Moore, *The Science of Melanin: Dispelling the Myths* (Silver Spring, MD: Venture Books/Beckham House, 1995), 4.

26. Moore, *Melanin*, 6–13; Robert Elliot Fox, "Afrocentrism and the X-Factor," *Transition*, issue 57 (1992): 22–23.

27. Moore, *Melanin*, 6.

28. Ibid., 15.

29. Stephen Howe, *Afrocentrism: Mythical Pasts and Imagined Homes* (London: Verso, 1998), 122–23.

30. J. Gordon Melton, "An Overview of the New Age Movement," *New Age Encyclopedia* (Detroit: Gale Research, 1990), xiii–xxxiii.

31. Moore, *Melanin*, 105–6.

32. Ibid., 106–7.

33. Portland Public Schools, ed., *African-American Baseline Essays*, rev. (Portland, OR: Portland Public Schools, 1988), S-41.

34. Mary Lefkowitz, *Not Out of Africa: How Afrocentrism Became an Excuse to Teach Myth as History* (New York: Basic Books, 1997); Clarence E. Walker, *We Can't Go Home Again: An Argument about Afrocentrism* (New York: Oxford University Press, 2001); Kwame Anthony Appiah, *In My Father's House: Africa in the Philosophy of Culture* (New York: Oxford University Press, 1992); Diane Ravitch, "Multiculturalism: E Plurbus Plures," *American Scholar* 59, no. 3 (1990): 337–54; Molefi Kete Asante and Diane Ravitch, "Multiculturalism: An Exchange," *American Scholar* 60, no. 2 (1991): 267–76; Craig L. Frisby, "One Giant Step Backward: Myths of Black Cultural Learning Styles," *School Psychology Review* 22, no. 3 (1993): 535–57; Janice E. Hale, "Rejoinder to '. . . Myths of Black Cultural Learning Styles': In Defense of Afrocentric Scholarship," *School Psychology Review* 22, no. 3 (1993): 558–61; Tina Q. Richardson, "Black Cultural Learning Styles: Is It Really a Myth?" *School Psychology Review* 22, no. 3 (1993): 562–67; Craig L. Frisby, Ò'Afrocentric' Explanations for School Failure: Symptoms of Denial, Frustration, and Despair," *School Psychology Review* 22, no. 3 (1993): 568–77; Bernard Ortiz de Montellano, "Multicultural Pseudoscience: Spreading Scientific Illiteracy among Minorities, Part 1," *Skeptical Inquirer*, Fall 1991, http://www.csicop.org/si/9111/minority.html, accessed 23 July 2004; Bernard Ortiz de Montellano, "Magic Melanin: Spreading Scientific Illiteracy among Minorities, Part 2," *Skeptical Inquirer*, Winter 1992, http://www.csicop.org/si/9201/minority.html, accessed 23 July 2004. Asante responds to many of these specific authors and their positions in *The Painful Demise of Eurocentrism* (Trenton, NJ: Africa World Press, 1999).

35. Paul M. Sniderman and Thomas Piazza, *Black Pride and Black Prejudice* (Princeton: Princeton University Press, 2002), 37.

36. Ibid., 23, 24.

37. Natalie Angier, "Patients Rushing to Alternatives," *New York Times*, 28 January 1993, Section A, 12.

38. Ibid.; Gina Kolata, "On the Finges of Health Care, Untested Therapies Thrive," *New York Times*, 17 June 1996, Section A, 1.

39. Sniderman and Piazza, *Black Pride*, 37; Wilson Jeremiah Moses, *Afrotopia: The Roots of African American Popular History* (Cambridge: Cambridge University Press, 1998), 32.

40. Moore, *Melanin*, 4.

41. Molefi Kete Asante, *Kemet, Afrocenticity and Knowledge* (Trenton, NJ: Africa World Press, 1990), 147.

42. Kunjufu, *Lessons from History*, 2.

43. Daima M. Clark, "Similarities between Egyptian and Dogon Perception of Man, God and Nature," in *Kemet and the African Worldview: Research, Rescue and Restoration*, ed. Maulana Karenga and Jacob H. Carruthers (Los Angeles: University of Sankore Press, 1986), 127.

44. For example, Molefi Kete Asante sees his work as being in opposition to "human insensitivity, interracial hatred, and cultural bias." Asante, *Afrocentric Idea*, vii.

45. Archie, "The Centered School," 98.

46. Ibid., 103.

47. Curriculum and Instruction Department, Portland Public Schools, "Portland Model," rev. 26 May 1993 [unpublished document]. Very similar information is reproduced on the Portland Public Schools website. See www.pps.k12.or .us/district/depts/essays.shtml and www.pps.k12.or.us/district/depts/philosophy .shtml.

48. Molefi Kete Asante, *Afrocentrism*, new rev. ed. (Trenton, NJ: Africa World Press, 1988), 2.

49. Asante, *Afrocentric Idea*, 10.

50. Asante, *Afrocentricity*, 39, 30. Even in the Afrocentric era, only about 25 percent of black women had natural hairstyles. Pamela Reynolds, "Home-spun Hair," *Boston Globe*, 25 October 1995, Living Section, 71.

51. Asante, *Afrocentricity*, 30.

52. Hilliard, Payton-Stewart, and Williams, *Infusion of African and African American Content*, xxi.

53. Asa Hilliard, *SBA: The Reawakening of the African Mind* (Gainesville, FL: Makare Publishing Company, 1998), 7, 8.

54. Jeffrey Louis Decker, "The State of Rap: Time and Place in Hip Hop Nationalism," *Social Text* 34 (1993): 53, 62, 64, 74, 76.

55. John Henrik Clarke, "Africa in the Ancient World," in *Kemet and the African Worldview: Research, Rescue and Restoration*, ed. Maulana Karenga and Jacob H. Carruthers (Los Angeles: University of Sankore Press, 1986), 49.

56. John Henrik Clarke, Foreword to *African World History Project: The Preliminary Challenge*, ed. Jacob H. Carruthers and Leon C. Harris (Los Angeles: Association for the Study of Classical African Civilizations, 1997), xvii.

57. Mary C. Waters, *Ethnic Options: Choosing Identities in America* (Berkeley: University of California Press, 1990), 17, 118.

58. Hilliard, *SBA*, 6, 16.

59. "The Association for the Study of Classical African Civilizations Atlanta Declaration," http:/www.ascac.org/atldeclaration.html, accessed 12 January 2005.

60. Asante, *Afrocentrism*, 39.

61. Asante, *Afrocentric Idea*, 18.

62. William J. Wilson, *Power, Racism, and Privilege: Race Relations in Theoretical and Sociohistorical Perspectives* (New York: Macmillan, 1973), 190.

63. Diane S. Pollard and Cheryl S. Ajirotutut, eds., *African-Centered Schooling in Theory and Practice* (Westport, CT: Bergin and Garvey, 2000), 43.

64. Although this invective is not as common as it was in the past, it can still be heard. See, for example, Peggy Peterman, "Racism Sheds Its Shame," *St. Petersburg Times* (Florida), 17 March 1989, 1D; Aurelio Rojas, "Turning a Blind Eye to Hate Crimes," *San Francisco Chronicle*, 22 October 1996, A1.

65. Quoted in Kerry Ann Rockquemore and David L. Brunsma, *Beyond Black: Biracial Identity in America* (Thousand Oaks, CA: Sage Publications, 2002), 14.

66. Hilliard, *SBA*, 35.

67. F. James Davis, *Who Is Black? One Nation's Definition* (University Park: Pennsylvania State University Press, 1991).

NOTES TO CHAPTER 6

1. William J. Wilson, *Power, Racism, and Privilege: Race Relations in Theoretical and Sociohistorical Perspectives* (New York: Macmillan, 1973), 50.

2. John Hope Franklin and Alfred A. Moss, Jr., *From Slavery to Freedom: A History of African Americans* (New York: McGraw-Hill, 1994); Manning Marable, *Race, Reform, and Rebellion: The Second Reconstruction in Black America, 1945–1990*, rev. 2d ed. (Jackson: University Press of Mississippi, 1991); Bob Hepburn, "Black Leaders in U.S. Sounding Conservative," *Toronto Star*, 23 April 1987, A15; Maureen Dowd, "Bush Says Dukakis Desperation Prompted Accusations of Racism," *New York Times*, 25 October 1988, Section A, 1; Lee Sigelman and Susan Welch, *Black Americans' Views of Racial Inequality: The Dream Deferred* (New York: Cambridge University Press, 1991), 53, 57; Joe R. Feagin and Melvin P. Sikes, *Living with Racism: The Black Middle-Class Experience* (Boston: Beacon Press, 1994), 321–23.

3. Charles M. Madigan, "Violent Crime Distorts Perceptions of Voters," *Chicago Tribune*, 27 August 1996, Section 1, 9.

4. See, for example, Diane S. Pollard and Cheryl S. Ajirotutu, eds., *African-Centered Schooling in Theory and Practice* (Westport, CT: Bergin and Garvey, 2000), 45–54, 67–80.

5. Quoted in Stephen Steinberg, "The Underclass: A Case of Color Blindness," *New Politics* (Summer 1989): 46.

6. Michael B. Katz, "Introduction: The Urban "Underclass" as a Metaphor of Social Transformation," in *The "Underclass" Debate: Views from History*, ed. Michael B. Katz (Princeton: Princeton University Press, 1993), 16.

7. Hannibal Tirus Afrik, "Rites of Passage Convention Set," *New Pittsburg Courier*, 8 July 1995, A7. Afrik is a Council of Independent Black Institutions activist (see chapter 4). Many Black Power activists and organizations have

changed with or have been changed by the times. I will point to some other Black Power Pan-Africanists who have become Afrocentrists in chapter 7.

8. Jawanza Kunjufu, *Hip-Hop vs. MAAT: A Psycho/Social Analysis of Values* (Chicago: African American Images, 1993), iii.

9. Ibid.

10. Jawanza Kunjufu, *Restoring the Village, Values, and Commitment: Solutions for the Black Family* (Chicago: African American Images, 1996), 145.

11. Carol Ascher, "School Programs for African-American Males . . . and Females," *Phi Delta Kappan*, June 1992, 777; see also Pollard and Ajirotutu, *African-Centered Schooling*, 45–54, 67–80.

12. Michael D. Harris, "Africentrism and Curriculum: Concepts, Issues, and Prospects," *Journal of Negro Education* 61(3), 1993: 307. Harris was the author of the *African-American Baseline Essay* for Portland Public Schools, ed., *African-American Baseline Essays*, rev. (Portland, OR: Portland Public Schools, 1988).

13. Watson and Smitherman, *Educating African American Males*, xvi.

14. I am certain that if asked directly, Afrocentrists would admit that racial discrimination is a problem in American society. However, the fact that it is so regularly omitted from their discussions of social problems indicates that it is not at the forefront of their thinking about these problems. Afrocentrists see white supremacy at work whenever someone opposes Afrocentrism. See, for example, Molefi Kete Asante, "Multiculturalism: An Exchange," *American Scholar* 60(2), 1991: 267–76; Mary Lefkowitz, *Not Out of Africa: How Afrocentrism Became an Excuse to Teach Myth as History* (New York: BasicBooks, 1997), xii; Jacob Carruthers, "Reflections on the History of African Education," *Illinois Schools Journal* 77(2), 1998: 13–21.

15. See the Afrocentric rites of passage text by Nathan and Julia Hare, *Bringing the Black Boy to* Manhood: *The Passage* (San Francisco: Black Think Tank, 1985); William Julius Wilson, *The Truly Disadvantaged* (Chicago: University of Chicago Press, 1987).

16. Carol Ascher, "School Programs for African-American Males . . . and Females," *Phi Delta Kappan*, June 1992, 778–79; Watson and Smitherman, *Educating African American Males*, 24.

17. Christopher Jencks and Paul E. Peterson, eds., *The Urban Underclass* (Washington, DC: Brookings Institution, 1991), v.

18. Ibid., v. Emphaisis added.

19. Ibid., 84.

20. Ibid., 28, 94–95.

21. Jencks and Peterson, *The Urban Underclass*, 76, 94–95; Jeff Grogger and Mike Willis, *The Introduction of Crack Cocaine and the Rise in Urban Crime Rates* (Cambridge, MA: National Bureau of Economic Research, 1998); Daniel Cork, Seminar abstract for "Crack Markets and the Diffusion of Guns

among Youth," presented to the Statistics Department of the University of Washington, 2 February 2000, http://www.stat.washington.edu/www/seminars/archive/2000/winter/cork.shtml, accessed 20 July 2004.

22. Jencks and Peterson, *The Urban Underclass*, 94.

23. "After the Riots: Excerpts from Vice President's Speech on Cities and Poverty," *New York Times*, 20 May 1992, Section A, 20.

24. James Forman, Jr., "Saving Affirmative Action," *The Nation*, 9 December 1991, 746.

25. "The Welfare Bill: Text of President Clinton's Announcement on Welfare Legislation," *New York Times*, 1 August 1996, Section A, 24.

26. *Newsweek*, 46; Portland Public Schools: Multicultural/Multiethnic Education Task Force, *Multicultural/Multiethnic Education in Portland Public Schools* (Portland, OR: Portland Public Schools: Curriculum and Instruction Support Services, 1993), 5; John J. Miller, "Afrocentrism in the Suburbs," *National Review* 45(18), 20 September 1993, 58; Donald Leake and Brenda Leake, "African-American Immersion Schools in Milwaukee: A View from the Inside," *Phi Delta Kappan*, June 1992, 784; Kimberley R. Vann and Jawanza Kunjufu, "The Importance of an Afrocentric, Multicultural Curriculum," *Phi Delta Kappan*, February 1993, 490–91.

27. John P. Hewitt, *The Myth of Self-Esteem: Finding Happiness and Solving Problems in America* (New York: St. Martin's Press, 1998), xi, 51; Daryl Michael Scott, *Contempt and Pity: Social Policy and the Image of the Damaged Black Psyche, 1880–1996* (Chapel Hill: University of North Carolina Press, 1997), 187–88; Wendy Kaminer, *I'm Dysfunctional, You're Dysfunctional: The Recovery Movement and Other Self-Help Fashions* (Reading, MA: Addison-Wesley, 1992), 36; Peggy Orenstein, *School Girls: Young Women, Self-Esteem, and the Confidence Gap* (New York: Anchor Books, 1994), xviii.

28. W. E. B. Du Bois, *Black Reconstruction in America, 1860–1880* (Cleveland: World Publishing Company, 1935), 8–9.

29. Brown v. Board of Education, 347 U.S. 483 (1954), http://caselaw.lp.findlaw.com/scripts/getcase.pl?court=US&vol=347&invol=483, accessed 20 July 2004.

30. Note the variety of terms used by William E. Cross, Jr., in *Shades of Black: Diversity in African-American Identity* (Philadelphia: Temple University Press, 1991), ix–x, 190.

31. bell hooks, *Rock My Soul: Black People and Self-Esteem* (New York: Atria Books, 2003), 162, 164; see also x–xi.

32. Cornel West, "Nihilism in Black America," in *Race Matters* (New York: Vintage Books, 1993), 26–27.

33. Ibid.

34. Ibid.

35. Ibid., 20, 24, 26–27.

36. E. Franklin Frazier, *Black Bourgeoisie* (New York: Free Press Paperbacks, 1957).

37. Risasi Dais, "I.S. 113 Educator Fired for Teaching Truth to Black Students," *New York Amsterdam News*, 15 February 2001, 22.

38. Jean S. Phinney, "When We Talk about American Ethnic Groups, What Do We Mean?" *American Psychologist* 51, no. 9 (1996): 918–27; Jean S. Phinney, "The Multigroup Ethnic Identity Measure: A New Scale for Use with Diverse Groups," *Journal of Adolescent Research* 7, no. 2 (1992): 167–71; Clovis L. White and Peter J. Burke, "Ethnic Role Identity among Black and White College Students: An Interactionist Approach," *Sociological Perspectives* 30, no. 3 (1987): 322–23.

39. Cross, *Shades of Black*; Jean M. Twenge and Jennifer Crocker, "Race and Self-Esteem: Meta-Analyses Comparing Whites, Blacks, Hispanics, Asians, and American Indians and Comment on Gray-Little and Hafdahl (2000)," *Psychological Bulletin* 128, no. 3 (2002): 371–408.

40. James S. Jackson et al., "Race Identity," in *Life in Black America*, ed. James S. Jackson (Newbury Park, CA: Sage Publications, 1991), 238–53; Phinney, "When We Talk"; Veita L. Sanders, "Variables Affecting Racial-Identity Salience among African Americans," *Journal of Social Psychology* 139, no. 6 (1999): 748–61.

41. Phinney, "When We Talk"; J. R. Porter and R. E. Washington, "Minority Identity and Self-Esteem," *Annual Review of Sociology* 19 (1993): 139–61; Phinney, "Multigroup Ethnic Identity," 167–71; Twenge and Crocker, "Race and Self-Esteem."

42. Molefi Kete Asante and Diane Ravitch, "Multiculturalism: An Exchange," *American Scholar* 60(2), 1991, 274; Claude M. Steele, "Race and the Schooling of Black Americans," *Atlantic Monthly*, April 1992: 68–72; Jennifer Crocker and Jason S. Lawrence, "Social Stigma and Self-Esteem: The Role of Contingencies of Worth," in *Cultural Divides: Understanding and Overcoming Group Conflict*, ed. Deborah A. Prentice and Dale T. Miller (New York: Russell Sage Foundation, 1999), 385–86.

43. Gerald David Jaynes and Robin M. Williams, Jr., eds., *A Common Destiny: Blacks and American Society* (Washington, DC: National Academy Press, 1989), 377.

44. Ibid., 348–50.

45. Based on the unlikely but not impossible assumption that the greatest gains within the 1980s might have continued, the black seventeen-year-old NAEP averages would be equal to the white averages in 2004. The white average score on the NAEP tests has changed little since testing began. From 1980 to 1988, the black seventeen-year-old reading score average improved 31 points to 274. In 1999, the white seventeen-year-old reading score average was 295, a difference of 21 points from the 1988 black average. From 1982 to 1990, in

mathematics the black seventeen-year-old-score average increased 17 points to 289. In 1999, the white mathematics average was 315, 26 points above the 1990 black average. From 1982 to 1986, the black science average increased 18 points to 253. In 1999, the white science average was 306, 53 points above the 1986 black average. Office of Educational Research and Improvement, National Center for Education Statistics, *NAEP 1999 Trends in Academic Progress: Three Decades of Student Performance* (NCES 2000-469) by J. R. Campbell, C. M. Hombo, and J. Mazzeo (Washington, DC: U.S. Department of Education, 2000), 31–38.

46. David C. Berliner and Bruce J. Biddle, *The Manufactured Crisis: Myths, Fraud, and the Attack on America's Public Schools* (Cambridge, MA: Perseus Books, 1995), 140.

47. Ibid., 13, 26, 24–27, 139–40.

48. Karenga and Carruthers, *Kemet,* 180.

49. *Newsweek,* 46.

50. Molefi Kete Asante, *Malcolm X as Cultural Hero and Other Afrocentric Essays* (Trenton, NJ: Africa World Press, 1993), 124.

51. For applications of Afrocentrism to social and psychological ills, see Molefi Kete Asante, "Afrocentrism and the Question of Youth Violence," in *Malcolm X as Cultural Hero and Other Afrocentric Essays* (Trenton, NJ: Africa World Press, 1993), 117–24; Karenga, *Black Studies,* 285–97; Linda James-Myers, *An Afrocentric World View: Introduction to an Optimal Psychology* (Dubuque, IA: Kendall Hunt, 1988); Carol Ascher, "School Programs for African-American Males . . . and Females," *Phi Delta Kappan,* June 1992, 777–82.

52. This insightful phrase is used by Carol Ascher in "School Programs," 780.

53. Ascher, "School Programs"; Watson and Smitherman, *Educating African American Males.*

54. Watson and Smitherman, *Educating African American Males,* 51.

55. Watkins, "Womanism," 278.

56. Asante, *Afrocentric Idea,* 4.

57. Asante, *Afrocentrism,* 29.

58. Quoted in Russell Jacoby, "'The Most Radical Afrocentric Ideologue Is Culturally an American,'" *Chronicle of Higher Education,* 30 March 1994, B5.

59. Watson and Smitherman, *Educating African American Males,* xviii–xix.

60. Quoted in Alan Wieder, "Afrocentrisms: Capitalist, Democratic, and Liberationist Portraits," *Educational Foundations* (Spring 1992): 35. Wieder identifies three types of Afrocentrisms, but only the "capitalist Afrocentrist" is a widely published Afrocentric educator. This is just one reason why I see the "capitalist" strain as far more influential than the others.

61. Doug Henwood, "Income Classes around the World," *The Nation,* 29

March 1999, 10; Greg J. Duncan et al., "Poverty Dynamics in Eight Countries," *Journal of Population Economics* 6(3), 1993: 215–34.

62. Quoted in Jim Myers, "'Black' May Be Replaced by 'African-American,'" *USA Today*, 16 January 1989, 9A.

63. Jonathan Kozol, *Savage Inequalities: Children in America's Schools* (New York: HarperPerennial, 1992).

64. Watson and Smitherman, *Educating African American Males*, 23–34; Ascher, "School Programs," 779; Marlene Marie Archie, "The Centered School: An Afrocentric Development Project for Urban Schools" (Ph.D. diss., Temple University, 1997), 14.

65. See Diane S. Pollard and Cheryl S. Ajirotutu, eds., *African-Centered Schooling in Theory and Practice* (Westport, CT: Bergin and Garvey, 2000), 33–123.

66. Tonikiaa Orange, "The Beliefs of the Constitutents of Malcolm X Academy, an African-Centered School, on What Makes It Effective in Educating African-American Children" (Ed.D. thesis, University of Pittsburg, 1991), 133.

67. Archie, "The Centered School," 76.

68. Kenyatta, *Implementing Afrikan-Centered Education*, 18.

69. Archie, "The Centered School," 55–56; Donald Leake and Brenda Leake, "African-American Immersion Schools in Milwaukee: A View from the Inside," *Phi Delta Kappan*, June 1992, 785. This décor is also present in Oakland. See Shawn Alexander Ginwright, "Identity for Sale: The Afrocentric Movement and the Black Urban Struggle in Oakland Public Schools" (Ph.D. diss., University of California, Berkeley, 1999), 218.

70. Barbara Seidl, "You Know Children, Our History Didn't Begin with Slavery" (Ed.D. thesis, University of Wisconsin, Milwaukee, 1996), 27–28.

71. Orange, "Malcolm X Academy," 133.

72. Ginwright, "Identity for Sale," 206–7.

73. Archie, "The Centered School," 94, 132; Orange, "Malcolm X Academy," 105–6.

74. Watson and Smitherman, *Educating African American Males*, 55–78; Orange, "Malcolm X Academy," 122–23; Leake and Leake, "African-American Immersion Schools," 785.

75. Watson and Smitherman, *Educating African American Males*, 71–72; Kenyatta, *Implementing Afrikan-Centered Education*, 50–54.

76. Seidl, "You Know Children," 67.

77. Archie, "The Centered School," 87.

78. Ibid.

79. Portland Public Schools, *African-American Baseline Essays*.

80. Watson and Smitherman, *Educating African American Males*, 62.

81. Seidl, "You Know Children"; Kevin Bushweller, "Separate by Choice," *American School Board Journal*, October 1996, 36.

82. Pollard and Ajirotutu, *African-Centered Schooling*, 45–54, 67–80.

83. Seidl, "You Know Children"; Watson and Smitherman, *Educating African American Males*, 55–77; Archie, "The Centered School."

84. Watson and Smitherman, *Educating African American Males*; Ascher, "School Programs."

85. Karenga and Carruthers, *Kemet*, 86, 128.

86. Watson and Smitherman, *Educating African American Males*; Ascher, "School Programs"; Donald O. Leake and Brenda L. Leake, "Islands of Hope: Milwaukee's African American Immersion Schools," *Journal of Negro Education* 61, no. 1 (Winter 1992), 27.

87. Seidl, "You Know Children"; Watson and Smitherman, *Educating African American Males*; Archie, "The Centered School."

88. Watson and Smitherman, *Educating African American Males*; Leake and Leake, "Islands of Hope."

89. Alan Wieder ("Afrocentrisms") and Gary Rivlin are two of the few observers to recognize that Afrocentrism is not a challenge to American society. Rivlin observes, "the grand irony of African-centered schools" is that "teaching widely branded as too radical is, boiled to its essence, conservative: respect, responsibility, community." Gary Rivlin, "Eyes on the Prize," (Chicago) *Reader*, 23 May 1997, 31.

90. "Broad Coalition Seeks 'African American' Name," *Jet*, 16 June 1989, 53.

91. "Jackson and Others Say 'Blacks' Is Passe," *New York Times*, 21 December 1988, Section A, 16.

92. "Jesse, Late Is Better than Never!" *Muslim Journal*, 6 January 1989, 8; Al Giordano, "No Rush to 'African-American,'" *WJR: Washington Journalism Review* 11, no. 3 (1989): 13.

93. Jackson had recently waged an impressive campaign for the Democratic presidential nomination. Tom W. Smith, "Changing Racial Labels: From 'Colored' to 'Negro' to 'Black' to 'African American,'" *Public Opinion Quarterly* 56 (1992): 509.

94. "Jackson and Others."

95. Don L. Lee, *From Plan to Planet: Life Studies; The Need for Afrikan Minds and Institutions* (Chicago: Institute for Positive Education, 1973), 45.

96. Ruth W. Grant and Marion Orr, "Language, Race and Politics: From 'Black' to 'African-American,'" *Politics and Society* 24, no. 2 (1996): 137–52; Mary C. Waters, *Ethnic Options: Choosing Identities in America* (Berkeley: University of California Press, 1990), 147–68.

97. For some recent discussions about distinguishing "African Americans" from other blacks, see Rachel L. Swarns, "'African American' Becomes a Term for Debate," *New York Times*, 29 August 2003, Section 1, 1; Sara Rimer and Karen W. Arenson, "Top Colleges Take More Blacks, but Which Ones?" *New York Times*, 24 June 2004, Section A, 1.

98. Giordano, "No Rush"; Smith, "Changing Racial Labels," 510; "Most Blacks Prefer 'Black' to 'African-American,'" *Society* 28, no. 4 (May–June 1991): 2–3.

99. Stanley Lieberson and Kelly S. Mikelson, "Distinctive African American Names: An Experimental, Historical, and Linguistic Analysis of Innovation," *American Sociological Review* 60 (1995): 928–46; Roland G. Fryer, Jr., and Steven D. Levitt, "The Causes and Consequences of Distinctively Black Names," National Bureau of Economic Research Working Paper Series, Working Paper 9938, http://www.nber.org/papers/w9938.pdf, accessed 24 July 2004.

100. A rough count of African-naming books was obtained from a World-Cat keyword search of "African" and "names." African-naming books published or reprinted in the United States in the 1980s and 1990s were counted.

101. Liberson and Mikelson, "Distinctive American American Names"; Fryer and Levitt, "Causes and Consequences."

102. Joseph K. Adjaye, "The Discourse of Kente Cloth: From Haute Couture to Mass Culture," in *Language, Rhythm, and Sound: Black Popular Cultures into the Twenty-First Century*, ed. Joseph K. Adjaye and Adrianne R. Andrews (Pittsburg: University of Pittsburg Press, 1997), 23–39; James Anderson, "Crazy for Kente Cloth," *Emerge* 2, no. 1 (1990): 68; Vincent Thompson, "McDonald's Goes Afrocentric," *Philadelphia Tribune*, 5 April 1994, 1-B; Florence Fabricant, "Off the Menu," *New York Times*, 12 October 1994, Section C, 2.

103. Emil Wilbekin, "A Detailed Guide to an Afrocentric Lifestyle," *Emerge* 7, no. 10 (1996), 83.

104. Ibid.

105. Kenneth M. Jones, "Say, Brother: Dread Comes from the Heart," *Essence*, October 1985, 8; Wilberkin, "Detailed Guide"; Erica Johnson, "African American Women Embracing Natural Hairstyles," *Oakland Post*, 28 February 2001, 1B; Pamela Reynolds, "Homespun Hair," *Boston Globe*, 25 October 1995, Living Section, 71; Kaylois Henry, "Going Natural," *St. Petersburg Times* (Florida), 23 September 1992, Floridian Section, 1D.

106. I discuss US Organization in detail in chapter 4. Elizabeth Pleck, "Kwanzaa: The Making of a Black Nationalist Tradition," *Journal of American Ethnic History* 20, no. 4 (2001): 3–28; Scot Brown, *Fighting for Us: Maulana Karenga, the US Organization, and Black Cultural Nationalism* (New York: New York University Press, 2003), 53–55, 88–91, 94–95.

107. Pleck, "Kwanzaa," 3–4.

108. Quoted in Pleck, "Kwanzaa," 14.

109. Naomi Marcus, "Island of Stolen Souls," *New York Times Uprfont*, 4 October 1994, 10–12; Tom Masland, "'And Still I Rise!'" *Newsweek*, 6 September 1999, 71–72; Edgar Sanchez, Synopsis [*Sankofa*], http://dickinsg.intrasun.tcnj.edu/sankofa/s-synopsis.htm, accessed 5 June 2004; Klaus de Albuquerque,

"Daughters of the Dust: The Making of an American 'Classic,'" *Reconstruction* 2, no. 2 (1993): 122–25; Franklin and Moss, *From Slavery to Freedom*, 487; Martha Bayles, "Malcolm X and the Hip Hop Culture," *Reconstruction* 2, no. 2 (1993): 100; "Paperback Best Sellers," *New York Times*, 13 December 1992, Section 7, 32.

110. Jeffrey Louis Decker, "The State of Rap: Time and Place in Hip Hop Nationalism," *Social Text* 34 (1993): 53, 62. See the Malcolm X photograph at http://www.malcolm-x.org/media/pic/mg44.jpg, and the Boogie Down Productions restaging at http://www.musicmatic.de/B/BoogieD3a.jpg, accessed 25 July 2004.

111. Decker, "The State of Rap," 53, 62, 64, 74, 76.

112. "Ohio Players, Bobby Womack, and Hugh Masekela Headline African Festival of the Arts," *African Spectrum* 2, no. 6 (2000), http://www.african-spectrum.com/2000/09/front/f3.html, accessed 25 July 2004; Alan M. Kriegsman, "DanceAfrica to Make Its First National Tour," *Washington Post*, 10 May 1995, Style, C4; Ian McCann, *The Complete Guide to Bob Marley* (London: Omnibus Press, 1994), xiii; Joel Whitburn, *Joel Whitburn Presents Top R&B Singles, 1942–1999* (Menomonee Fall, WI: Record Research, 2000), 284.

"The foreign-born black population of the United States doubled between 1960 and 1970, and increased by more than two and a half times between 1970 and 1980," states Rachel Buff, "'Mas' in Brooklyn: Immigration, Race, and the Cultural Politics of Carnival," in *Language, Rhythm, and Sound: Black Popular Cultures into the Twenty-First Century*, ed. Joseph K. Adjaye and Adrianne R. Andrews (Pittsburg: University of Pittsburg Press, 1997), 227. Buff also discusses tensions between black Americans and West Indians, on 227. See Mary C. Waters, *Black Identities: West Indian Immigrant Dreams and American Realities* (New York: Russell Sage Foundation; Cambridge, MA: Harvard University Press, 1999) for a discussion of second-generation West Indians. West Indians have been accepted by black Americans in the past but usually when they associated with black Americans as blacks, not as West Indians.

113. Nobles, "Ancient Egyptian Thought," 113.

114. Asante, *Afrocentricity*, 57; Molefi Kete Asante, interview by Avery Brown, *This Way Out International Gay and Lesbian Magazine*, 25 May 1995, http://www.qrd.org/qrd/www/culture/black/articles/asante.html, accessed 5 June 2004.

115. Marlon T. Riggs, *Black Is . . . Black Ain't: A Personal Journey through Black Identity* (San Francisco: California Newsreel, 1995), videorecording.

116. Robert F. Reid-Pharr, *Black Gay Man* (New York: New York University Press, 2001), 166.

117. View the Brothers United in Support Symbol at http://www.tpan.com/mocha/bus/retreat.html, accessed 25 July 2004. *BLACKlines*, April 2000, 9, 21,

36. "Adodi," *BLACKlines*, 2 January 2003, http://www.windycitymediagroup
.com/gay/lesbian/news/ARTICLE.php?AID=1156, accessed 25 July 2005.

118. Michael Janofsky, "Federal Parks Chief Calls 'Million Man' Count
Low," *New York Times*, 21 October 1995, Section 1, 6; Tony Kornheiser, "No
More Marches by Poor People," *Plain Dealer* (Cleveland, Ohio), 24 October
2000, 9B; "Women March for Family Unity," *Pittsburg Post-Gazette*, 26 October 1997, A-1.

119. Louis Farrakhan, *The Million Man March: A Day of Atonement and a
Proclamation of Exodus* (Chicago: Final Call, 1995), videorecording.

120. "Women March"; Michael Janofsky, "At Million Woman March,
Focus in on Family," *New York Times*, 26 October 1997, Section 1, 1.

121. Farrakhan, *Million Man March*; "Women March"; National Million
Man March/Day of Absence Organizing Committee, *The Million Man March/
Day of Absence: Mission Statement* (Los Angeles: University of Sankore Press;
Chicago: Third World Press; Chicago: FCN Publishing Company, 1995), 12;
Janofsky, "Million Woman March."

122. Michael O. West, "Like a River: The Million Man March and the
Black Nationalist Tradition in the United States," *Journal of Historical Sociology* 12, no. 1 (1999): 92.

123. Imamu Amiri Baraka, ed., *African Congress: A Documentary of the
First Modern Pan-African Congress* (New York: William Morrow and Company, 1972), 96, 99.

124. Farrakhan, *Million Man March*; National Million Man March/Day of
Absence Organizing Committee, *Mission Statement*.

125. Michael H. Cottman and Deborah Willis, *Million Man March* (New
York: Crown Trade Books, 1995), 79.

126. "Register for the Million Man March," leaflet, n.d.

127. Michael A. Fletcher and DeNeen L. Brown, "'We Are Countless in
Unity': Hundreds of Thousands Flock to Philadelphia for Million Woman
March," *Washington Post*, 26 October 1997, Section A, 1; Tracie Reddick,
"One Woman Finds Million Ways the March Fell Short," *Tampa Tribune* (Flor-
ida), 2 November 1997, Baylife, 1.

128. Fletcher and Brown, "'We are Countless in Unity.'"

129. Ibid.

130. "Women March."

131. Reddick, "March Fell Short"; DeNeen L. Brown, "My Bumpy Ride
Back from a Day of Sisterhood," *Washington Post*, 2 November 1997, Out-
look, C1.

132. Mario A. Brossard and Richard Morin, "Leader Popular among
Marchers; But Most Came to Support Black Family, Show Unity, Survey Finds,"
Washington Post, 17 October 1995, Section A, 1; Joseph P. McCormick, II,

"The Messages and the Messengers: Opinions from the Million Men Who Marched," *National Political Science Review* 6 (1997): 145–46; Joseph P. McCormick, II, "A Report on the Findings from the Million Woman March Survey," draft, unpublished paper, March 1998, 8. The national median household income in 1996 was $35,172. U.S. Census Bureau, "Table 4. Median Household Income by Type of Household: 1969, 1979, 1989, 1993, and 1996," http://www.census.gov/hhes/income/mednhhld/t4.html, accessed 12 July 2004.

133. Joseph McCormick, II, and Sekou Franklin, "Expressions of Racial Consciousness in the African American Community," in *Black and Multiracial Politics in America*, ed. Yvette M. Alex-Assensoh and Lawrence J. Hanks (New York: New York University Press, 2000), 327; McCormick, "A Report," 11, Table 3.

134. McCormick, "Messages and the Messengers," 147; McCormick, "A Report," 13.

135. Chris Booker, "The Million Man March Revisited: A Leadership Void Contrasts with Grass-Roots Initiative," http://www.pressroom.com/~afrimale/mmmrev.htm, accessed 5 June 2004; Victor Volland, "Speakers at Rally Urge Black Women to Vote," *St. Louis Post-Dispatch* (Missouri), 25 October 1998, Metro, D2.

136. For a recent example, see "The Cosby Show," *Economist*, 10 July 2004, 30. See also Gertrude Ezorsky, *Racism and Justice: The Case for Affirmative Action* (Ithaca, NY: Cornell University Press, 1991), 57–60.

137. Hilliard, *Maroon*, 74.

138. Ibid., 130–32. Emphasis in original.

139. The editors of the *Economist* write, "American history is full of examples of impoverished immigrants (Jews a century ago, Asians today) who have made it from the inner city to the Ivy League." "Cosby Show."

140. Mary C. Waters, *Ethnic Options: Choosing Identities in America* (Berkeley: University of California Press, 1990), 147–68.

141. Waters, *Ethnic Options*, 129–68; Mary C. Waters, *Black Identities: West Indian Immigrant Dreams and American Realities* (New York: Russell Sage Foundation; Cambridge, MA: Harvard University Press, 1999), 94–139.

142. Jawanza Kunjufu, *Restoring the Village, Values, and Commitment: Solutions for the Black Family* (Chicago: African American Images, 1996), 145.

143. Ramona Edelin, "Talk of a Serious Cultural Offensive," *Chicago Defender*, 31 December 1988, 20. Emphasis in original.

144. Wilson Jeremiah Moses best appreciates the complexity of motives and themes in black nationalist thought. This idea of an integrationist black nationalism is inspired by his *The Wings of Ethiopia: Studies in African-American Life and Letters* (Ames: Iowa State University Press, 1990).

145. Ameritech and Allen Bradley are business partners of the Malcolm X Academy in Milwaukee (see www.milwaukee.k12.wi.us/048.htm).

146. Adolph L. Reed, Jr., *W. E. B. Du Bois and American Political Thought: Fabianism and the Color Line* (New York: Oxford University Press, 1997), 163–76.

NOTES TO CHAPTER 7

1. William Brink and Louis Harris, *The Negro Revolution in America; What Negroes Want, Why and How They Are Fighting, Whom They Support, What Whites Think of Them and Their Demands* (New York: Simon and Schuster, 1964), 67. See also Gary T. Marx, *Protest and Prejudice: A Study of Belief in the Black Community*, rev. ed. (New York: Harper and Row, 1969), 233–41.

2. Marx, *Protest and Prejudice*, 237.

3. Ibid., 233–41.

4. The Inter-University Consortium for Political and Social Research website can be searched to see most of the datasets available to the author. http:// www.icpsr.umich.edu/index-medium.html.

5. For a detailed discussion of these problems, see Howard Schuman, Charlotte Steeh, Lawrence Bobo, and Maria Krysan, *Racial Attitudes in America: Trends and Interpretations* (Cambridge, MA: Harvard University Press, 1997), 58–98. For the potential impact of different data collection methods, see Allyson L. Holbrook, Melanie C. Green, and Ion A. Krosnick, "Telephone versus Face-to-Face Interviewing of National Probability Samples with Long Questionnaires: Comparisons of Respondent Satisficing and Social Desirability Response Bias," *Public Opinion Quarterly* 67(1), Spring 2003: 79–125.

6. Howard Schuman and Shirley Hatchett, *Black Racial Attitudes: Trends and Complexities* (Ann Arbor: Institute for Social Research, University of Michigan, 1974), 4–18.

7. The data collection for the study began in 1993 but was not completed until 1994.

8. For information on Jesse Jackson's relationship with Louis Farrahkan, see John Hope Franklin and Alfred A. Moss, Jr., *From Slavery to Freedom: A History of African Americans* (New York: McGraw-Hill, 1994), 542–43, and Michel Marriott, "Black Muslim Leader Endorses Jackson," *Washington Post*, 20 November 1983. For a glimpse into Jackson's black nationalist past, see his speech in Imamu Amiri Baraka, ed., *African Congress: A Documentary of the First Modern Pan-African Congress* (New York: William Morrow and Company, 1972), 22–32. Two other good examples of the melding of black nationalism with integrationism are Reverend Al Sharpton and Reverend Benjamin Chavis. There are some aspects of Reverend Al Sharpton's activism that put him in the civil rights camp, but others that would put him in the black nationalist camp. One black politician once accused him of trying to start a race war which would be a more nationalist thing to do. The Reverend Benjamin Chavis also

seemed to incorporate civil rights and black nationalist tactics. In 1997 he officially became a black nationalist and a member of the Nation of Islam. James
Barron, "Black Official Faults Tactics of Sharpton," *New York Times*, 2 March
1988, Section B, 1; Michael Finnegan, "Farrakhan Fills Harlem Post with Fired
Leader of NAACP," *Daily News* (New York), 21 November 1997, 48.

9. The fifteen cities are: Baltimore, Boston, Chicago, Cincinnati, Cleveland,
Detroit, Gary, Milwaukee, Newark, New York (Brooklyn only), Philadelphia,
Pittsburgh, San Francisco, St. Louis, and Washington, D.C. Angus Campbell
and Howard Schuman, *Racial Attitudes in Fifteen American Cities*, in *Supple-
mental Studies for the National Advisory Commission on Civil Disorders* (New
York: Frederick A. Praeger, 1968), 11, note a.

10. Political scientists believe that the Los Angeles riots were a factor in the
strong nationalism of this period. Michael C. Dawson, *Black Visions: The
Roots of Contemporary African-American Political Ideologies* (Chicago: University of Chicago Press, 2001), 132–33.

11. For example, the 1968 Fifteen-Cities result that 5.7 percent of blacks
desired a black nation is not statistically different (the 95 percent confidence
interval ranges from 4.9 to 6.5 percent) from the results of a 1968 national survey by CBS News which found 5 percent of blacks desiring a separate country.
Here there is also a difference in the wording of the questions. Marx, *Protest
and Prejudice*, 226. My comparison of the means, medians, and standard deviations of the full 1993 national sample with the 1993 urban respondents on the
black nationalist questions analyzed found both groups to be very similar. See
also Paul M. Sniderman and Thomas Piazza, *Black Pride and Black Prejudice*
(Princeton: Princeton University Press, 2002), 16, 49.

12. John H. Bracey, Jr., August Meier, and Elliot Rudwick, eds., Introduction to *Black Nationalism in America* (Indianapolis: Bobbs-Merrill, 1970), lix;
Rod Bush, *We Are Not What We Seem: Black Nationalism and Class Struggle
in the American Century* (New York: New York University Press, 1999), 41;
Errol A. Henderson, "War, Political Cycles, and the Pendulum Thesis: Explaining the Rise of Black Nationalism, 1840–1996," in *Black and Multiracial Politics in America*, eds. Yvette M. Alex-Assensoh and Lawrence J. Hanks (New
York: New York University Press, 2000), 340.

13. For example, see Bush, *We Are Not*, 99.

14. William Brink and Louis Harris, *Black and White: A Study of U.S.
Racial Attitudes Today* (New York: Simon and Schuster, 1967), 9.

15. Ibid., 260–61, 262–63, 264–65.

16. Ibid., 260–63.

17. Robert A. Brown and Todd C. Shaw, "Separate Nations: Two Attitudi-
nal Dimensions of Black Nationalism," *Journal of Politics* 64(1), February
2002: 22–44.

18. See U.S. Census Bureau, "Historical Poverty Tables," http://www.census .gov/hhes/poverty/histpov/hstpov1.html, accessed 18 December 2004.

19. Sniderman and Piazza, *Black Pride and Black Prejudice*, 38–44, 59–60.

20. Carol Ascher, "School Programs for African-American Males . . . and Females," *Phi Delta Kappan*, June 1992, 777–82.

21. Jennifer Hochschild, *Facing Up to the American Dream: Race, Class, and the Soul of the Nation* (Princeton: Princeton University Press, 1995).

22. Elijah Muhammad, *Message to the Blackman in America* (Chicago: Muhammad's Temple No. 2, 1965), 35–37, 56–57, 195–96, 203; Claude Andrew Clegg, III, *An Original Man: The Life and Times of Elijah Muhammad* (New York: St. Martin's Press, 1997), 235–65, 283; John Woodford, "Testing America's Promise of Free Speech: Muhammad Speaks in the 1960s, a Memoir," *Voices of the African Diaspora* (Fall 1991), 8, 11, 12.

23. Wilson Jeremiah Moses, *The Golden Age of Black Nationalism, 1850–1925* (New York: Oxford University Press, 1978).

24. Robert A. Hill and Carol A. Rudisell, eds., *The Marcus Garvey and Universal Negro Improvement Association Papers* (Berkeley: University of California Press, 1983), lii.

25. Ibid., lix.

26. Ibid., li.

27. Kwame Anthony Appiah, *In My Father's House: Africa in the Philosophy of Culture* (New York: Oxford University Press, 1992), 3.

28. Moses, *The Golden Age of Black Nationalism*, 7.

29. Maulana Ron Karenga argued for "concrete programs" in "The Black Community and the University: A Community Organizer's Perspective," in *Black Studies in the University: A Symposium*, ed. Amstead L. Robinson, Craig C. Foster, and Donald H. Ogilivie (New Haven: Yale University Press, 1969), 37. He mentions his second dissertation in his *Introduction to Black Studies*, 2d ed. (Los Angeles: University of Sankore Press, 1993), 50.

30. Haki Madhubuti, *Enemies: The Clash of Races* (Chicago: Third World Press, 1978), 184, see also 184–90. Emphasis in original.

31. Gary Rivlin, "Eyes on the Prize" (Chicago) *Reader*, 23 May 1997, 31.

32. Haki Madhubuti, *Claiming Earth: Race, Rage, Rape, Redemption; Blacks Seeking a Culture of Enlightened Empowerment* (Chicago: Third World Press, 1994), 165–66.

33. Molefi Kete Asante, "Systematic Nationalism: A Legitimate Strategy for National Selfhood," *Journal of Black Studies* 9, no. 1 (September 1978): 115–28.

34. See Molefi Kete Asante, *Afrocentricity*, new rev. ed. (Trenton, NJ: Africa World Press, 1988), 98–99; Russell Jacoby, "The Most Radical Afrocentric Ideologue Is Culturally an American," *Chronicle of Higher Education*, 30 March 1994, B5.

35. There were still Pan-Africanists of the Black Power variety in the 1980s and 1990s. K. Agyei Akoto, who is affiliated with the Council of Independent Black Institutions, is one example. See K. Agyei Akoto, *Nationbuilding: Theory and Practice in Afrikan Centered Education* (Washington, DC: Pan Afrikan World Institute, 1992). Kwame Ture (Stokely Carmichael) and his All-African People's Revolutionary Party is another. See "Kwame Ture, 'Black Power' Activist," *Chicago Sun-Times*, 16 November 1998, 58. And there are still Pan-Africanists today.

36. Ben Martin, "From Negro to Black to African American: The Power of Names and Naming," *Political Science Quarterly* 106, no. 1 (1991), 83–107; Jennifer Jordan, "Cultural Nationalism in the 1960s: Politics and Poetry," in *Race, Politics, and Culture: Critical Essays on the Radicalism of the 1960s*, ed. Adolph Reed, Jr. (Westport, CT: Greenwood Press, 1986), 45–48.

37. Wilson Jeremiah Moses, *Afrotopia: The Roots of African American Popular History* (Cambridge: Cambridge University Press, 1998).

38. Wilson Jeremiah Moses, ed., *Classical Black Nationalism: From the American Revolution to Marcus Garvey* (New York: New York University Press, 1996), 2.

39. Norman Kelley, "The Specter of Nationalism," *New Politics* 6, no. 1 (1996): 13.

40. Herbert J. Gans, "Symbolic Ethnicity: The Future of Ethnic Groups and Cultures in America," *Ethnic and Racial Studies* 2(1): 9.

41. Ibid., 3.

NOTES TO CHAPTER 8

1. Many scholars maintain the physical appearance versus culture distinction but accord differing amounts of importance to it. Some feel that it is a trivial distinction while others feel that it is of great importance. Some define race as a subset of ethnicity and some see ethnicity as a subset of race. However, most of these differing conceptualizations still maintain a biology-culture distinction, which is my concern. See Richard D. Alba, "Ethnicity," in *Encyclopedia of Sociology*, 2d ed., ed. Edgar F. Borgatta and Rhonda J. V. Montgomery (New York: Macmillan Reference, USA, 2000), 841; Chris Smaje, "Not Just a Social Construct: Theorising Race and Ethnicity," *Sociology* 31, no. 2 (1997): 309; Michael Omi and Howard Winant, *Racial Formation in the United States: From the 1960s to the 1990s*, 2d ed. (New York: Routledge, 1994), 20–23, 54–56; Pierre van den Berghe, *The Ethnic Phenomenon* (New York: Elsvier, 1981), 28–29, 240–41; Richard Williams, *Hierarchial Structures and Social Value: The Creation of Black and Irish Identities in the United States* (Cambridge: Cambridge University Press, 1990), 2; Nathan Glazer, "Black and Ethnic

Groups: The Difference and the Political Difference It Makes," *Social Problems* 18 (Spring 1971): 447.

2. Edward J. Park, "Racial Ideology and Hiring Decisions in Silicon Valley," *Qualitative Sociology* 22, no. 3 (1999): 223–33; Johanna Shih, "'. . . Yeah, I Could Hire This One, But I Know It's Gonna Be a Problem': How Race, Nativity and Gender Affect Employers' Perceptions of the Manageability of Job Seekers," *Ethnic and Racial Studies* 25, no. 1 (2002): 99–119; Joleen Kirschenman and Kathryn M. Neckerman, "'We'd Love to Hire Them, but . . .': The Meaning of Race for Employers," in *The Urban Underclass*, ed. Christopher Jencks and Paul E. Peterson (Washington, DC: Brookings Institution, 1991), 203–32.

3. Glenn Loury, "The Real Thing," interview by Ira Glass, WBEZ's *This American Life* (August 27, 1999, Episode 138).

4. Edge, "You Mean Black Folks Created Rock 'n' Roll? Yes," *YSB* 4, Issue 9 (31 July 1995): 96; Gil Griffin, "They Rock Your World," *YSB* 4, Issue 9 (31 July 1995): 95; Peter Watrous, "Living Colour Breaks Racial and Rock Stereotypes," *New York Times*, 24 April 1989, Section C, 15; Paul Rogers, "Against the Colour Code," *Independent* (London), 24 October 1991, Arts Page, 24.

5. John Shelton Reed and Dale Volberg Reed, *1001 Things Everyone Should Know about the South* (New York: Doubleday, 1996), 190.

6. Melville J. Herskovits sees more West African influence than there actually is and exaggerates their importance, but he does provide a good sense of the range of retentions. Melville J. Herskovits, *The Myth of the Negro Past* (Boston: Beacon Press, 1958), 32.

7. Everett C. Hughes, "The Study of Ethnic Relations," in *The Sociological Eye: Selected Papers* (New Brunswick, NJ: Transaction Books, [1971] 1984), 153–54. This essay was originally published in *Dalhousie Review*, vol. XXVIII, no. 4, January 1948.

8. Quoted in Allan G. Johnson, *The Blackwell Dictionary of Sociology* (Cambridge, MA: Basil Blackwell, 1995), 356.

9. Oliver C. Cox, *Caste, Class and Race: A Study in Social Dynamics* (New York: Monthly Review Press, 1948), 319.

10. See, for example, Mary C. Waters, *Ethnic Options: Choosing Identities in America* (Berkeley: University of California Press, 1990); "Survey Brief: Assimilation and Language" (Washington, DC: Pew Hispanic Center/Kaiser Family Foundation, March 2004), http://www.pewhispanic.org/site/docs/ASSIMILATION%20AND%20LANGUAGE-031904.pdf, accessed 8 October 2004.

11. Frederik Barth makes these points in his discussion of ethnic groups. He writes, "The important thing to recognize is that a drastic reduction of cultural differences between ethnic groups does not correlate in any simple way with a reduction in the organizational relevance of ethnic identities." He also observes, "Where ethnic groups are organized in political confrontation in this way, the

process of opposition will therefore lead to a reduction of the cultural differences between them." In other words, if two groups compete for dominance within the same political system and adhere to the same rules of competition as one would see in what is referred to as ethnic politics, they show that they are culturally similar to each other. They are competing for something that they both value and doing so in accordance with one set of norms for competition. This type of conflict requires cultural similarity, even as it can foster strong feelings of difference. Frederik Barth, Introduction to *Ethnic Groups and Boundaries: The Social Organization of Culture Difference*, ed. Fredrik Barth (Boston: Little, Brown and Company, 1969), 32–33, 35.

12. Stefano Luconi, *From* Paesani *to* White Ethnics: The Italian Experience in Philadelphia (Albany: State University of New York Press, 2001), 17–56, quotation from 30.

13. U.S. Census Bureau, "Overview of Race and Hispanic Origin" by Elizabeth M. Grieco and Rachel C. Cassidy (Washington, DC: U.S. Census Bureau, 2001), 2, http://www.census.gov/prod/2001pubs/c2kbr01-1.pdf, accessed 9 October 2004.

14. Richard Jenkins, "Ethnicity Etcetera: Social Anthropological Points of View," *Ethnic and Racial Studies* 19, no. 4 (1996): 816.

15. Ibid.

16. Stephen Cornell and Douglass Hartmann argue strongly that an asserted identity is an ethnic identity, but they also argue that ethnicity can be imposed. It is easy to misread them as saying that race is imposed while ethnicity is asserted, as Vilna Bashi does. Ultimately, for them the only clear distinction between race and ethnicity is the physical appearance distinction. Other scholars do make the asserted-imposed, race-ethnicity distinction. See Stephen Cornell and Douglas Hartmann, *Ethnicity and Race: Making Identities in a Changing World* (Thousand Oaks, CA: Pine Forge Press, 1998), 35; Ellis Cashmore, "Ethnicity," in *Dictionary of Race and Ethnic Relations*, 3d ed. (London: Routledge, 1994), 102–7; Vilna Bashi, "Racial Categories Matter because Racial Hierarchies Matter: A Commentary," *Ethnic and Racial Studies* 21, no. 5 (1998): 961.

17. Cornell and Hartmann, *Ethnicity and Race*, 25–34; Richard Jenkins, "Rethinking Ethnicity: Identity, Categorization and Power," *Ethnic and Racial Studies* 17, no. 2 (1994): 197–223.

18. Cornell and Hartmann, *Ethnicity and Race*, 103–8.

19. Tom Smith, "Changing Racial Labels: From 'Colored' to 'Negro' to 'Black' to 'African American,'" *Public Opinion Quarterly* 56 (1992): 504, 508–9.

20. For example, Dona Richards states that there is much truth in the idea the blacks have rhythm, love to dance, and can sing. "The Implications of African-American Spirituality," in *African Culture: The Rhythms of Unity*, ed. Molefi Kete Asante and Kariamu Welsh Asante (Trenton, NJ: Africa World Press, 1990), 223–24. See also chapters 5 and 6.

21. Cornell and Hartmann, *Ethnicity and Race*, xvii, 39–41, 68–71; Richard Schaefer, *Racial and Ethnic Groups*, 8th ed. (Upper Saddle River, NJ: Prentice Hall, 2000), 384; Luconi states that Italian immigrants were "generally short and dark-skinned" in *From* Paesani, 40; Oliver C. Cox, *Caste, Class and Race: A Study in Social Dynamics* (New York: Monthly Review Press, 1948), 319.

22. Alain F. Corcos, *The Myth of Human Races* (East Lansing: Michigan State University Press, 1997), 135.

23. Francisco J. Gil-White, "How Thick Is Blood? The Plot Thickens . . . : If Ethnic Actors Are Primordialists, What Remains of the Circumstantialist/Primordialist Controversy?" *Ethnic and Racial Studies* 22, no. 5 (September 1999): 790.

24. Gil-White, "How Thick Is Blood?" 789–820; Waters, *Ethnic Options*.

25. Schaefer states that racial groups have "obvious physical differences." Schaefer, *Racial and Ethnic Groups*, 6–7.

26. This finding is based on my analyses of the 1984 National Black Election Study, the 1993 National Black Politics Study, and the 1996 National Black Election Study. See the Appendix for more detailed information about the datasets.

27. Kathleen Cleaver recalls that in Jim Crow Tuskegee, Alabama, "Many people on our side of town would have been mistaken for white in any other part of the country. . . . I figured out who was who by geography: if they lived in our part of town, they were black. It didn't matter what their color was." Kathleen Neal Cleaver, "The Education of Kathleen Neal Cleaver," interview by Susie Linfield, *Transition*, Issue 77 (1998): 177. Gunnar Myrdal found that "a white woman associating with Negroes was considered to be a fair-skinned Negro because Southern men could not believe that a real white woman would want to go about with Negroes." Michael Banton, *Race Relations* (New York: Basic Books, 1967), 61. See also Davis, *Who Is Black?* 56.

28. Cornell and Hartmann, *Ethnicity and Race*, xvii, 41; see also 39–41, 68–71.

29. Schaefer, *Racial and Ethnic Groups*, 384.

30. I address the reasons for this dismissal in some detail in my doctoral dissertation. Algernon Trevor Michael Austin, "The Racial Ideologies of Blackness in Twentieth-Century Black Nationalism; Towards a More Sociological Understanding of Race and Ethnicity" (Ph.D. diss., Northwestern University, 2001), 41–49.

31. Christian A. Meissner and John C. Brigham, "Thirty Years of Investigating the Own-Race Bias in Memory for Faces: A Meta-Analytic Review," *Psychology, Public Policy and Law* 7(1), March 2001: 3–35; F. Bedford, "Cross-Racial Eyewitness Identification," http://www.u.arizona.edu/~bedford/expertwitness.htm, accessed 9 October 2004.

32. In Malaysia, the Chinese and the Malay are seen as two different races.

Charles Hirschmann, "The Making of Race in Colonial Malaya: Political Economy and Racial Ideology," *Sociological Forum* 1, no. 2 (Spring 1986): 330–61; Eugene K. B. Tan, "From Sojourners to Citizens: Managing the Ethnic Chinese Minority in Indonesia and Malaysia," *Ethnic and Racial Studies* 24, no. 6 (November 2001): 949–78.

33. Frank M. Snowden, Jr., *Before Color Prejudice: The Ancient View of Blacks* (Cambridge, MA: Harvard University Press, 1983); Gary L. Morrison, "Loulan Beauty: Encountering the Xinjiang Mummies," *World Order* 32(2) (Winter 2000–01): 33–38; Peter Stern, "The White Indians of the Borderlands," *Journal of the Southwest* 33, no. 3 (1991): 262–81; James Axtell, "The White Indians of Colonial America," *William and Mary Quarterly* 32, no. 1 (1975): 55–88; Kenneth W. Porter, "Chapter One: Their Best Soldiers Are Black," in *The Black Seminoles: History of a Freedom-Seeking People* (Gainesville: University Press of Florida, 1996), 3–12; T. H. Breen and Stephen Innes, *'Myne Owne Ground': Race and Freedom on Virginia's Eastern Shore, 1640–1676* (New York: Oxford University Press, 1980).

34. Hirschmann, "Race in Colonial Malaya"; Tan, "From Sojourners to Citizens."

35. Marvin Harris, Josildeth Gomes Consorte, Joseph Lang, and Bryan Byrne, "Who Are the Whites? Imposed Census Categories and the Racial Demography of Brazil," *Social Forces* 72(2), December 1993: 451–62.

36. Park, "Racial Ideology and Hiring Decisions"; Shih, "Employers' Perceptions"; Kirchenman and Neckerman, "'We'd Love to Hire Them, But. . . .'"

37. As Joane Nagel has observed, Omi and Winant's *Racial Formation in the United States* is a good example of Americans generalizing specifics of American "racial" and "ethnic" relations. She writes, "While color constitutes a powerful ethnic boundary in the United States, any broad understanding of ethnic and racial relations in America or elsewhere cannot ignore the reality and volatility of nonsomatic boundaries, for example, among black Africans in Nigeria, Uganda, or Zaire, or among white Europeans in Northern Ireland, Belgium, or Spain." Joane Nagel, "Book Review: Racial Formation in the United States: From the 1960s to the 1980s," *American Journal of Sociology* 93, no. 4 (1988): 1025–27. See also Glazer, "Blacks and Ethnic Groups."

38. To the examples discussed in chapter 1 we can add Omi and Winant's statement, "Race will *always* be at the center of the American experience." This statement can be interpreted to make race transcendental rather than social. *Racial Formation*, 5.

39. See David R. Roediger, *The Wages of Whiteness: Race and the Making of the American Working Class* (London: Verso, 1991); Noel Ignatiev, *How the Irish Became White* (New York: Routledge, 1995); Matthew Frye Jacobson, *Whiteness of a Different Color: European Immigrants and Alchemy of Race* (Cambridge, MA: Harvard University Press, 1998).

40. Roediger, *The Wages of Whiteness*, 133–36; Joe R. Feagin and Clairece Booher Feagin, *Racial and Ethnic Relations*, 5th ed. (Upper Saddle River, NJ: Prentice Hall, 1996), 99–130.

41. Quoted in Feagin and Feagin, *Racial and Ethnic Relations*, 105.

42. Ibid., 107–8.

43. Roediger, *Wages of Whiteness*, 146.

44. Feagin and Feagin, *Racial and Ethnic Relations*, 105–6; Waters, *Ethnic Options*.

45. Michael Banton, "Discarding Park's Axiom," *Ethnic and Racial Studies* 26(3), May 2003: 549.

WITHDRAWN
PUBLIC LIBRARY OF
BROOKLINE

CPSIA information can be obtained
at www.ICGtesting.com
Printed in the USA
LVHW091029061119
636418LV00005BA/818/P